To my frien

Helen Lacey
with sincere affection-
Eudora Bundy Ferry

YUKON GOLD

YUKON GOLD

Pioneering Days in the Canadian North

Eudora Bundy Ferry

An Exposition-Lochinvar Book

Exposition Press   *New York*

EXPOSITION PRESS INC.

50 Jericho Turnpike   Jericho, New York 11753

FIRST EDITION

0-682-47279-4

Contents

Cheechako

1911 — 1912

1. Into the Unknown

MY TRAIN FROM CALIFORNIA pulled into the Portland station, and there was Cousin Dina herself, gray-haired and smiling, and adequate-looking even for eight o'clock of a hot July morning.

"How long can you stay in Portland?" she asked, while our heels were tapping along the marble floor on the way to the taxi stand. "Your telegram didn't tell me. So you're actually going north to be married in Dawson?"

"My boat sails from Seattle in two weeks, Dina, and I'll have to do a lot of shopping before that. I couldn't do much while I was teaching, you know."

During the process of getting ourselves and my luggage into the taxi, the conversation was left dangling. On the way to Dina's apartment we talked about the school in Marysville where I had been teaching and about her job as a private secretary. It was evident that Dina did not wish to discuss my personal plans in the presence of the taxi driver.

When we were seated at her breakfast table by a window overlooking the city, she leaned back in her chair.

"Now tell me more," she urged, "about your fiancé and how this whole thing came about." She had a right to catechize me as my only available close relative, who had acted for many years *in loco parentis*.

"My fiancé is Douglass Ferry, and we have known each other from the days when we were both students at Stanford. Doug is an engineer with the Yukon Gold Company, a Guggenheim corporation with extensive mining operations in the Klondike area near Dawson." I was buttering a piece of toast and looked up to meet the questioning in Dina's kind eyes.

"Isn't it customary for a man to do the traveling to his own wedding?" she asked. "Why can't Douglass come to Portland instead of your traipsing off into that remote place? Aren't you afraid to go away up there all by yourself?"

"Not when I know that Doug is there waiting for me," I answered. "You see, Dina, it's a matter of climate and geography. During the summer the mining goes on twenty-four hours a day, and Doug can't leave. The only way into Dawson in winter is by sleigh over the ice of the frozen Yukon, too rugged a trip for a woman. Several brides-to-be have gone in during the summer to be married in Dawson. Besides, you know I am quite accustomed to traveling alone."

"Hmm. I went as far as Skagway last summer. But what about the rest of the way into Dawson?"

I opened my handbag and brought out a colored map Douglass had sent me. My journey had been clearly inked in by him, from Seattle to Skagway through the Inside Passage, then over the White Pass Railroad to Whitehorse, then by steamer down the Yukon River to Dawson. Three thousand miles in all, it did seem rather lengthy. At Dawson, Doug had sketched in a log cabin, smoke curling from its roof, and marked it HOME.

Dina studied the map and the log cabin. I gave her my best brand of disarming smile.

"I'll have to do enough shopping to last for at least two years. Prices are high in Dawson and things are scarce."

Dina picked up her dishes and started for the kitchen.

"I am still pretty skeptical," she admitted. "What will you need? Let's see your list. Count on me for any help you need."

"After I telegraph you the date, will you send out the wedding announcements? I'll arrange for the engraving and leave you plenty of stamps."

"Glad to," agreed Dina cheerfully.

Two weeks later Dina and I were hurrying along the Alaska Steamship Company dock in Seattle, the dusk of the late northern twilight gathering about us.

"Sure you haven't forgotten anything?" Dina asked, as we approached the steamer *Jefferson,* due to sail at ten o'clock and now taking on passengers and cargo.

"No," I answered. "I almost forgot warm pajamas for the

boat, but here they are." I hugged the parcel under my arm as we walked the length of the lighted ship.

Passengers and their visitors were going aboard. Chatter of farewell mingled with the rumble of winches as rope-net slings of trunks and freight were lowered into the hatchways. While most of these people were going on a vacation, I was embarking on the biggest adventure of all time, hazardous by the look on Dina's face. We found my stateroom and emptied our arms of bundles.

Thank you for everything," I said, feeling that the imminence of departure had already separated us. "I'll telegraph you the date for the announcements."

Tears in her eyes, Dina hugged me, I kissed her, and she was gone. Left alone, I was glad to lie in my berth, listening to endless footsteps along the corridor, while all the noises incident to the sailing of a passenger ship went on about me.

I introspected luxuriously, Dina's skepticism or not, taking the leap into the unknown, wearing pajamas which, I discovered, were several sizes too large for me. The material was a tan and brown plaid, the wide stripes running crosswise, slightly reminiscent of a convict's suit. I was blond, and my color was blue. That they did nothing for me was an understatement. Even their design was intimidating. They had been my last purchase before the closing of the stores, in sudden remembrance that nights on the boat would undoubtedly be cold. The material was excellent, and thinking how well they would wear, I had grabbed them from a table heaped with garments and told the clerk to wrap them up.

But they were warm! I lost my hands in the sleeves and went on thinking. Let's see . . . I had brought Doug's wedding ring, a gift for Hoyt Perring, who would be Doug's best man, and also one for Margaret Strong, at whose house we would be married. I had bought a heavy wool sweater to wear on the boat and enough matching yarn to crochet a beret . . . My mind went on and on.

It was almost sailing time, when my roomate appeared, a

Seattle girl with quiet manner and good-looking clothes. Her name was Margaret, and she put on a pretty pair of pajamas which fitted her.

Next day the air was sharply clear, the sea blue or jade against the black-green of the conifers which rose from the water's edge in endless serrated ranks as the *Jefferson* carried us farther and farther north along the Inside Passage. Margaret and I sat in the sun on the upper deck, while before us passed the most spectacular panorama on the North American continent. Meanwhile I made fine time in crocheting my beret, keeping my fingers busy and catering equally to my esthetic enjoyment and my grandmother's precepts about idle hands.

While the routine of shipboard life went on around us, even to the interest in a bride and groom who kept to themselves and looked beatified, I began to sense the mystery of this country we were entering, this country which was to be my universe.

Ordinarily one travels miles to see a single mountain or a white waterfall, but here they passed in unending procession. The mountains thrust their tops high into ice and eternal snows; their bases, clad in green forests, were washed by the waters of that thousand-mile fiord and reflected in its shimmering expanse. Almost every ravine framed darkly a waterfall which flung itself in white tumult from enormous heights into the quiet sea. Spreading glaciers, ancient before any time known to man, had eventually crept down to the waters of the fiord, where they cast off bergs in desolate thunder from a vertical wall of ice. The bergs moved slowly and majestically, a mysterious, white fleet.

Since the weather was bright and clear, the captain decided to put into Taku Inlet and give us a view of the glacier itself. At a safe distance the *Jefferson* hove to in order to give us the full effect. The perpendicular face of Taku was almost two hundred feet high and a mile wide. Masses of ice hung from the eroded surface, ready to crack off at the slightest disturbance. A cold wind came from the titanic ice mass, as we heard the sound of waterfalls and an occasional muffled boom from the moving glacier.

Several loud blasts from the *Jefferson's* whistle produced enough vibration to loosen an overhanging fragment or two which crashed into the sea, sending waves which rocked our boat with their force, and detonations reverberating back into the mountains. We watched until the bergs stopped thrashing and settled deeply into the water. We had seen the beginning of an iceberg, but of its finish no one would ever know.

We stopped briefly at Metlakatla, at Ketchikan, Wrangell, and also at Juneau, capital of Alaska, on our way to Skagway. We reached Skagway and the end of our journey at five o'clock in the morning. According to Doug's directions, I was to go to the Pullen House for breakfast. I was saying goodbye to Margaret, when I heard my name being paged along the dock.

"Telegram," the messenger announced when I had identified myself. "Sign here, please."

Startled, I tipped him. What in the world . . .? I withdrew to the rail and opened the envelope.

"Call at Wells Fargo for a package and bring it in with you," I read. It was signed "Margaret Strong." I put the telegram in my handbag and hurried off the boat.

It was a tradition that Mrs. Pullen, proprietor of the Pullen House, would meet every boat that came into Skagway, riding side-saddle on a handsome sorrel horse and wearing a green riding habit and conventional stiff hat. Most incongruous against this crude background, but an arresting sight. Many were the signatures of notables who had dined at her hotel and left their names adorning its walls.

"Help yourself," she told me at breakfast, as she showed me how to skim the cream from a pan of milk sitting on the table. The rich cream crinkled at the edges of the skimmer as I pushed it along the pan. There was all the cream one could wish, for coffee and cereal, a tradition at this hotel. It was the last real cream I was to see for many a day.

The Wells Fargo office was not open yet. Fortunately, it was close to the station from which my train would soon leave for Whitehorse. I decided to spend the intervening time in exploring Skagway.

Numerous bright flower gardens and neat log cabins served to counteract the tumbledown wreckage of the old days when roisterous Skagway held twenty thousand people, during the gold rush of '98. Behind the town rose the wall of mountains, the grim and terrible barrier the gold seekers had to surmount on foot and over which we, too, must pass to reach the interior. In contrast, lying to the south, was Lynn Canal, shining in the morning sun. Skagway, gateway to the North!

A lack of historical background made this Alaska-Yukon area a new country, a land of the present. As I walked along the streets of Skagway with its plank sidewalks and buildings of logs I came across one building bearing the sign ARCTIC BROTHERHOOD. That sign, more than the air, fresh as the morning of the world, made me realize where I was. I was actually within the arctic region, at the top of the world. Even here men were brothers, much more so than in some other places, I was to learn later.

My tailored woolen suit was none too warm as I looked at the wares in the famous Kirmse jewelry store, seeing my first gold-nugget jewelry as well as articles of polished fossil ivory, a reminder that mastodons once roamed here, when the climate was tropical.

Time was passing, and I hurried to claim my package from the express office. After a bad half hour during which I telephoned here and there to find the agent, he finally came and I signed for the package, with a few minutes to spare. I must not miss that train, for it connected with the Dawson boat that evening at Whitehorse.

The agent told me the small package was valuable, so I put it safely in my handbag and ran for the train. I would know no peace of mind until it was delivered to its owner, who I assumed was Peggy Strong. I was glad to do this small favor for her.

We were all day on the train—old-timers returning from the States, miners, businessmen, a few tourists, and myself. A women who was sitting across the aisle came over to sit by me and introduced herself.

"I am Mrs. Edwards," she told me, "and this is my daughter, Bessie." Mr. Edwards was the agent for the White Pass and Yukon Transportation System at Dawson, and I was destined to know them well.

Mrs. Edwards pointed out the old "mushers trail" far below us in the canyon along which the gold seekers of '98 had walked the many weary miles up the western slope and climbed the final steep barrier, the White Pass, to the head of navigation and the Yukon River.

An unbelievable railroad, the White Pass was blasted out of solid rock and cost more per mile than any other railroad in existence. It provided the only means of entering the Inside, as the Alaska-Yukon interior is called, unless one went the long way around by way of St. Michael and the lower Yukon River. On one side of the track there arose a wall of mountains, while on the other there fell away an abyss so deep that a stream looked like a shining thread alongside the old trail of '98. After the steep descent from those magnificent heights we lunched at Lake Bennett. Then I began to feel the impact of that vast solitude and see what Dina had meant. The chill in the air was a foreboding of the North. The world I had known seemed indeed to have dropped below the horizon behind us, leaving us high and remote in this untamed and uninhabited waste, but with a lure so strong that it invariably calls back those who swear they have left it forever. No longer in Alaska, we were now in the Yukon. With a long way yet to go, I was still on my way home.

For many miles the train followed the shore of Lake Bennett; then it detoured around the dangerous Whitehorse Rapids of the Yukon River where so many gold seekers had lost their outfits and some even their lives. At Whitehorse, I saw again the little log cabins, typical of this country, and the bright flowers of an arctic summer. The waterfront was crowded with river boats and the huge barges used for hauling freight.

I ate my dinner at a little restaurant, feeling somewhat apart from the tourists who would stay overnight at Whitehorse and return the next day to Skagway for the return trip on the

Jefferson. After dinner I picked up my suitcase and started for
the boat. It was waiting at the dock, a stern-wheeler named,
appropriately, the *Dawson*. The distance was not much more
than going across the street. Politely raising his cap, a Scan-
dinavian-looking man offered to carry my suitcase. I thanked
him, realizing that a tip would be an insult. Perhaps he would
even turn out to be our neighbor.

We went aboard, and I had begun the last part of my long
journey. Surrounded by my secret aura of knowledge that I
was going home, despite Dina's misgivings, I went about in this
strange far place undisturbed by the clamor of the loading boat,
as contented and secure as a kitten in a basket.

They laughed at me when I asked for a key to my stateroom. I was mindful of the package I carried in my handbag.
Finally with the combined efforts of the whole crew, from
captain to purser, a key was found and given to me as a concession to the fussy ways of outsiders. About ten o'clock I
locked my door, put the handbag with its valuables under my
pillow and fell asleep listening to the slow chuff-chuff of the
wood-burning engine as the *Dawson* caught the current and
churned down the river in the broad daylight of a summer
night. The trip would take two days. I was to make the whole
journey from Seattle to Dawson in eight days, a record for time.

The *Dawson* was pushing a freight barge ahead of her loaded
with mining machinery and other commodities, making the
navigation of the dangerous Five Finger Rapids a tricky business. I could easily see why so many adventurers attempting it
in small boats had lost their lives here in the gold-rush days.
We passed swiftly through a channel so narrow that one could
almost touch the high walls of rock on either side.

During the hours I spent on deck I became acquainted with
Mr. and Mrs. John Burns of Calgary, the bride and groom of
the *Jefferson*, who were going to Dawson, and saw again the
Edwards. I watched for towns whose names I had seen printed
large on the map and found them to consist of a few huts,
several people, and many dogs, barking and hoping for scraps
thrown out from the galley.

At frequent intervals the boat would stop for "wooding up."

The crew members would race ashore with wheelbarrows to load wood which had been previously cut and stacked ready for the boats. Cord after cord was taken aboard, and then we were off again, taking utilities where they were found to be. The wood lay undisturbed until picked up by the steamer's crew.

As the *Dawson* dropped mile after mile behind her, running with the current, the banks of the Yukon would be covered with a growth of firs, and farther on a great mass of fireweed would flash a pink flame of color. Again the high-cut banks would glide by, a medley of browns and ochers always dominated by the swirling waters of the great river. Something in me responded to this country, and I felt at home in it. I already was a part of the North.

The vastness and the solitude became a living fact that was ever with us. The hardy souls who lived in those few hamlets along the river must have been on very good terms with themselves, because there was no escape by means of the usual diversions. Perhaps just the business of living in this stern land kept them so occupied that there was no time for introspection. The whole summer would be spent in preparation for the long winter with the river the main artery of life.

About noon of the second day we rounded a great turn in the river. To the right the Klondike River added its waters to the Yukon and just beyond its *débouchure* lay Dawson, spread for two and a half miles on a low flat which rose in a succession of hills behind the town to a mountain known as the Dome. On one of the hills above the town a huge scar of bare rock gave evidence of a landslide many years before, which had reputedly buried an Indian village in its path, forever making a landmark for Dawson. On the opposite bank the mountains rose high again, sheltering Dawson in a pocket along the half-mile-wide river.

As we approached I could see people gathered along the waterfront. The *Dawson* warped up to the dock and made fast, and the engines were still. Our solitude had given way to the activity of this remote city, one of the most northerly capitals of the world.

I was on the upper deck, my heart beating fast, looking for

a special someone in this crowd of strangers. Passenger after passenger left, including the Burnses and the Edwardses, but I saw no one I knew. Finally a woman who proved to be Margaret Strong called out heartily, "There she is!" and started toward the boat to meet me.

Margaret, clear-eyed and friendly, clasped my hand in her cordial one, giving me her friendship and loyalty without question.

Doug was in charge of operations on Hunker Creek, she told me, and would have to wait until Fred Morris, another company engineer, could drive over from a distant camp to take over while Doug was in Dawson for the wedding. Then Doug would take the team and drive the twenty miles into Dawson, arriving in time for dinner. From that minute I realized that COMPANY FIRST would be the rule of our lives. There would be no setting aside of duty for personal plans.

Margaret at once became Peggy. Her husband, Art, was there with his hearty laugh and twinkling dark eyes. Art was in charge of the "Big Ditch," the eighty miles of flumes, pipelines and ditches which fed the company's twenty-two hydraulic mines. The three of us walked to the Strongs' house, Art carrying my suitcase. My trunks would be cleared through customs later.

As I walked along I found that Dawson was built along a succession of benches parallel with the river and rising to the mountains back of the town. The intersecting streets rambled from the river back to the hills, finally losing themselves in grassy trails. The main business streets had wide plank sidewalks and substantial wooden buildings. The streets were unpaved.

The signs on the buildings intrigued me: Bank of British North America, North American Trading and Transportation Company, Northern Commercial Company, Canadian Bank of Commerce. I was in the North, and that North was Canadian; there could be no mistake about that.

The Strongs were Doug's best friends, and they proved to be mine. Peggy had arranged for me to stay with them until the wedding, and my bags were put in the tiny room usually occupied by their two-year-old son, Charles. Their house was neat and attractive, facing a park around which were built the gray-painted buildings of the Territorial Government. Now I was a "cheechako," a newcomer in this forbidding land. I had to prove myself equal to it, but with Doug to back me up I felt sure I could learn to cope with whatever lay ahead, where no quarter is given to cowards.

At lunch I laid the package I had brought beside Peggy's plate.

"Here is the package from Wells Fargo," I said, glad to be rid of it.

Peggy was busy tying a bib on little Charles. "It belongs to Doug," she answered. "You can give it to him tonight." So I was not rid of it after all. I put it back in my handbag.

That afternoon we made plans for the wedding, including sending the telegram to Dina. The ceremony would be performed by the Anglican bishop, I. O. Stringer, Bishop of the Yukon. Mrs. Stringer would be the only guest. Afterward there would be a reception, to which Peggy had invited all the Strongs' Dawson friends to meet their "house guest" (they knew nothing of the wedding). As we made our plans I could see that Peggy was quite capable of coping with any situation as well as being lots of fun.

Doug arrived about six, having left his team at the Pinkerton stable downtown. The minute he stepped into the room, browned by the sun, bringing with him an atmosphere like a clean wind in a pine forest, I knew that everything was all right—that I could do any coping that was necessary, backed by his confidence and good judgment.

"You're *here!*" he exulted, and crossed the room in about two strides.

Then we sat down on Peggy's sofa and began to talk as fast as we could. I produced the package I had brought in.

"Here you are," I said. "I'm certainly glad to have that responsibility off my mind. To guard it, I had the only stateroom key on the boat."

He laughed. "It's yours. Here, let me put it on for you. There was such an enormous duty on it that I shipped it back to Skagway and let you bring it in yourself."

I had brought myself a solitaire diamond ring, a stone that Doug had inherited. The rest of the evening I tried not to be conscious of my finger.

Hoyt Perring came in later on. I had heard much of Hoyt as one of the Strongs' and Doug's closest friends. Possessed of wit, friendliness, and generosity, Hoyt was a favorite everywhere, his husky laugh ringing out infectiously.

While they were in town the two men were staying at the company dormitory, known as Wholoomoloo Cottage. Here the bachelors could enjoy the luxury of hot showers, good meals, and a recreation room with card tables, a piano, books, and magazines.

The next day Doug cleared my trunks and attended to errands, while Peggy and I baked cakes and made ready for the wedding that evening. I also took the time to write letters, including one to Christina Rose, a close friend in Berkeley, telling her where I was and why.

Bishop Stringer was not used to a double-ring ceremony, but he improvised one, performed for the first time in all his widely extended diocese, from Whitehorse to Hershel Island. My ring was made from gold which Doug himself had panned from several of the most noted creeks of the Klondike; he had had it fashioned at Dawson.

I wore my traveling suit. My attendant was Peggy. Art gave away the bride. Mrs. Stringer, our only guest, wore pink chiffon and a flowered hat, looking much more like a bride than I did. The stalwart and distinguished bishop, hero of numberless adventures in his travels through the Arctic wilderness, gave superlative dignity to the service.

After the ceremony friends began to arrive and were properly surprised to meet Mrs. Ferry, a name I was just getting used to myself. These people were the "Ping-pongs." How the name originated, I never heard, but they formed a definite social stratum in the town. They included the Government set, employees of the two banks, the engineering and office forces of the big mining companies, the leading lawyers and professional men, the Royal Northwest Mounted Police, heads of the big commercial companies, and various others.

They asked, "How do you like the North?"

I knew they expected me to say something pleasant and meaningless that they would enjoy hearing. If I said what was true, that the whole scene was too new for me to estimate its nuances as yet—so how could I know how I liked it?—they would have thought me too serious or very dull.

I smiled, and said, "Oh, it's wonderful," and everybody smiled in return, and we were all very comfortable and light-hearted about it. (As a matter of fact, I hadn't even gotten accustomed to their canned milk!)

Actually, something had happened to me during the course of that long trip, something I was never to forget. The North had silently claimed me, and like it or not, I realized that I was forever bound.

Someone suggested, "Why don't we telephone the Burnses?" Found at a picture show, they eventually came. Except for Mrs. Edwards and Bessie, they were the only ones I knew among the throng at the reception.

Mrs. Burns said she wished she had known sooner that I was coming in to be married: then I could have shared some of the attention they had received on the *Jefferson*. She took my hand in hers and asked, "Is this little hand going to be able to do all it will have to do in this hard country?" as if half to herself.

"Why, of course," I answered, "the answer is yes." That was pure bravado, but we cheechakos must show the right spirit.

It was broad daylight when we left for our cabin, at 10 P.M. The spirited team Doug had driven to town had been in the stable for two days and were so restive that Art had to hold their heads while Doug leaped into the buckboard and seized the reins. They were hard to hold while I was helped in, and then we dashed off.

We drove along the Klondike River, past the machine shops

and other buildings of the company plant to Hunker Creek and then up Hunker to Gold Bottom and the camp. While handling the mettlesome team just as simple routine, Doug told me the history of the various claims along that twenty miles, passing several camps and night shifts of company workmen, last of all the drill crew at Gold Bottom, where Doug was in charge. It was still daylight, the men near the road looking at us with expressionless faces as their boss drove by. When we reached our cabin about two miles farther on, we discovered a collection of old shoes tied to the back of the buckboard with wide white ribbons.

2. Honeymoon-on-Hunker

WE NAMED OUR CABIN Honeymoon-on-Hunker. It was rented from two old prospectors and contained four rooms. We had sorted out and discarded most of their belongings, including a big hunting rifle which Doug said was used to hunt moose, and put them all in a bedroom off the kitchen. We now had three rooms left to use: living room, bedroom, and kitchen. A fence of peeled saplings set us apart from the rest of the wilderness; our front steps and door sill were slabs of bedrock. Across the front of the cabin there stretched a piece of canvas supported by poles to serve as a porch. This was HOME, at the end of that journey sketched on the map, and the smoke from its chimney rose fragrant and free.

The furniture was mostly homemade; the cookstove of cast iron and fairly good. On the kitchen floor was linoleum, so ragged and old, the dirt so ground in, that I never could get it really clean. In the front room were several bearskin rugs and one of caribou hide which was forever shedding gray hairs. Doug had told me that the caribou migrated from place to place looking for food and certain plants. They formed immense herds which would take days to pass a given spot. They had been photographed crossing the Yukon River on those migrations. To assist the caribou in swimming, their hair contains tiny air cells; perhaps it was these cells that made the hairs so lively on my floor.

The old prospectors were hunters too, and their walls were adorned with several caribou heads and a really impressive moose head with huge antlers. I should think the moose's neck would have ached at the end of the day carrying those antlers around! Besides these, there was a large stuffed owl that lived on a shelf in the corner.

The back of the cabin was built into the hillside, an excellent provision for warm floors. The windows at the back of the living room and the bedroom, although four feet from the floor on the inside, were at ground level outside. Something came in the open bedroom window one morning and awakened me by running across my face. I never discovered whether it was a squirrel or just a mouse. After that I tacked netting over the window.

When I realized that Doug had to walk a quarter of a mile to a spring for all the water we used, I soon learned to be very careful of it. He carried it in two "John D's," or five-gallon kerosene tins, suspended from his shoulders by a Chinese water yoke, as he plodded up the hill trying not to spill it on his clothes. We cleaned out an empty barrel we found and placed it at a corner of the cabin to catch any rain water, and by that means add to our supply.

We did not need to use the two kerosene lamps I found in the cabin, for daylight lasted until nearly midnight. When my trunks came I added some bits of bright fabric, a few pictures and books and my sewing basket to make a little island of home in the midst of alien objects, dirty walls, the caribou hairs, the tin dipper, and the bucket of water. We loved that little cabin because it was the beginning of a structure of living. Happiness was within it and brimmed out over the hills.

Then washday came, as it must to all cheechakos, to Mrs. Ferry at Honeymoon-on-Hunker. The equipment was a galvanized tub on two chairs, a washboard, and my two hands (see remark by Mrs. Burns), plus soap and water, the latter of course carried by Doug and heated on the top of the cookstove. Against these cleansing agencies was heaped the laundry, including sheets, towels, and other heavy items. About the heaviest thing I had been used to washing was my hair.

Doug poured a bucket of water into the boiler on the stove.

"I'm going to help you, Bunny. You just let this get hot while I take a quick run over to the camp. I'll be back." (My Stanford friends had called me by my last name, Bundy, which Doug had shortened to Bunny).

He arrived in time to help wring out the sheets and towels and hang them on the line. We were just finishing this part of it, when a car drove by. Automobiles were so rare in the country that Doug immediately took notice.

"Ye gods, Bunny, that's Thomas with O. B. Perry, the general manager from New York!" Doug was out of the yard and down the path to the camp before I had quite recovered from my surprise. I finished hanging out the washing and went back into the cabin. Now there was the little matter of mopping the kitchen floor. Afterward I felt that I should be called up for a citation, at least.

About five o'clock Doug came back. "We're going to dinner at the hotel," he announced, "as soon as you are ready."

The Gold Bottom Hotel was just about a mile downstream from our cabin. I dressed, feeling that I had indeed earned a vacation.

"Tell me about the visitors," I called to Doug, who was reading in the front room.

Doug laughed. "You should have seen my complete *savoir-faire*, talking to the gentlemen while my hands were all crinkled up from that washing!"

"Did they guess?"

"Of course not. Thomas—the resident manager, you know, you met them at the wedding—Thomas was too busy telling O. B. Perry about the new plans to notice anything about me. O. B., you know, is the Big Fellow from New York, who earns a salary greater than that of the President of the United States, although he's only about thirty-five. He is going to be at the hotel tonight, and another engineer too, Frank Short. He is keen; you'll hear from him, someday, too."

The dingy little hotel seemed like a palace to me, I was so tired. The dinner tasted wonderfully good, as we talked to the two engineers. Of course, they asked me how I liked the country. I was ready with my answers, and I noticed that they watched me closely. A discontented wife was no asset to the Yukon Gold Company.

Wherever men have prospected for gold, there is glamor over the hills. The glint of colors in a pan is enough and romance follows in its trail. The whole legend of the Klondike gold rush was filled with fascination for me. The stampede and the men who made it were just a memory now, since machinery had taken over, although many individual miners remained.

Hunker Creek, a tributary of the Klondike River, was rich in auriferous gravels. It was a part of the large holdings, bought for a good price, of the Guggenheims. Their corporation, the Yukon Gold Company, was operating nine dredges when I came to Dawson and twenty-two hydraulic mines. One of these dredges was at Gold Bottom. Before any of the operations started, the company had invested $17,000,000, and now the dredges and hydraulic mines were busy producing the gold, which was melted and cast into bars, to bring back into the company coffers the millions already spent.

The company housed and fed its men well. They paid top wages, and there was not a man in the combined forces of office and field who would not have given all he had to see the work through. In fact, I began to think that instead of marrying Doug, I had married the Yukon Gold Company, for that was what he actually was. I was sure that if I should tell him I was dying he would say, "Can't you possibly put it off until tomorrow, Bunny? I have a company trip today."

Since there were only the summer months in which field work could be done and since all the jobs were running full time, I soon caught the feeling of "Company First" myself. I was secretly proud of Doug's loyalty and decided it was that giving his best which made up the moral fiber necessary for a man to withstand the hardships of the country and not have it get him down in the last analysis.

Originally a peat bog, all this area remained frozen to an unknown depth the year around. Under the shallow topsoil, one came in many places to a muck which was about 60 per cent ice. Beneath this was frozen gravel, then frozen bedrock. Before it could be dredged, this frozen ground had to be thawed. The thawing was done by means of steam carried through pipes which were drilled into the frozen ground ahead of the dredge. Years later the method of thawing by means of cold water was adopted.

There were many things for me to learn—facts, in neat, hard little pellets, bombarding me. I had never been a factual person, as Doug definitely was. It was very good for me to have to listen to these clean-cut statements and to true up my mind to accurate data.

All the dredges and mines were "cleaned up" at intervals, I learned. The gold was removed in the form of an amalgam with mercury and taken in locked cast-iron buckets to the assay office at the company plant on the Klondike River near Dawson, to be retorted, melted, and cast into bars, which would be shipped Outside by boat.

Many a time Doug and Hoyt drove from one of the dredge camps to the plant, a cleanup of anywhere from $35,000 to $50,000 beneath their feet. Robbery was the last thing they would ever have thought of, since the Mounted Police had the country so well organized.

"Did I ever tell you," Doug asked me one day, "about the absent-minded assayer? Probably not, since he left before you came in."

"Tell me," I prompted, "what he did to merit such a title."

"One day"—Doug needed no urging—"he started to Dawson with a cleanup from all the dredges. That means nine bars, you know. They lay on the floor of the buckboard, held there by their own weight. They weren't even covered up, this fellow was so carefree in his methods. Once at the Dawson office, the man forgot to hitch his horse and walked into the office carrying one of the extremely heavy bars. While he was inside, something frightened his horse. When he returned for another bar, horse and buckboard and gold had vanished."

Doug looked up to enjoy my shocked horror. "And then?" I asked.

"Everyone in the office dashed out to hunt for the missing rig. They finally located it in the residential district, where a man had caught the horse. There was one bar left on the floor of the buckboard. Where were the rest? Someone reasoned that as the horse had turned the corners in his flight, the bars had slid off the buckboard. So they back-tracked along its probable course, finding all the bars, some in the downtown area, others farther out, where it would have been easy for anyone to take them.

"Once more the gold was loaded and taken back to the office. The men were so certain they would find the gold that they had not even thought of consulting the police!"

Doug was busy one afternoon weighing the gold samples from the drills—a few grains in a tiny glass vial. They had been secured by washing and panning the core from a drill pipe, a few feet at a time. Since those few grains represented about a hundred dollars in capital outlay and their value would determine the value of the ground being prospected, there must be no mistake in weighing and computing.

On the table were the gold scales, tiny weights, and a camel's-hair brush with which was removed every vestige of gold dust. Doug did this easily, singing gustily as he weighed and brushed and figured, his browned hands, still the smooth hands of a boy, moving with nice precision among tweezers and weights. This was only the beginning. His real work, estimating the value of a piece of ground, involved elaborate computations and other complicated engineering problems which I could not even grasp. Doug's estimate on that particular parcel of ground was $750,000. Mr. Thomas, months later, jokingly accused Doug of having occult powers—what the dredge recovered differed from Doug's estimate by just thirty-six dollars!

Suddenly there was a knocking at the door and the sound of men's voices. Doug let them in, five or six of the office force from Dawson, all full of jovial camaraderie and good humor at the prospect of a trip into the camps and a day away from the office. May Norton, a recent bride, had alerted me to expect callers some day.

"We have brought you a wedding present from the force," one man announced, putting some large parcels on our tiny living-room table. "Congratulations and all that sort of thing, you know." We made them all sit down, and Doug brought out cigarettes while I started to open the parcels. The men laughed and told jokes as I brought to light a sterling-silver tea and coffee service in the Queen Anne pattern with a silver-mounted mahogany tray, there being no silver trays in Dawson at the moment, as well as a silver-embossed water pitcher. While everybody exclaimed at the beautiful silver, I rushed to the kitchen to heat water for tea and prepare something to eat.

We served the tea from the new teapot in the English Coalport china that was a wedding gift from Art, Margaret, and Hoyt. The moose and the caribou and the owl looked on with great interest. Could they have spoken, they probably would have said what the miner did who was asked to a friend's house for Christmas dinner. He had been living on his claim and using tin dishes for so long that when he saw the table set with china which had just come in from the Outside, he ejaculated, "My God, human dishes!"

Some of our callers had never seen tea served with lemon, as this is not an English custom. In order not to hurt anyone's feelings, they helped themselves to both cream and lemon, the cream being canned milk, of course. The results were peculiar and curdled, but nobody cared as there was plenty of tea. We were young and laughter came easily and winter was a long way off yet.

At that time Doug was operating a camp of about fifty men at Gold Bottom, while he was testing a certain piece of ground. There were four drill crews, six shaft-sinking crews, teamsters for hauling wood and water, and so on. One of the drill runners working there at Gold Bottom was Henry Henderson, a man of about twenty. Henry was one of three brothers, sons of Bob Henderson, the original discoverer of gold in the Klondike, according to one school of thought (another insisted that the right belonged to George Carmack). The Canadian government thought enough of Bob Henderson's priority to grant him an annuity for life on the strength of his discovery.

The three sons, Grant, John, and Henry, all worked for the Guggies. Henry was the one destined to be associated with our lives later—for over thirty years, in fact. In Dawson he worked on the drills and also as one of the cleanup men for all the dredges, a responsible position, handling all the gold that was produced.

In later years he took on more and more responsibility, until he was dredgemaster for many years on different operations where Doug was in charge. Trustworthy and loyal, there never was anyone quite like Henry. Doug depended on him and was never disappointed.

"Bunny, Bunny, come quick!"

The insistence of that stage whisper brought me running from the front room, where I was dusting, to the kitchen. Doug was in the back bedroom taking the big moose gun, a .44 repeater, off the rack on the wall and finding it, fortunately, loaded.

"Keep your eye on that grouse." He pointed to the road. "I want to get him for your dinner."

We had been talking about grouse for days and Doug hoped I could taste it, the best game fowl in the country. I ran to the window. A single grouse was walking along the road, unafraid, colored so much like dust that I had to look carefully. Only the sense of something in motion told me where it was.

"Such a big gun," I objected, incredulous.

"It's this or nothing. No other gun around." Doug was creeping as carefully as a cat out of the kitchen door and along the edge of the cabin.

There came a sudden loud report. Doug speeded forward to a fluttering in the road. I had visions of seeing just a few remaining feathers. There stood Doug in the doorway, grinning, holding a headless grouse by the feet. He had neatly clipped off its head with the one huge bullet from the gun.

The moose on the wall looked smug. The same gun had got him, but his head had been saved.

That was the best meal we ever had at Honeymoon-on-Hunker. I cooked the grouse according to the directions for cooking chicken in my brand-new cookbook. Even the best cookbooks, it seemed, did not contain directions for cooking grouse or even ptarmigan!

The noise of the operating dredge was the leitmotif of all our summers in the North. Its ponderous machinery, electrically driven, made such a gamut of sounds that one could easily get the impression of a symphony, from the strident violins to the deepest tones of bass viol and drum. That music was part of our lives, together with a gravelly stream bed, green willows growing alongside, and the clear sound of water running over rocks. Add to these the flame of fireweed, the smell of wood smoke in the clearings, the tang and freshness of northern air, eternal daylight in a limitless sky, incredible distances to the horizon, and you have a few ingredients of an Arctic summer.

Every day I ranged the hills, both upstream and down, to the spot where the drills were working. While I watched the men and listened to the clank-clank of the descending drill bit, I would find smooth pieces of silvery birch bark on which to write little love notes to Doug. Impassively he would take them from my hand, glance down his aristocratic nose at them, and give some order to the men. Equally sphinx-like, he would write an answer, usually witty and delightful, and pass it to me as he walked by. It was just as secretive and exciting as

Yukon River. Klondike River mouth, upper left corner.

Steamer on Yukon River.

Midnight sun.

Mountains and stream, White Pass Railroad.

Cabin in winter near Acklen Trail above Dawson.

Miner's cabin in winter.

Winter scene in Dawson.

Street scene in Dawson, looking toward Yukon River and cliffs on opposite bank.

Dawson at 70° below zero. Water vapor in air condenses into fog.

Transportation in winter. "Over the ice" into Dawson.

Dog team on ice of Yukon River.

Dog takes a break on the ice.

Steamer with scow on Yukon River.

"The Plant" (Guggieville). Klondike River in background.

Sleighing in winter. Chester A. Thomas seated to left of driver.

The Yukon Gold Company. Main office at right, Northern Commercial Company at left.

Mining in the Yukon.

passing notes under the eyes of the teacher in school, and the men never once found out about it.

On my walks I found hills, verdure, the good earth, just as I had found them anywhere else. I decided that wherever they go men have learned to do the same things: to take comfort from the sun and food from the earth. All lands are basically the same. It is the necessities of climate, the differing languages and customs, that make some lands alien, while others seem like home.

I brought back treasures of wild cranberry, kinnikkinnick, or other leaves to decorate the table or brighten up our living room. There were priceless discoveries free for the taking. Salmonberries and raspberries were hidden from sight under the leaves, and I learned that the thing to do was to get down underneath the branches and look up. There, suspended in a canopy of sun-lighted leaves, would hang the little ruby globes, each one a jewel awaiting its destiny while the humming of insects accented the stillness.

I preserved some of the berries with a thrifty satisfaction, making them into jam and juice. There was a slight drawback, however; the jam remained liquid while all the juice jellied in the bottles!

Before the summer was over, I had become a fair housekeeper in the ways of the North. I could endure the taste of canned milk and storage eggs, I was not dismayed by the washing, and I had become quite proficient in Indoor Golf, the name I invented for mopping the floor. More than that, I had learned the threefold nature of the great god Pan—dish, dust, and frying. There was not much for me to do and there was unlimited time in which to do it. Everything was rough, elemental and on a big scale, punctuated by the clanking drills and the thundering dredge. The limitless freedom and release from everything little and absorbing that had once seemed to be so important gave us a new set of values. In this country, all importances are scaled down from the one primal necessity, survival.

On August 13 we had a frost. The days were perceptibly shorter. Some weeks later, after it had grown dark one evening, Doug called to me, "Bunny, come out and see the northern lights."

People in Dawson had told me to be sure to see them when they appeared in the fall. As a child in northern Michigan, I had seen pale traces of the northern lights in our winter skies. As I hurried outdoors I was thinking, "I've seen all this before, but I suppose to a Californian like Doug it seems like something wonderful."

To a Californian or to anyone else, what I saw when I stepped from my door to the open hillside was beyond description. The darkened sky, spread before us in its entirety, was flashing with luminous, gauzy banners which fluttered in waves of unearthly light. As those incandescent streamers flared up to the zenith in concentric arcs, subsided and flared again, I could imagine I heard a faint swishing sound, as of silk upon silk. Arched overhead in a complete 180 degrees the illumination spread, shimmered and receded in continuous, undulating movement as if a chiffon scarf of infinite proportions were being shaken across the heavens. We were being given a titanic display of something beyond our ken, a riddle of the universe for which there was no known answer. When we had seen it to our fill, we turned and went speechless into the house.

By September the kinnikkinnick was running a red flame along the hills, and the frost had turned the cranberry bushes to gold and bronze. The talk turned to going back to town. Soon the summer work would be terminated, the office and engineering forces working night and day to get out the yearly reports and close the books for the season. In October the last boat would leave Dawson, the river would freeze over, and by November the winter program would begin.

One day the word came. It was the middle of September. I packed all evening and the next morning. At noon the company dray took our belongings, and that afternoon we rode into Dawson with Mr. Thomas in his automobile. We were to be the Thomases' house guests for a few days while we looked for a place to live during the winter. We had been told that houses were very hard to find.

As we left the cabin the moose, the caribou, and the owl stared imperturbably into space. It was as if we had never been there. We walked down the bedrock steps to the waiting automobile and were whirled away. Honeymoon-on-Hunker remained while we went on, a symbol of the many houses we were to occupy and leave behind us in the years of our mining life. But we would always remember it. Never again would we have a moose head, some caribou, and an owl.

Those hills we left would be given over to silence and the snows while the ptarmigan changed from brown to white, as would the foxes and the rabbits. The weasels, blanched all but the tips of their tails, would become the stealthy ermine. Then the dark and bitter arctic winter would come silently down upon the land, as low over it swung the brilliant stars and nowhere could there be found any respite from the cold.

3. Winter Comes

WE WERE READY TO APPRECIATE to the utmost the luxuries of the Thomas menage. Their house was steam-heated and well furnished, even to a piano. It possessed a lawn and a garden where a few late flowers and vines persisted in spite of the frosts. The Thomases were a Stanford glamor couple of an earlier day than ours; he, handsome and heroic in size; she, tall and good-looking, carrying with ease her share of the responsibility of their position. The ability of their Chinese chef, Frank, was well-known and exceptional. We found Mrs. Thomas to be the capable mother of two small daughters as well as a very thoughtful hostess.

Probably the first thing we noticed in the guest room was a dish of fresh fruit on the table. *Fresh fruit!* Then Mrs.

Thomas said casually, "Would you like a bath before dinner?"

That was the ultimate of hospitality in Dawson, to be able to offer a guest a bath in a real bathtub with running water. In contrast to our galvanized tub on the kitchen floor in front of the oven door for warmth with sheets hung on chairs to keep out the draft and soap on a saucer on one of the said chairs, this was more than hospitality. It was gaudy ostentation.

Only three or four houses in Dawson were equipped with year-round running water. To prevent their freezing in winter, the water pipes had to be linked to parallel pipes of live steam which must be kept constantly hot. In addition, the water must be kept moving through the pipes continually and thence through an insulated outlet all the way to the river. Not many people could afford to do that, even if it were possible mechanically. Instead, when cold weather started, the town as a whole was served by the "water works," a sleigh or wagon, according to the condition of the streets, which delivered to all householders ten gallons a day in two five-gallon tins. The water supply was kept in a wooden barrel which was periodically emptied and cleaned.

The smiling Frank served our dinner, while C.A.T., as all the men called him among themselves, teased us and told jokes and Mrs. Thomas provided the tactful counterbalance to the conversation. In the simplicity of Honeymoon-on-Hunker I had almost forgotten there were such things as finger bowls. As I lifted mine off the dessert plate I realized that formality was going to be a part of our lives, a small oasis of ceremony in the wilderness.

That evening Mrs. Thomas entertained a group from the office and engineering staffs and their wives. It was heavenly to be able to play the piano again. I found some of the latest music, and so I played hits from *The Pink Lady* and *The Chocolate Soldier*, while everybody sang. Each person there, it seemed, was striving for gaiety, trying to push aside the realization that he was indeed on top of the world, geographically if not psychologically, and that winter was close at hand.

After a few days at the Thomases we moved over to the Strongs', a cabin not yet being available. As we reached the Strong domicile Margaret was just coming in from paying a formal call. She was arrayed in a black velvet hat with a pale-blue ostrich plume and a black fur coat over her blue dress. She carried a card case and white gloves, tokens of gentility, and as she swept into the doorway she looked hardly less than regal, as befitted the wife of a Guggie engineer in Dawson!

Doug, with his pipe, and Art, his deep voice filling the room, talked of company business while Margaret and I were being domestic. At the last minute Margaret had decided to ask in some friends for dinner and bridge.

"We'll have the rest of that roast, sliced," she decided, "and potato salad." She was whisking about the kitchen while I beat oil, drop by drop, into the mayonnaise. "The secret of potato salad"—she put Charles in his high chair—" is *plenty of salt.*" All this I tabulated away in memory for future use while Charles watched us from his chair.

During the evening the main topic of discussion was finding a house for the Ferrys to live in during the winter. "Found anything yet, Doug?" one of the men asked.

"Doug is out in the field all day, making tests on the dredges for gold recovery—may lead to some redesigning," Art explained, "so the business of hunting houses is mostly up to Eudora."

"There aren't many choices," one of the women said. "The houses deteriorate so fast and then they are torn down for firewood."

"Why do they deteriorate?" I asked.

"Frost. It raises and lowers the ground during the winter until floors are uneven, chinking falls out between logs and cracks appear around doors and windows. Then the house is no longer weatherproof. Dawson was once the largest log-cabin town in the world, but it keeps dwindling every year."

"There is a little house up on the next street that is vacant," Margaret said. "I just heard about it late today. We'll take a look at it tomorrow."

With that encouragement, I felt much more cheerful. The house was close to town, it was reputed to be warm, and it was just about what we would need.

We looked at the house the next day. It stood close to its neighbors, on the flat at the foot of the hill up which the streets of Dawson rambled. We should have grabbed it, but we didn't. We wanted to live on a hill! Refusing the good house, small and conveniently located and checked for warmth, we turned ourselves hopefully loose in a practically houseless Dawson. I thought many times later of how Margaret could have had a good laugh at our expense. She didn't, for two reasons: she was too good a sport about it, and she was not there later on that winter.

After days of practically hopeless search I was beginning to feel twinges of despair as well as being slightly on the defensive with Margaret. One afternoon Doug called up from the office.

"Will you meet me at four o'clock to look at a house?"

Would I! Together we walked up the hill on First Street, bordering the Yukon River. Doug told me as we covered the six or seven blocks from town that the house had never been rented, that it belonged to an official of the Northern Commercial Company and had been borrowed that summer by one of the men in that office for himself and his mother, who had been visiting him. After she left, in a few days, the house was to be offered for rent.

By that time we had reached the place. The house, a log cabin, had stood unoccupied for several years, Doug told me, so I mustn't expect too much. There it stood, snug, neat, and inviting. I loved it from the first minute I saw it. It stood on the edge of the bluff overlooking the river with a peerless view both ways. I was enchanted.

We knocked. The present tenant admitted us, showing us all over the house. There were seven large airy rooms, with above-average furniture for Dawson. The woodwork was painted white instead of being finished in the dark varnish prevalent in town. The wallpaper was white with leafy scrolls in dark red, which color was carried out in the Brussels carpet. Some really handsome lace curtains hung at the windows. It was by far the most attractive room we had seen in Dawson.

We found that the dining room had a substantial golden-oak extension table and six chairs, as well as a sideboard and a handsome brass chandelier, the only one in town. In the other rooms an electric cord hung from the ceiling, the bulb shaded by various devices. In the kitchen there were painted shelves and table and a very good steel range. Off the kitchen was a cache big enough to hold firewood, while shelves provided space for food storage. Off the living room was a small bedroom containing a bird's-eye maple bed and dresser. The clothes closet was just a shelf, curtained off. Outside the front door was a storm shed big enough to hold several days' supply of wood for the heater.

We were just as attracted to that house as we had been repelled by the other one. Before we left it was ours, at twenty dollars a month! We walked back to Margaret's excited and jubilant, bursting in on her.

"We have a house, we have a house!"

Margaret was just as delighted as we were, and I will say for her that never once in all the time that followed did she say, "If only you had . . ." and so on.

We moved in. We hung Indian baskets of wandering Jew, the one plant that would withstand the winter; we set up our Lares and Penates; we put our books on the shelves and our belongings in the cupboards. We considered ourselves very attractive, and we wanted everybody to see our new house. There were many callers, and the boys from the office came in the evening, and all was very, very merry for a while. . . .

The days were exciting and vivid as I settled our possessions and looked out at the long stretch of the shining river below us. Often during the sunny hours in the middle of the day Margaret and I, with others, would take long walks, including one to Moosehide, the Indian village several miles below Dawson on the river. The Moosehide Trail wound along the cliff high above the river and was one of the most scenic in the vicinity.

On September 29, Mrs. Thomas decided to go Outside for the winter. Mr. Thomas would follow when the season was closed. I was to keep her plants for her—the familiar hanging baskets of wandering Jew—but best of all, she offered me her piano for the winter. Margaret Strong gave a large farewell party for Mrs. Thomas and some of the others who were going Outside. We who were staying behind began to feel just a whisper of the shut-in sensation as we saw them leave.

At the last minute before the freeze-up, the Strongs decided to go Outside too. There wasn't much time left, so several of us offered to help Margaret pack. Every day, as I walked to Margaret's, the rime was so thick on the sidewalks that it caught and held to the nails in my heels. At every step I would have to unstick my shoe from the sidewalk. Yet if I dressed adequately I was very comfortable, whereas I had expected to shiver every minute after I landed in the North.

The day came when the *Prospector* pulled away from the dock, and we waved good-bye to Art and Margaret and little Charles, feeling bereft and sad. That was the last boat up the river, and we were Inside for the winter. Mme. Laliberite and I walked back to straighten up Margaret's house for closing. She was a charming Frenchwoman whose husband was in the government service and related to the premier of Canada. As we walked along she said, "My dear, you must be sure to provide yourself with a pair of heavy black woolen tights to wear when you go outdoors in the winter. This cold, it seizes you right in the legs!"

I promised, since Margaret had given me a list of things I must have to dress warmly for winter. The order was already on its way to one of the big mail-order houses in eastern Canada, in fact. Doug had the most amazing array of winter clothing to wear when he had to take long drives or be out on field trips. Both of us had to have substitutes for leather shoes to wear during the coldest weather. He had pacs (half boots) of various kinds and Indian moccasins. I bought a pair of felt shoes with felt soles which would not let in the cold as leather would.

Our fur coats were typical of the North—Doug's a raccoon, lined with heavy quilted satin; mine a northern muskrat, very soft and heavy. We both had caps which could be pulled down over our ears, and very warm gloves.

Margaret had told me that all the wives of Guggie engineers had to learn to stay alone. That was a part of the discipline of the North and was taken as a matter of course. We wives were perfectly safe. Some houses in Dawson did not even possess a door key, thanks to the fear of God that the Mounted Police had put into the region.

Now it was my turn. Faced with the loneliness as well as the responsibility of the house in cold weather, I tried to look cheerful when Doug announced that he must make a trip lasting several days.

For him it involved a long, cold drive, whereas I could stay snugly by the fire if I wanted to. Before he started out, he put on an incredible amount of clothing, until he resembled some strange monster as he went out the door. Before he closed it, he announced, "I'll be at Twenty Below on Bonanza." Then he vanished into thin air so far as I was concerned. I could not visualize where has was until much later, when I learned that *below* and *above* referred to claims numbered each way from the discovery claim and had nothing to do with the thermometer or the map.

While Doug was away, I busily wrote letters, including one to Christina, ordering Doug's Christmas present. I also visited Mrs. Caldrick, a congenial neighbor across the street; and Mrs. Caldrick introduced me to Mrs. Gus Johnson, who was to prove a lifelong friend. The days were growing shorter and shorter, and things began to point toward winter and the long night. The evening skies took on that pale, greenish hue which is the harbinger of cold. Regularly each day I flitted out the front door and into town, to break the acute sense of being alone. There was always some little thing to get for the house which involved a lot of shopping around to find. I had not yet learned what fun it is to rustle things.

Rustling consisted in unearthing or finding an object left

behind by former inhabitants as useless and utilizing it through one's own ingenuity. In all my life I have never found a hobby so thrillingly exhilarating as rustling. Nothing one buys and pays for begins to have the appeal which clings to the smallest rustled possession—some tiny treasure which we have fitted into our daily lives and found priceless beyond all proportion to its intrinsic value.

Then came the day when Doug unexpectedly walked into the house. He was home again, and it mattered nothing whether the days were long or short or how the thermometer stood.

Winter schedules for the office started in November. The hours were from nine to four-thirty with Saturday afternoons and Sundays off. Our cache was filling up with frozen berries which I had gathered during the summer, half a caribou, some moose which had been given to us, and a few ptarmigan and grouse. The greatest treat of all was a saddle of mountain sheep. All these hung frozen from the rafters, and we cut off what we needed from time to time and thawed it out for cooking.

At 25 below the nights were clear, the stars brilliant. The North Star seemed almost overhead. Often the northern lights played their fanfare of color and light as we gazed awestruck while we braced ourselves for the fierce stab of the cold. All thermometers were of the spirit type, as mercury freezes at 40 below, which is just a starter for a real arctic cold snap. Finally I found it more comfortable to shut off the bedroom during the day; this plan also afforded us quite a saving in fuel. We undressed by the heater in the living room, and at the last moment opened the bedroom door and made a dash for the bed. Icy sheets? Yes, but not so icy as the usual variety, because we used sheets of fleecy cotton flannel. Our blankets were leased from the company at ten dollars a pair and were heavy enough to have served singly. We had two pairs in reserve for the very coldest weather yet to come. We also had a pair Doug had bought from the Northwest Mounted Police with their huge monogram embroidered in the center of each.

Now, as if to test our mettle, came the episode of the collapsing bed, the handsome bird's-eye maple bed of which we were so proud. One evening when I had gone in to open the covers and to bring out our night clothes to warm them by the stove, the bed simply fell apart. It was of the old-fashioned variety, the high headboard composed of several wide interlocking panels. These had become loosened by the dryness of many summers as well as the cold of the winters until they no longer held together and all the glue had long since vanished from them.

I deposited the night things in a heap on the couch in the living room and went back to look at the disaster, pulling on my heavy sweater as I went. The panels in the headboard were resting askew, still partly attached to the bedpost at one side. I realized that all it needed was one touch to collapse.

This situation certainly called for a coper, which Douglass had every intention of being. He took one look and waded in.

The room was so cold that my hands were quickly numb. Never have I been at my best when slightly congealed. Had I been alone, I should probably have shrugged my shoulders and found an easy way out, like sleeping on the couch until a man could come the next day and repair the bed. Just at the moment there was not a trace of the sourdough in my being; I was all cheechako, and a pretty poor one at that.

Not so Douglass. This was a challenge, slight to be sure, to his ability to cope. He seized one of the panels, while I held on to the opposite side, and fitted it into place. The minute we let go it slid down again smoothly, like a fish over a waterfall. We tried bracing, sneaking up on the loose panels unawares, firmness, collaboration, everything. As soon as we had one piece fitted the bed fell apart somewhere else.

I was learning, too, something about the vocabulary a man can acquire in the North. Finally I gave up, I was so cold.

"Let's let it go for tonight," I suggested weakly.

Doug took one look at me; I suppose I was a little blue around the mouth. He ordered me out into the living room and shut the door. I started to weep, I was so tired, and hopping mad besides. Doug went out to the cache for a rope.

When he came back, he sneezed. One of my recollections of earliest childhood had been my mother's ladylike sneeze, at its loudest a delicate *a-chiff*. When Doug's sneeze rent the air, it could have been heard a block and was followed by a trumpeting into his handkerchief that would intimidate the hardiest. This done, he went alone into that frigid room where the two of us had been unable to do the job. He wrestled singlehanded with that recalcitrant bed amid whams, bangs, and sulphurous language. Minutes later he opened the door and gestured for me to look inside. The bed was lashed together and hogtied, completely conquered and firm as a fortress.

"I always was pretty good with a rope," he admitted modestly. Doug had often told me about his youth on his father's cattle ranch in southern California, but I had not realized that roping a steer and roping a collapsing bed had anything in common. The rope stayed on all winter and the bed gave us no more trouble.

The weather grew colder and colder. From the bottom of my trunk I hauled out the heavy cross-barred pajamas I had worn on the boat coming in and looked at them dubiously. Certainly they were not chic, but oh, how warm they were!

After that there were two pajama-clad figures, well shod in eiderdown bed socks tied around the ankles in a sort of Foreign Legion effect, that crept into that frigid and securely roped bed.

By that time we knew that our cabin was playing us false. Its exterior was still as seductive as ever, but it had a cold nature. In fact, it leaked cold at every joint. The years it had stood vacant had brought about an unseen yawning where the chinking had fallen out between the logs. The embankment around the outside was loose and cracked. All the cabins in Dawson had this floor insulation of earth, about a foot wide and high enough to come above floor level. Along the top were usually planted flowers in summer, which gave a gay effect to the cabin.

Doug worked after hours and on Saturdays, going over every inch of the outside of the cabin. We hung the double windows we found in the cache using torn strips of old blanket as padding between the window and frame, to keep out every breath of cold. Then I sealed up all the cracks on the inside of the windows with strips of paper. The theory was that if it was airtight, one could keep even a tent warm.

All we could do was not enough. The cabin grew colder and colder. Soon the windows were covered with a thick hoarfrost on the inside so that we could not see out. My ink bottle froze on the bookshelf and regularly as I dusted each morning I pulled the couch pillows loose from the wall to which they had frozen during the night. In the cold bedroom our clothes froze to the wall where they were hanging.

We closed off the back bedrooms and that part of the house became a no man's land. We could still use the kitchen, but the floor was very cold.

November 30 and Thanksgiving found the thermometer at 35 below zero, and a big evening dinner party scheduled at Wholoomoloo for those of the office and engineering forces who had remained Inside. E. E. McCarthy, acting resident manager in the absence of Mr. Thomas, was to be our host.

Formal attire in the evening was a must in Dawson, and that meant white ties and tails for the men. Over our evening clothes we wore boots and mittens, mufflers and caps, then our fur coats, for the cold was vicious and we had a walk of six or seven long blocks from our house to the dorm.

We crammed the heater as full of chunks as it would hold, closed the dampers, and set the heavy filled teakettle over the lid. Often, fire smoldering in a stove with no draft will produce gas forceful enough to blow the lid off the stove. Then the liberated gas and extra draft will make a fire fierce enough to result in a red-hot stove. It was not an uncommon thing for Dawsonites to clamp down the lid with a full kettle of water and several flatirons.

When we were all ready, we fortified our courage and started out the door. Mme. Lalibertie was right!

The cold air rished into the room behind us in a cloud of frost. We felt the familiar icy blow which I called the blistering cold and buried our noses in our fur collars while it searched every less protected spot and harried us. With lowered heads and arms hugging closely to us, we started down the hill. Conversation was not an accompaniment to our winter walks. Silently, so as not to waste breath or take the cold air into our lungs, we made our way along the snowy path down the hill, our footsteps creaking in the snow.

The steam-heated air of Whoolomoloo encouraged us to unwrap and ease the tension of skin and muscles which accompanies resistance to the cold. Noise and laughter came from the dining room, but we must first go to our dressing rooms and remove our wraps.

Suave and smiling, the perfect host replacing the exacting boss, Mr. McCarthy seated us at a long table in the dining room. As the newest bride I had the seat of honor at the head of the table next to Judge McCaulay, chief justice of Yukon Territory. Mrs. McCaulay was Outside for the winter. At the other end of the table Mr. MacCarthy presided; perhaps twenty guests, all told, enjoyed the occasion. The table was most elaborate with finest linen, silver, and crystal. There were branched silver candelabra flanking a huge silver bowl of hothouse grapes, and no detail of correct service had been overlooked.

I was to learn that lavish display was characteristic of the Klondike, where millions had been made and spent, and this opulence extended also to the Thanksgiving dinners given by the Guggenheims. The food was even more astonishing. There were a great many courses, including soup, fish, salad, the turkey, and dessert, and each was accompanied by its correct wine. It seemed incredible that we could be looking at clusters of fresh grapes, but when course after course came in revealing fresh vegetables, salad delicacies, fruit, and the turkey itself, I found myself full of questions. The answer was that these comestibles were brought in by horse-drawn covered sleighs from Whitehorse and that inside the sleighs were heating stoves kept burning constantly to prevent the freezing of the perishable freight.

I thought of how long that trip had seemed to me when I made it by fast boat in the summer. There were five hundred miles of winter trail—the drivers sleeping overnight in roadhouses, changing horses three times a day and battling the cold every hour they were driving. It seemed to me that we should have been more grateful instead of saying merely, "Oh, how *nice*," and making away in a short time with what it had taken so many weary hours to bring to us.

Some of us were called on for toasts, including me. At the end of the dinner we gave Mr. McCarthy a toast with Highland honors. I had seen that ceremony before, but here it was exceptionally colorful and impressive as we stood on our chairs and clinked our glasses over the table with the guest opposite to us. The beautiful table, the colorful evening gowns, the black and white of the men's attire, all combined to make a scene long to be remembered as we drank to our host.

We lingered over the dinner table, telling stories and jokes. Then there was music and singing in the big recreation room. We put it off as long as we could, but we finally had to come to the point of leaving, resuming the overshoes and furs and saying the last goodbyes. Then, steeling our resolution, we stepped out from the warmth and the cheer to the other side of the door where the clear star-glitter of the silent arctic night and the savage cold were waiting.

After walking uphill, fighting the cold, there was something sweet and friendly that rushed to meet us as we unlocked the door and put it between us and the frozen world outside. The fire in the heater had held. Doug put in another chunk and opened the drafts. The stove soon glowed red around the middle. Our stiffened fingers and feet were warmed and finally the room attained a livable temperature. Our first Thanksgiving in the North was past, and the next big day on the calendar would be Christmas.

4. Society and Malemutes

"HAVE YOU DECIDED ON YOUR day At Home, Eudora?" Margaret asked me as we sat sewing one afternoon.

"Goodness, must I?"

"Oh, yes. Dawson society is founded solidly upon the conventions. If you go back far enough, you come smack up against the peerage and royalty, who take no nonsense from you or anybody else. So make up your mind."

"The last Friday in the month," I temporized, "just to put off as long as possible. What do we do?"

"You add the date to the lower left-hand corner of your calling card. We'll start out by leaving our cards at a few places. Let's see—there are two At Homes this week. That will give you a chance to see how the thing is done and what they serve. You leave two of your husband's cards and one of your own, as you already know, of course."

"Why all the formality?" I asked.

"I suppose so that we will not revert. All British colonial settlements do the same thing. Even if you talk to your neighbor over the back fence in the morning, on her 'Day' you must appear at her door with your white gloves and your card case. If you are not high society, you won't know it."

We did attend two At Homes that week, and I noted the teapots, hidden in their huge cosys, the very black English tea, and the many kinds of sandwiches and cakes. We partook, teetering our saucers on our knees, conversed politely and of course gossiped, leaving the prescribed cards as we departed. It all looked fairly simple.

My first At Home day arrived while Doug was away on one of his trips. A cateress kept the tea hot and the cups washed in the kitchen while I received in a robin's-egg-blue dress with a train, my favorite dress. The entire top half was all-over lace I had bought in Brussels. It was dyed exactly the color of the

skirt and overlaid with chiffon of the same color. A blue bow
in my hair completed the ensemble.

What if I wouldn't live up to all the rules and be a dis-
grace to Doug and the Yukon Gold Company? With a smile
warm enough to offset the chill of trepidation in my fingers,
I greeted the many callers who knocked at my door. Among
them were Mrs. Edwards and Bess, whom I had not seen since
our wedding.

The callers wanted to be friendly, and look me over too,
a happy mixture of altruism and plain everyday curiosity. If I
could have heard them, the comments probably would have
been interesting. Long afterward I did hear one from a woman
who became one of my closest friends, Mrs. Frank Osborn.

"I thought you were putting on a lot of dog." She laughed.

"Oh, no," I assured her, "I was only trying to be sure that
I was doing everything according to Hoyle and the sacred
British tradition."

"No mistakes," she assured me. "By the way, did anyone
tell you about the baskets?"

"I don't think so," I answered, puzzled.

"If for any reason a hostess does not want to receive, she
hangs a basket on her door. The callers simply leave their cards
in the basket and that way the social accounts are kept straight."

"I shall be on the watch for a basket after this," I promised.
And once I had occasion to hang a basket on my own door
when I was sick with a cold.

It was while I was preparing for that first day At Home
that I had my initial encounter with a Malemute. These fierce
sled dogs of the North, when not in harness, were allowed to
range at will, and since they were always hungry, nothing
was safe from their prowling. In fact, I had been warned that
if the kitchen door was open, they would come in and steal
the roast right out of the oven.

Since we lived close the river, we saw many of them, going
and coming along the Moosehide Trail over the ice. As long
as a man was on foot he was safe, but alas for him if he lost
his footing.

A neighbor across the street was returning home one afternoon and turned aside out of the path for a dog team and its driver. When he left the path, his foot went down into soft snow, and he fell headlong. In an instant the whole team was upon him, and he was severely bitten before the driver could beat the dogs off with his whip. Doug warned me repeatedly to give the dogs a wide berth.

While I swept our living room in the mornings, I usually left the front door open for ventilation. I timed myself by the school bell. When it stopped ringing, I had aired the house long enough. This particular day of the At Home, I wanted the carpet to look especially bright, so I scattered dry snow over it to help collect and settle the dust. I went into the dining room and when I came back there was a huge Malemute standing in the middle of the living room. His natural inquisitiveness had led him to investigate the open door. We stood and looked at each other. I waved the broom.

"Get out," I ordered sternly. He did not move.

I came closer, brandishing the broom at his head. "Out!" I demanded.

He didn't move. I practically had to shove him out the door with the broom. Fortunately, I had never been afraid of dogs and thought the whole incident very funny.

When I told Doug about it, he told me the Malemute did not understand me.

"All you have to do is to tell him to 'mush.' He doesn't know what 'get out' means."

"What does he think 'mush' means?" I asked.

"Oh, 'get along,' or something equivalent. All the drivers say that, and it's regulation dog-team usage. The next time, you try it."

A few days later the incident repeated itself. A very large and grinning Malemute and I met on the bearskin rug in the living room. He stood his ground.

"Mush!" I said sternly.

He turned instantly and trotted out. With a feeling of great triumph, I shut the front door. No Malemute could put over any funny business on me. Just learn a few of the tricks, and it is perfectly simple to live anywhere!

That was not the last I was to hear of Malemutes, however. Doug and I decided to give a dinner party during the time remaining before Christmas. The guests invited, I spent a long time with the cateress in planning the menu. There were so many things we couldn't buy. We finally decided on soup, a roast, root vegetables we could buy fresh, and a salad. For a spot of green with the salad, I intended to wash carefully and place on the plates some sprigs of wandering Jew.

I had no qualms about the dessert. It was to be a very special frozen pudding of which Doug and I were extremely fond, containing eggs, macaroons, almonds, maraschino cherries, and whipped cream. There was a special English brand of canned cream called Fessel's, which really would whip and which I had bought at three cans for a dollar. It was arranged that I would have the pudding made beforehand, and the cateress would come in to cook and serve the rest of the meal.

I opened the olives, fixed the celery, polished the silver and set the table. A big fire in the range made the kitchen fairly habitable as I blanched and salted almonds and cooked the custard for the pudding, ground up the macaroons and cut the cherries. I had some of each ingredient left over after the recipe was measured out, even an extra can of cream.

When everything was combined, a most generous amount, the hot pudding smelled very good. There was a large chopping block right by the outside door of the cache and I decided to set the pudding on that to cool and ultimately to freeze, a process which would not take very long. Dinner was still a good hour away, and I went on with my preparations. The last thing I would do before dressing for dinner would be to bring the pudding into the cache, where it would remain frozen until we were ready to serve it.

When the time came, I stepped outside. The fenced-in yard was vacant and still. The pudding pan lay upside down in the snow, polished clean and entirely empty. I was so stunned that the full implication did not occur to me for a minute or so. At first all I could grasp was that dinnertime was approaching and apparently I had no dessert, unless it had crawled out of the pan and hidden coyly around the corner.

Malemutes! Of course, that was it, the sly, thieving brutes! I hadn't heard the slightest sound. They had jumped over the fence and eaten every drop of it.

After the first shock had passed, I seized the pan and flew back into the kitchen. My guests had to have dessert and that dessert was strictly up to me, Malemutes or no Malemutes.

"I hope you burned your tongues *good and hard!*" With this malediction I had to be satisfied. Now for action.

Thank God for those leftover ingredients! I assembled them as hastily as I could, whipping the cream so vigorously as if it too were a Malemute. When I put the second batch out to freeze, high up on a shelf inside the cache this time, I prayed to all by Lares and Penates that it would freeze hard in the time remaining.

The cateress came and I explained things to her.

"We can lag a little on the dinner, Mis' Ferry," she suggested hopefully.

So we lagged a little—a few extra jokes, a lingering over the serving—and when the pudding finally came on the table, it was not quite so hard as it was supposed to be. It could not be sliced but had instead the consistency of soft ice cream. Nevertheless, it was delicious.

Our guests greeted my explanation with much hilarity. It was certainly a cheechako trick to put anything in the line of food outside of the house and ever expect to see it again. So they teased me a lot, even while they liked the pudding.

Later in the evening we played charades. Our side had the word *handkerchief*. It was not hard to guess the syllable *ker*, when the usually impressive and unapproachable Mr. McCarthy came in on all fours, a bearskin rug covering him. He began to howl (a Malemute can't bark) and pretended to eat an imaginary pudding from a tin pan set on the floor.

Almost every evening after office hours the sound of Doug's axe could be heard in the little side yard which held the woodpile and the chopping block while he split a supply for the kitchen range. In that same yard was a barrel into which I threw discarded tin cans.

There was one thing to which I always objected definitely and that was throwing dishwater out in the back yard, there being no provision for disposing of it otherwise. I invented the scheme of pouring it into empty tin cans, setting the cans outside for quick freezing, and then putting the ice-filled cans into the barrel for the garbage man to haul away. Any garbage I could not burn was disposed of in the same way. I had reckoned without what was to me the unknown factor, the Malemute.

One evening after dinner we heard a terrific racket in the side yard. Tin cans were falling in cascades while mysterious bumps and rushes accompanied the clatter. Then there was silence.

Doug went out to investigate. It took time because he had to protect himself from the cold first with cap, mittens, and arctics; even to satisfy our curiosity, he hardly cared to freeze. By the time that was done and Doug on his way, the yard was empty except for tin cans scattered far and wide, and an up-turned barrel. Doug straightened the barrel, replaced the tins and came in again, looking grim.

"Malemutes."

He hung up his mackinaw and cap and sat down to take off his arctics. "They are after what you froze in those tins. Always hungry."

"They couldn't get the cans open," I suggested.

"Oh, yes, they could. With their teeth. Did I ever tell you about the crate of ham and bacon that one family had in their cache for the winter? The Malemutes broke the window, jumped in and tore open the crate and scattered hams and bacon all over Dawson!"

"The fence is more than shoulder-high. How did they get into our yard?" I wanted to know.

"All winter I have been shoveling snow out of there to get at the woodpile and throwing it over the fence. Made a perfect ramp. They just walked up to the top of the fence and jumped over. Probably jumped on the woodpile to get out. There wouldn't be any other way."

By the faraway look in his eyes, I knew he was planning on just how he would handle the situation if they ever came again.

They did come, several times, but always by the time Doug could put on his warm outer clothing and get out, the clatter had subsided and the dogs were gone—until one night.

The woodpile had diminished, and it was harder for the Malemutes to get out by jumping first on the wood and then over the fence. So one was still in the yard when Doug stepped into it and faced the brute, threatening it with a stick of wood.

"Bet you here's one Malemute that won't come back," he called to me as he lunged at it with the wood. The Malemute made for the fence corner but couldn't quite jump the fence. He scurried here and there ahead of the shouting man who brandished his weapon with fierce battle cries as well as throwing a few chunks just for the heck of it. Several times the Malemute turned on Doug. Had he slipped in the dark and uneven footing, it would have been all up with him; but he didn't, and the panicky Malemute finally, in one last desperate leap, cleared the low woodpile and scrambled over the fence to freedom. Never again did a Malemute come into the yard!

Not long after the Malemutes' last call Doug invited me to drive to Bonanza with him. Since the weather was mild, all of 15 above zero, I accepted. I packed a lunch and filled the thermos bottle with hot coffee. Then we filled the heater and put on so much clothing that we felt clumsy and could hardly walk around. The sleigh was well provided with fur robes, which we tucked under and over ourselves to keep out any wind.

Our team jingled briskly out of town and along the frozen Klondike River toward Bonanza Creek. My spirits were high. I was to find out what 60 Below on Bonanza meant, while Doug was busy mapping out a session with the foreman at that plant.

Sixty Below on Bonanza was no different from anything else I had seen on the creeks—just another log cabin surrounded by hills, solitude, and snow. Somehow I could never cure myself of the habit of building up glamor and mystery around the unknown. I was never entirely disappointed. Some small source of unexpected delight usually came to light, and sometimes, although rarely, I was really transported by the unexpected. Serendipity!

This time there was something waiting for me too. We entered the foreman's cabin, where we would eat our lunch and where I would remain to keep warm while the two men tramped around outside and discussed figures and other vital and concrete matters which had a direct though remote connection with the abstractions handled in the Dawson office, expressed in long columns of figures and pages of statistics, all leading to the final test, profit.

While they were about their manly and congenial doings, I, left alone, looked about the cabin. It had no ceiling. The roof was supported by rafters of unpeeled logs and crossbeams of heavier logs, all hand-hewn. I knew it must be cozy and warm overhead and decided that if I ever had such a cabin I would build a gallery up near the roof for my bed. Against the log walls were nailed shelves for supplies and dishes.

The furniture was all homemade, and there was a sheet-iron heater like ours and a cookstove.

Everything was neat and fairly clean. This man had evidently made the discovery that order in his possessions and a routine of keeping clean had their advantages.

There were no books, magazines, or pictures, nothing of any recreational value, in evidence—just the paraphernalia of working, eating, and sleeping. But this man remained cheerful and normal. I had seen him, and I knew.

When lunch time came, our host gave us a corner of his long table for our own. We poured out our hot coffee into his thick white ironstone cups, typical of all frontier camps. He looked at the hot liquid with puzzlement.

"This is something new," Doug explained, "a vacuum

bottle. Mrs. Ferry brought it in with her from the States. It keeps coffee hot for hours."

Coffee? All the way from Dawson? No, it was not to be believed. He shook his head and turned away, probably regretting that such promising young people were such incredible liars. He couldn't say what he thought, however, to one of the bosses, so he kept still.

Then he supplied a little magic of his own and that was the delight that made the day. He produced a delicious fresh pie for us and asked us to share it with him.

Knowing he had few facilities for baking, I asked how come.

He explained that once a week he went to Dawson, where his wife and family were living, and stocked up on supplies. Before each of his visits his wife would bake enough to last him a week—bread, cake, and pies. She froze them while they were still steaming hot and packed them for him. He kept them outside in a securely locked cupboard until he was ready to use them. Brought in and thawed, each article was as fresh as it was the moment it was frozen. Knowing we were coming, he had thawed out a pie.

There it stood, juicy and inviting. Taking a knife the like of which I had never seen for size, easily two feet long, its blade three or four inches wide, he cut, delicately and precisely, three pieces, one for each of us. As long as I live I shall never forget that scene: the earnest expression of the man over his task, the beautiful fresh pie, the gargantuan knife, the exquisite delicacy of the carving, the great satisfaction in consuming the pie.

All this after we had so blatantly tried to fool him with our trick bottle too!

Another short session over business after lunch, and then it was time to go. All bundled up again, we climbed into our cutter. The brief light of noonday was already giving way to dusk as we skimmed jingling along toward Dawson and home.

There was no real daylight now. The sun was approaching the winter solstice, when for six weeks it did not appear at all above the horizon. During that period it was dark all day except for a sort of twilight at noontime. Added to the duskiness was the frost in the air. When the thermometer dropped beyond 35 below, all the moisture in the air congealed into frost which closed in on us with a chilly, foggy blanket, shutting out visibility farther than a few feet away.

The sun was gone, and we must make up for its light and warmth in other ways. Keep the dark and the cold outside ourselves and our houses—that was the idea. Whether the cheer we needed came from a bottle or our own ingenuity was up to us.

Win or lose, the battle was on. Winter had arrived.

5. Christmas

DRESSED VERY WARMLY, we set out early one afternoon before it should grow too dark. Doug carried a light axe, and we started up the road toward the Catholic church and the top of the hill where there were some open fields and a tree for Christmas might possibly be found. We soon left the road and started across lots.

Panting and laughing, we plowed through the snow, almost waist-deep in places. I floundered and fell several times and finally was stuck immovably in the snow until Doug came to pull me out. We went on and on. At last we found just the right tree, not too tall and of pleasing symmetry. It did not take long to cut it, and then came the task of getting it home. Doug carried the butt over his shoulder and let the tip drag behind him. Retracing our steps was easier than breaking trail and before long we had the tree at our front door, where it stood braced against the corner of the cabin until Doug could make a standard for it.

To other people it might have looked like just a tree. To us it was significant and symbolic, practically sacred. Our first Christmas tree, it stood at the head of a long line of trees to come among all the other Christmas traditions we would create for our family.

We placed it in the corner of our living room and decorated it as lavishly as we felt we could afford, prices in Dawson being what they were. Strings of cranberries and popcorn and dabs of cotton snow helped, together with small gifts and unlighted candles. The mysticism of the Christmas season had entered our dwelling, and the scent of spruce carried us back to a dim ancestral past.

Then came the baking of Christmas goodies, the making of cranberry sauce and other traditional food. Mrs. Coldrick made English puddings and cherry cake and delicacies from marzipan, a secret recipe in her family. She brought us some of these confections, rich and delectable, to add to our Christmas luxury. Every little while I would skip across the street to see what new delights she was concocting.

We hung a wreath of artificial holly on the front door and put red candles in the candlesticks. Christmas was going to be fun this year.

The most coveted invitation of the whole winter was a card to the Midnight Mass on Christmas Eve at the Catholic church. It stood, white and impressive, a beacon high on the bluff along the river where it could be seen for miles, a monument to its builder, Father Judge, the first Catholic priest in Dawson, who had also established the Catholic hospital and school. Admission had to be by card because the church could not possibly hold all who wished to attend. Doug had been given cards for us and we planned to go.

That evening we felt as if it were indeed the middle of the night when church time approached. It had been dark for so many hours that the world seemed to be enfolded in the very depths of endless night and the sun only a dream forgotten.

Our cabin was on the street which led to the church, and since it was only about four feet from the living room wall to the sidewalk, we could hear the people walking up the hill long before we were ready to go ourselves. There was no other sound, as it was far too cold to talk. The footfalls crunching on the snow were soft and continuous as the silent procession passed our door.

We put on our wraps and stepped out into the night to join the long line of churchgoers. The sky scintillated with stars, myriad and low-hanging. The cold struck to our very marrow as we dug our chins into the fur of our collars and curled our shoulders forward instinctively to ward it off. We became one with the line of muffled figures trudging uphill. Never had we felt so remote from gaiety and the warmth of sunlight as at this moment, when the sun we had not seen for weeks was at its farthest southern reach. From our hilltop in the dark and cold, the world seemed to flow down and away from us in every direction. We stood, indeed, at the lonely top. Only the stars kept watch. The silence, which was a force in itself, was only emphasized by the mournful howls of the Malemutes on the hills beyond us as they lamented their exile from the sun.

Some need was in each soul that climbed the hill that night, something strong enough to call us from our warm houses to the rigors of that walk, something that the church symbolized. Whether it was light, or music, or companionship, or something infinitely deeper, it took us, each bringing his own exigency, to that door.

We reached the church, bulking amorphous in the dark, and entered, grateful for the warmth and dazzled by the lights, and found ourselves seats. The interior was simple and unimpressive, the walls of tongue-and-groove lumber, varnished, the altar conventional and simply decorated. I was not interested in the decorations, however; the congregation was the focus of my attention.

Within this sanctuary were Indians, poorly dressed; teamsters from the creeks, wearing rough mackinaws; miners in coonskin coats; fine ladies in Canadian mink and jewels; government employees; engineers; Royal Northwest Mounted Police in their scarlet coats; a saloonkeeper; a former dance-hall girl; a doctor who had come from nobody knew where, his past closed off like a book that has been destroyed; and ourselves, people who were young and observant and eager, the new life that had flooded Dawson with the coming of the big mining companies. Row upon row we sat, each with his own reason for coming.

From the choir loft at the back of the church the organ broke the stillness; and the service had begun. The chorus of the regular choir was augumented by two truly fine voices—that of Mrs. MacDougall, beautiful wife of the gold commissioner, who had been trained in eastern Canada and in Europe, and that of Charles MacPherson, dominion land surveyor for our company, who possessed a full baritone. Several violins accompanied the organ. Never had the great traditional music of the church been given to a more appreciative audience or amid more striking incongruities, the development of the religious and musical tradition of a highly cultivated environment being poured out into an atmosphere both crude and remote. It found ready reception there and transported its listeners to the Bethlehem scene, equally remote and of like simplicity.

In the pauses between the words of the priest and the musical parts of the service, we could hear plainly the ululations of the Malemutes on the hills.

The last note was sung, the spell broken. We were dismissed, bemused by the deep sense of Christmas that possessed us. There was no talk, no laughter, as we filed out, felt again the impact of the cold, made our way down the hill. Doug and I were luckier than the rest; we did not have far to go.

Since we were seated fairly well at the back of the church, we were among the first to leave the building and were home before most of the crowd had reached our cabin. We wished each other Merry Christmas, and Doug opened the drafts of the heater to warm the room. As usual I went into the bedroom to get our night clothes to warm them by the heater, the crossbarred pajamas among them. I spread them out on the couch and put our slippers under the heater just as a hearty knock came on the front door mingled with the sound of voices and stamping feet.

With a strangled exclamation of dismay I scooped up slippers and night clothes in both hands and disappeared into the bedroom just in time as Doug opened the door to admit Charles

MacPherson, the soloist, and several of the boys from the office. Though not having lighted a Chesterfield, I returned nonchalantly to the living room to find Doug serving them punch, a punch of his own making.

This punch was one of the most fantastic concoctions I have ever sampled. It was a triumph of Doug's ingenuity and fondness for salvaging things which might otherwise be thrown away. Its base was a syrup I had made from wild cranberries, which was too bitter to use. This he had embellished with other berry juices and Scotch. The cranberry killed the taste of the Scotch and the result was unique. Doug called it his Klondike Killer, and the boys were entranced by it.

I was still embarrassed by the close call we had had. When plump and genial Charlie MacPherson shouted "Merry Christmas!" to me as I entered the room, I returned the greeting and patted him on the shoulder as I did so. I saw Doug grinning at me from behind Charlie and realized that I was due for some teasing for having become so unnerved as to paw the guests. Ordinarily I would no more have put my hands on a guest than I would have brushed his hair!

Noel—our first together—was spent just as Christmas should be spent, at home around our tree. Since we were going to dinner at the Morrisons' at seven that evening, we had a luxurious sense of leisure and expectancy all day.

For the dinner we dressed in our most elegant. I wore the elaborate blue dress with the train, and Doug was correct in white tie and tails. Of course, there was the usual carrying of footgear and wearing felt shoes while we walked the mile and a half to the Morrisons', but we were accustomed to it by this time and thought nothing of it.

Eileen Morrison, as their sister-in-law, had access to the Thomas equipment and had in fact been given the suggestion by Mrs. Thomas that she use whatever she wished for her Christmas dinner. None of the rest of us could have approached such magnificence of crystal and silver as greeted us at Eileen's house that day. The table, set for ten, was midway between dining room and living room. It was lavish with the combined Thomas-Morrison assets and lavish is really the word, for Eileen had received many gorgeous wedding presents herself and was using them as well as what she needed from the Thomas home.

We were quite formal, seating ourselves decorously under the watchful eye of the serving woman imported for the occasion. The boys were relieved: they would not have to wash the dishes. After many a dinner in Dawson the men would remove their swallow tail coats, roll up their shirt sleeves, and do dishes. Then they would resume their coats to play bridge or whatever else was provided for entertainment.

In each napkin at the left of the service plate was folded a dinner roll. One of the boys was feeling just a little self-conscious. The table was a bit overpowering, and also he was initiating his first full-dress suit. Up to that time he had managed with a dinner jacket at evening affairs. When he flipped open his napkin and unexpectedly the roll bounced to the floor, he jumped up from his chair to retrieve it, exclaiming wrathfully, "*Who did that?*" thinking someone had played a trick on him.

This incident was passed over with hilarity and things went smoothly afterward, although the serving woman looked scandalized. It was apparent that she would have to steer this party into the proper channels, for hadn't she served at the most high-toned homes in Dawson and shouldn't she know what was what?

She did, too, serving with correct severity, even so far as to lean over and hiss into George Morrison's ear, "That's *enough*," when he was heaping the mashed potatoes generously on one of the plates.

It was a magnificent dinner from anyone's point of view. George and Eileen had certainly overlooked no bets in the menu. We were all enjoying it fully, when the boy of the dinner roll, now quite at ease, leaned back in his chair and said dreamily, "I can't help thinking what a good lunch the Morrisons are going to have tomorrow!"

It was at this Christmas dinner that Eileen and I traded the big news that by the next Christmas there would be new mem-

bers in our family circles and one more for whom to hang up
the Christmas stocking. We didn't tell the rest for a while, but
each had the other's confidence. We had been brides within a
few weeks of each other, and now we would have our babies
at about the same time.

The time came when the kitchen was so cold that we did
not use it at all. I cooked our meals on top of the heater and
washed and ironed in the dining room. Our water barrel was
moved into the dining room just around the corner and not four
feet from the heater. The barrel froze from the outside toward
the center until there was just a little core of water left, hardly
big enough for me to lower the dipper in. I had to wear my
felt shoes in the house and my heavy sweater over my dress.

The old year faded into darkness and became a part of the
past. Although the coldest weather was yet to come, we could
now begin to anticipate the return of the sun and spring.

That New Year's Eve was one the boys in the company
would never forget. On January first all the claims owned by
the company had to be restaked, a tremendous undertaking.

This claim-staking had been planned for over a year, and it
was like a big military campaign in its exactness. The company
owned thousands of claims, covering an area of about a hundred
miles in extent. These claims had been bought from individual
miners who had usually staked them by pacing out the distance
for five hundred feet along the stream bed. The claims went
from rim to rim to the base of the hills and were most in-
accurately measured. Above the creek claims were the bench
claims and above these, the hillside claims. On the company
map they looked for all the world like a gigantic crazy quilt.

In order to acquire contiguous holdings for the operation
of hydraulic mines, ditch lines and dredges, the company bought
up those claims by the thousands. When correctly surveyed by
Charlie MacPherson, they were found to overlap in places. In
others, fractions were found that had to be accounted for,
which threw the whole business into confusion. A great deal of
engineering and bookkeeping was required to keep track of all
this maze, as it was necessary each year to show that assessment

work had been done on them and to swear in assessment work on those that had already been worked in order to keep the claims in good standing so they could not be jumped.

By a resurvey of the entire company holdings, MacPherson had incorporated into the regular claims all the fractions. He simplified the boundaries and greatly reduced the number of claims by utilizing a recent law which permitted a Dominion Land Surveyor to extend or enlarge former claims so that one creek claim could now include several bench and hill claims. However, these new claims had to be restaked over the old ones and this done in entire secrecy on New Year's Eve, after midnight.

Getting together a crew meant that every man on the winter payroll was included: all the office force, engineers, teamsters, thawing foremen, dredge watchmen, men employed at the plant, drill crews, and so on. These men had to be taught how to find the claim stakes in the dark. Each crew was responsible for a certain locality. They were taken to the different locations, and each man was given his claim or claims to stake.

Staking a claim involved locating a claim stake at each corner of the four sides of a given parcel of land. On the stakes was written the locator's name, the date, and other data. That the whole thing went off without a hitch and in utter secrecy was a credit to the organization and the work that went into the planning. No wonder it took a year to get ready.

These scores of men, dressed against the cold and clumsy in layers of socks, mittens, coats, scarfs, and footgear, scrambled around their boundaries in the dark, locating the stakes by means of little homemade lanterns known as "bugs," warily, lest they meet a jumper at any moment who might try to sew up the claim for its nuisance value alone.

It was as free men that they went out that night to meet a challenge. There was no talk of overtime; such an idea was unheard of. Loyalty to the company was the idea and everybody fell to and did the job. The men were out all night. Doug came home at 5 A.M. and slept nearly all day. To the everlasting credit of all concerned, be it said that not one word had leaked

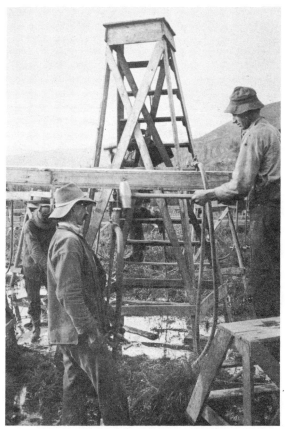

Getting ready to put steam pipes into ground for thawing.

Bonanza Creek, showing dredge tailings.

Hauling wood to the camps. Wood held in slings.

Hydraulic mining in the Klondike.

White Pass Railroad in winter.

Inside passage.

Frozen in! Yukon riverboat in winter.

Thawing ground by steam.

Drilling for gold samples.

Gold dredge in operation on Hunker Creek.

About half a million dollars in gold bricks. (Klondike, 1913.)

Mrs. Osborn's house in Dawson, John's birthplace, which cost $30,000 to build.

Honeymoon-on-Hunker.

The cold cabin.

The cold cabin.

Mrs. Thomas' piano.

That cold cabin and the Malemute's woodpile.

out, and the world in general was totally ignorant of what had gone on that night.

In order to leave the house quiet for Doug to sleep, I went calling with Ruth McFarland. One of our visits was at the home of Mrs. W. A. Thompson whose husband, one of the Dawson physicians, had an imposing background of degrees from British and Canadian colleges and was also physician for the Mounties.

Right then I knew where I wanted to live the following winter. We would go to the creeks as usual for the summer and come back to town in the fall. I wanted to live in that very house, Mrs. Thompson's. That was not coveting, for she had said that they were going to move during the summer. The house was just right for size, very attractive, and *on a hill*, this time east instead of north of town. Best of all, *it was warm*. I said nothing at the time but resolved to keep it in mind.

That evening Doug felt rested again, and we went to a basketball game in the big, drafty D-three-A's building. It was easy for the players to keep warm, but for us spectators it was another matter, especially our feet. I was glad when it was over and we started home through the dark streets. Since it was so far to our house, Doug suggested that we stop halfway and get warm at Wholoomoloo.

The boys crowded around us eagerly. "Mrs. Ferry, will you play the piano for us?"

We started our group singing, and finally, during a lull, one of the older men, called Sandy, said, "Mrs. Ferry, you still look cold. I think you should have a hot toddy."

"Thank you, no," I said. "We must be going."

He went to the kitchen to prepare one for me. I had never had a hot toddy so did not know what to expect.

Triumphantly, he returned with a steaming hot drink. "Try this," he said, almost smacking his lips.

I took a sip. Was this the Scotch everybody was talking about? It was simply nauseating! I took another sip, determined to be game if it killed me. Sandy watched me; I took another sip. Each taste was worse than the last. I couldn't swallow another drop, so I sat and held the glass.

Sandy asked, "How do you like it, Mrs. Ferry? Does it suit you?"

"You taste it," I said impulsively and held out the glass to him.

He took a swallow. "Ye gods!" he exploded and rushed the glass to the kitchen. Returning, he said he did not see how in the world I had downed as much as I did. He had made the toddy with hot water, lemon, Scotch, and—*salt!*

No further mention was made of toddies.

6. The Year Turns

DESPITE ITS EARLY REPUTATION as a roaring gold camp, Dawson was a British outpost and more sophisticated than equally small towns in the States. Social drinking was an accepted part of the life there, although I saw little of it. Our immediate circle of friends was made up mostly of young people from the Outside who came from an environment where social drinking simply was not done and the cocktail party had not yet been invented.

Perhaps New Year's Day in Dawson would be as good an illustration as any other of the informality with which drinking was regarded.

On New Year's Day it was customary for the married women to keep open house, either singly or in groups. The young girls, "Junior Leaguers" of the Ping-pongs, would assist these hostesses in serving and taking care of the guests. That left the role of callers to the bachelors. The festivities started just after noon and often lasted until the next morning.

The men at Wholoomoloo Cottage were entertaining as usual. It was Doug's first winter in Dawson as he helped lay out fine cigars, rye, Scotch, and bourbon—all of the very best, because the freight rates were so high that it did not pay to import cheap goods of any kind.

The bank boys and others called, and finally the Guggies decided to do some calling of their own. So they just put up a sign saying, "Help Yourselves," left the doors open and started out.

When he first came into the country, Doug had heard so many tales of the heavy drinking that went on in Dawson that he decided never taking a drink at all would be easier to do than to draw the line after a few had been taken. He nearly had his neck broken by the men who tried to get him off the wagon, but in the end they gave up, and he used to act as Hebe, passing drinks to the others. So New Year's was to be no exception. Doug would call with the others but would not drink.

Unfortunately, a few days before, he had slipped on an icy sidewalk and sprained his ankle. After he tried to keep up with the rest, hobbling along with Hoyt, the boys happened to see a Yukon dog sled alongside a cabin they were passing. With whoops of delight, they appropriated it and set Doug on it. Some of them drew the sled, howling like Malemutes, while others guided it by the handles behind.

Shouting and yelling, they tore along the sidewalks, careening around corners at a dizzy speed and nearly throwing their passenger out. When they drew up at the next house on their list, the door was opened by a startled miss. Here came the men, sled, Doug, snow and all, right into the crowded room. They were greeted with unrestrained hilarity and *joie de vivre*, as everybody laughed and the hostesses passed the drinks and eatables.

There was a large bowl of highly fortified punch on the dining-room table as well as stiffer drinks offered by the host and hostess. Eatables were varied—small sweet cakes or fruit cake, with sandwiches if one cared for them.

Just about like a cocktail party in the States today, the occasion here combined chattering of guests with passing of drinks and food. However, the atmosphere was highly informal. The guests held hands in a circle and all sang "Auld Lang Syne" and other songs and ballads. The background of formality was there, but the rules had been temporarily discarded, as the man did who asked his wife, "If I know I shouldn't tip my soup plate, may I do it?"

This celebration lasted all night, but by midnight the Guggies were back in Whoolomooloo, having done all the calling they wanted to for that year. After having fulfilled all the obligations and making the rounds, it would take a pretty hardy man not to show the results of each host's generosity. So it was not surprising that the next day the rumor was abroad that Doug, the only Guggie on the wagon, had fallen off so hard that he had to be hauled around on a sled! Too bad to have the name without the game. He had not had even one drink.

For us who were not given to roistering, the long arctic night was a sort of challenge to our resourcefulness. We could find amusements and diversions with books and music and friends. Mrs. Thomas's piano was a lifesaver to me and to the boys at Whoolomooloo, who often would drop in for an evening of singing. I started some really serious study, since I had so many hours to practice.

From the Dawson Library, a depressing building covered with iron made to look like stone, came many a book I had never before had time to read. I started the *History of Architecture*, in several large volumes, bound in red, which would take months to finish, so I was all set for the winter.

To have a reasonably warm cabin and clothing, plenty of firewood stacked within easy reach, and a generous stock of provisions—this in the Yukon is wealth. Living was stripped down to the fight for survival and that in itself was enough to keep one busy.

About January 10 it began to grow really cold. The thermometer dropped to 45 below, and I stayed in the house, playing the piano and keeping close to the heater. There is nothing in the world colder than an unheated shut-off room, as I found when I made a necessary trip to the kitchen. The dining room cupboard was chilly enough to use as a storage place for food, cooked or otherwise, in everyday use.

The top of the sheet-iron heater was flat and large enough to accommodate several small pans at once. With a little careful planning I could cook quite acceptable meals. To boil potatoes or fry meat, I would have to speed up the fire, but canned vegetables or other food could be warmed with the ordinary heat. I was amazed at the number of things I found I could prepare by this most limited method.

The thermometer went to 50 below. The bedroom became too cold for any human being to sleep in, so we brought our bedding out and made up the bed on the wide living-room couch. It was pretty close quarters, but we kept warm, tucked up together like a pair of spoons under our blankets.

We were now sleeping, cooking and even eating in the living room like any old Sourdough on the creeks, since even the dining room was cold enough to freeze the water barrel. I did clean the room every day, thus making us better off than some of the Sourdoughs, at that.

The red spirit column in the thermometer slid down to 55 below. Doug froze his ears and his nose just going out into the storm shed to get an armful of wood for the heater. His ears had been frozen before and were very susceptible to frost, while the ancestral Ferry nose was of such proportions that it simply invited frostbite. He applied dry snow vigorously and circulation was restored. The endangered members eventually turned brown and peeled.

It seemed too cold for a cheechako to venture far afield, although Doug went to the office every day as usual. I visited Mrs. Coldrick across the street and found her doing what I had done, laying rugs on the floor to cover the space between the door and the sill and hanging a blanket over the front door to keep out any breeze that might come through the cracks around the edges. She fussed around volubly, a sweater over her dress, lamenting that such a little thing as I had to live through such cold weather. There was not so much of me to get cold, at least.

The following day I invited the Coldricks to dinner, which was to be cooked and eaten in the living room.

That day it dropped to 67 below, which is real weather in any country. The nails snapped in the walls like pistol shots and the telephone wires hummed and sang an endless accompaniment. The Coldricks came, bringing *Cyrano de Bergerac,* which we read aloud. I set the table on the small, square living-room stand, and we four crowded around it and were served from the top of the heater. In spite of these limitations we were very gay and envied nobody. As Doug used to say, "I would not change places with *one* of the millionaires I know!"

After the dinner there was only one way we could be comfortable while reading aloud. We each took a blanket or a comforter and lined our chairs, letting the extra length come down from the seat to the floor, behind our legs, to keep off the draft, very much as an invalid is ensconced in an armchair wrapped in blankets. Next we grouped our chairs in a circle just as close to the heater as we could get without scorching our shins. Then we were ready to spend the evening in comfort.

We took turns reading. Mr. Coldrick's turn found him smoking a cigarette, which he kept lighted by puffs between paragraphs. But alas, he grew so affected by the scene he was reading that he wept, and blinded by tears, burned a hole in his comforter with the cigarette. Fortunately, it did no serious damage and we read on, finishing the book. Every time I shook out that comforter with the burned place in the days to come, I thought of that evening.

Then the thermometer climbed to 40 below. We were very much relieved at that; when it rose to 17 above, we were almost lightheaded.

Those weeks of severe cold were long and hard to bear. One must know how to meet each situation in order to survive. A man out alone can freeze his hands or his feet almost instantly in some crisis, such as a broken harness strap, or by stepping into water running deceptively over ice and under concealing snow. Then he is helpless and must freeze.

Hundreds of things can happen, and the chances are always against survival. Fortunately, nothing like that ever came to us despite the many trips Doug made alone and in such weather. However, when it was 50 below or more, the horses were not supposed to be taken out as they were in danger of freezing their lungs.

When it was milder I walked down town quite often for exercise. I would meet Doug at the office at four and walk home with him. By that time it was as dark as night and so cold the streets were almost deserted. Anyone I would meet was so enveloped in furs that it was impossible for me to recognize even my own husband until he was face to face with me. Most of the men wore heavy northern coonskin coats—black and gray pelts, exceedingly handsome—and fur caps and gloves, which concealed all individuality and made them all look alike.

There were two men I could always recognize. Chester Thomas was one. His herculean six feet two, and commensurate breadth, clad in heavy furs, made him practically a landmark. The other man was the equally gigantic Gus Johnson, husband of my friend Mrs. Johnson, who, fur-enveloped and accompanied by his great Dane, Catto, took up the whole sidewalk and was a worthy descendant of his Viking ancestors.

These muffled figures passed and repassed in silence. One did not open his mouth unless he must. Breathing was done, at least by me, behind the furry protection of my collar which reached to my eyes. My tuque was pulled down to my eyelids and over my ears. The frost from my breath collected in a white rime all over the front of my coat and floated out before me, a white cloud in the air. This frost soon froze my eyelashes together so that I must keep one eye behind my coat collar to thaw it out while the other one froze shut, when the process would be reversed. Each passer-by wore the same coating of frost on his clothing and the same aura of frost surrounded him as he walked along. Our footsteps, creaking in the snow, were the only sound except for the soft footfalls of Indian dogs as some driver mushed down the street. Very rarely, a teamster atop a load of wood drove slowly along on creaking runners, he and his horses both white with frost while he beat himself with his arms to help him keep warm.

Sometimes the stars could be seen, or a pale moon, when

there was not too much frost in the atmosphere, but usually the sky seemed as remote as the rest of the universe. The mightiest, terrible living fact was the cold and the dark, and we were right in the center of it.

The women one met were equally impersonal, wearing their long fur coats and disguised in enveloping tuques, hoods, or fur caps. It was only by the realization that this furry pelt was wearing such a cap at one end of it and two feet at the other that one understood that the animal had moved out and a lady had moved in!

Since there was a newcomer on the way for the Ferrys, something had to be done about the tiny garments. Things had to be ordered all the way from Toronto or Ottawa and that took time and a half during the winter. I wanted to make most of the things myself, so decided not to wait until the Yukon was open to navigation in the spring but to send at once for the materials I needed.

I held a consultation with Ruth McFarland, whose young Ben had needed such an outfit not too long ago. Eileen Morrison was also getting pointers from Ruth. We hauled out our mail-order catalogues and went to work. Up to that time I had never lived in a locality where I was dependent on a catalogue and thus did not realize what I had missed. Mail-order catalogues were our recreation, our fashion guide, and our education. How else would we ever know the parts of a work harness needed by a Saskatchewan farmer or how to look chic in a set of long winter woolies?

Making out our orders was quite an involved task because there must be no mistakes, and it would be weeks before they would be filled and sent back to us. Finally the last total would be figured, the I's dotted and the T's crossed, the money order enclosed and the envelope ready to mail. I often thought of the great distances we sent our thoughts and our wishes from that post office in Dawson and how they were always transported safe and sound wherever we sent them, and how the answers always came back.

In the meantime, weather or not, someone would give a

party for the women, with afternoon tea at the close, or Doug
and I would be invited out for dinner or an evening of bridge
or, less often, music. There were few phonographs, so anyone
who could sing or play a musical instrument was not allowed to
blush unseen. One such evening we called at the MacDougalls,'
and she sang

> Come out, come out, my dearest dear,
> Come out and greet the May,

to my accompaniment on the piano, while the nails snapped
and the wires hummed in anything but Maytime weather.

As our windows wore a continuous coat of frost, shutting
us all the more indoors, we had to learn to draw on our own
resources or go through a sort of mental starvation. Doug and
I never suffered from that. We always had more projects on hand
than we could possibly attend to and the last thing we thought
of was boredom because of inactivity.

One Sunday we carried out a long-talked-of project, walking
the length of Dawson and up the hillside back of the Strongs'
house to call on Robert W. Service at his one-room cabin with
the moose antlers at the peak of the gable. I wanted him to
autograph the two books of his poetry that Doug had given me
for Christmas. *Songs of a Sourdough,* first published in 1907
and years later retitled *The Spell of the Yukon,* was one. The
other was his second book of verses, *Ballads of a Cheechako,*
which was published in 1909.

Both volumes had proved so successful that Service was able
to retire from his job as clerk in one of the Dawson banks and
to spend his time exactly as he pleased in his hillside cabin. He
wrote his first novel, *The Trail of '98,* after his retirement and
was at work on his third volume of poetry, *Rhymes of a Rolling
Stone,* when we called.

Service was modest and self-effacing and in those days his
fellow Dawsonites did not outdo themselves in his honor. Some
admitted that "he imitated Kipling rather well," but few realized
that he was becoming world-famous and would one day amass

a fortune in excess of those of most of the gold-rush characters he made so real in his pages. However, the log cabin we visited for an autograph from a modest bank teller is now preserved as a sort of shrine to the Kipling of the Klondike. The Daughters of the Empire had it restored and protected after the cabin was almost demolished by souvenir collectors. Today many tourists visit Dawson mainly to see the home of Robert W. Service, who means more to them, perhaps, than do the famous Klondike gold fields, which in their minds serve only as a background for the lives of Dangerous Dan McGrew, Sam McGee, The Lady That's Known as Lou, and others of his creations.

January had passed into February and Mrs. MacDougall gave a lovely Valentine bridge party. February passed into March. Before we knew it the time had arrived for the vernal equinox. Although there was still plenty of snow and the cold had abated but little, *the sun was shining again.* With the lengthening of the days came a brightening of the spirits. This was the time of year one had to be careful of snow blindness, when the newly returned sun shone so glaringly on the snow, reflecting into our eyes inured to darkness. We wore dark glasses when we were to be out any length of time. Strangely enough, the first mosquitoes started coming before the snow had left, those fierce little enemies so dreaded in this region where they bred in the marshes and bogs, swarming throughout the wilderness. In Dawson itself they were not so numerous.

On the second of March we heard from the Strongs that they would not return to Dawson but intended to remain in Seattle. Ruth McFarland and I went to their cold and silent cabin and packed all their possessions ready to send them at the first opportunity. It was a distasteful undertaking because we realized how much we had depended upon Margaret's serene courage and Art's smiling presence at our gatherings. As, packing, we handled each article we recalled events connected with it and the Strongs. After the goods were packed and stored, their cabin was rented to others and our last link with them was gone while we lived in Dawson.

By the end of March the weather had moderated until I

could open up the kitchen again. It was just like moving into a new house. Now we could be gentry again and use the living room for the things it was intended for. I hired a man to help wash the windows and clean the house. The long winter was a thing of the past and we were prisoners set free.

I began to think of new clothes, which I did every year just as soon as the robins returned. New things appeared in the stores at fabulous prices. Ruth McFarland astonished us by buying *two* new hats. She liked them both and could not decide between them, so Warren told her to get them both. It was the last word in extravagance, but Ruth acted as unconcerned as if it were an everyday occurrence. Secretly I knew she was gloating over having a husband who was not only handsome but also prodigal, as she tried them both on to show us how they looked.

It takes an arctic winter to make one appreciate the spring sunshine, just as the view from a mountain is more thrilling when one has actually climbed the mountain oneself instead of riding up under some other power. How good it was to see the sun shining in at the clean windows as I worked in the kitchen! Doug's birthday was March 29, and I had invited Hoyt to dinner and baked a birthday cake. Using the range again was as good as an adventure. Now I could bake bread again, and there would be no more calls by the baker at twenty-five cents a loaf. Our menu, also, became much more varied with the additional facilities.

7. Coming Events

By the first of April we were back on summer schedule with long hours in the field and infrequent visits home for Doug. On one of those visits we called on the newest bride. Garrison Costar, who had been Doug's assistant on several jobs, had just come back from a winter Outside bringing Clara, his bride, with him. Doug and I invited them to dinner at once. Clara Costar would be an addition to our group of Guggie wives, a pleasant, quiet little person with dark auburn hair and the clear pale complexion that goes with it. She had come into the North the hard way, by the winter trail, but did not look at all the hardy sort of person to stand such a trip.

Doug was now away by seven every morning and home very late in the evening when he came at all. Gone were the leisurely breakfasts and the Sundays at home, as well as the long evenings together. The little living room, holding us so closely all winter that it reflected all the departments of our living, now became just another room in our house. The piano went back to the Thomases, as they would soon be arriving home. Life was again swept into the hectic summer program.

The days grew longer and warmer; the snow disappeared from the streets and the sidewalks while still lingering in the shady spots and the gulches. Crocuses could be found in bloom as soon as the snow passed. Doug moved out to the plant on the Klondike River for the summer to be closer to the work, and I lived alone except for his brief visits to town.

Following his research for gold saving on the dredges, done in the fall, Doug had been working that winter on new designs for screen plates on the dredges, including substituting slots for round holes through which the gold would drop to the gold-saving tables. He also redesigned "save-alls" and their grizzly bars, a name which reminded me of wild animals instead of dredge parts. His first work now was to see about installing these new parts.

On April 16, Doug was given the job of superintendent of the thawing department. As well as being a nice promotion, this meant more salary, which we certainly could use. There were nine thawing plants, one for each dredge, scattered over an area involving about thirty miles of driving to cover those on Bonanza and El Dorado creeks, plus twenty miles to Hunker Creek in the other direction. Each plant was engaged in thawing the ground ahead of one of the dredges and consisted of a battery of 150-horsepower steam boilers, steam points, miles of insulated pipes, bunk and mess houses, and most important of all, a woodpile.

Much of the ground in the Klondike area is frozen the year around. The top layer of ground, five to thirty feet thick, referred to as muck, when thawed becomes a spongy bog of the consistency of mush, resting on a twenty-foot-thick stratum of tight gravel. Below this is the solid bedrock.

The steam points before mentioned were steel-shod pipes connected to the steam boiler by huge steam pipes and flexible hose. These miles of pipe were all insulated to conserve the steam carried through them to the points, which were driven into the ground with sledge hammers by men standing on tall stepladders. Gradually, as the ground thawed, the points were pulled up and moved to a new spot.

The spacing of these pipes had always been done in squares until Doug took over, when he introduced the plan of equilateral triangles. This proved to be much more efficient as well as saving the company 20 percent of the thawing costs. That was the way my old friend Vergil, of college Latin days, planted his fruit trees!

One nightmare on this job was the danger of burns. As the ground was thawed, it became a quaking mass of hot mud. Plank walks were laid out for the men to go about on, but they were careless and occasionally one would slip and his leg slide into this steamy mud. Burn remedies and first aid were carried at all the camps, and the company doctor had many a case to handle.

As superintendent of this department, Doug had the responsibility of about four hundred men and the buying and distributing of approximately thirty thousand cords of wood a year to the boilers. Contracting for and buying the wood was just one of the jobs in the thawing department, which spent about $750,000 one year on wood alone.

The wood must be inspected and measured before buying, contracted for, cut and hauled to its location. This location involved careful figuring, as there must be enough wood for each boiler ahead of the dredge, yet when the dredge arrived at that spot there must be no wood left over. The whole boiler system would then be moved to a place farther ahead of the dredge for the next thawing to begin. Thus the location of the woodpile was a strategic business. At one time a single pile contained three thousand cords of wood and was protected from fire by hose and water supply.

By the time Doug came on the scene, all the wood close to Dawson had been exhausted, forcing the wood contractors to go far afield to find their timber. That meant very long trips into the wilderness and a long haul to bring the wood to the property. Much of it was cut about one hundred miles above Dawson, floated down the Yukon in log rafts to Klondike City, across the Klondike River from Dawson, and there cut into the proper lengths. It was hauled out of there by a small railroad, spur tracks being built to the sites of the various woodpiles.

Doug devised a sling, working from a derrick arm, that would pick up a whole carload of wood at a time, raise it to the top of the gigantic woodpile, then trip itself, thus releasing the wood. Then the sling, swinging in the air like a giant trapeze, would be lowered for another load of wood.

There was continuous daylight, and it was nothing unusual for Doug to work eighteen hours a day most of the time that spring. Even then there was more to be done than he quite had time for. He would come home very late, having had his dinner at one of the camps, fall into bed and sleep exhausted until it was time to get up again at six, often muttering in his sleep while his subconscious worked on some problem.

He was furious when he came into town one night after discussing wood contracts with several dealers.

"One so-and-so offered me a bribe," he sputtered—"said if I would give him the contract he would give me a cut on each cord. The price to the company would be the same either way, but I would get about three thousand for myself. I almost threw him out of the office."

He glared over that for days. Nowadays when men expect and take such cuts merely as a matter of course, his attitude may seem quixotic, but so far as Doug was concerned, it simply wasn't done.

The company plant, on the Klondike River about a mile above its junction with the Yukon, was also known as Guggieville. It consisted of the machine shops, warehouses, stables, assay office, field office, cookhouse-bunkhouse, and several cottages, one of which we would occupy in the summer. It rumbled with activity all summer as men came and went in both directions up the creeks, up Hunker and Bonanza.

Meanwhile I had an engagement with the stork, and it was arranged that I was to live at the home of Mrs. Frank Osborn after Doug moved to the plant so that I need not be alone as much as I had been lately. There was started then a wonderful friendship which has lasted to this day.

Mrs. Osborn had trained at Brooklyn General Hospital, so she was qualified to take care of me right in her own home. We decided on that plan instead of my going to the little Dawson hospital which was understaffed and overcrowded although the nurses were excellent.

This fortunate arrangement was followed by another piece of good luck, the appearance in Dawson for the summer of a fine new doctor who had just finished a graduate course at Johns Hopkins. Dr. Clark was doing some special work for one of the companies there, and I was his only private patient. I had more confidence in him than I had in any of the other doctors because he had trained in the States, and recently, while some of the resident doctors had been in Dawson for years without going Outside.

Once the plans were decided upon, I packed the things to go to the creeks for the summer house and sent them out by Danny, a company teamster who made daily trips to Dawson for errands, meat, and various supplies. Then I packed my own and the baby's things and moved to Mrs. Osborn's. Her family consisted of Frank, her husband, a hardware man at the time, although later he became gold commissioner of Yukon Territory. He was patient, and good as the salt of the earth is good.

There were two small children, Franklin, seven, and Harriett, five—bright, attractive youngsters—and last of all, the black dog, Chummy. They adopted me without delay as one of them, and I liked them all.

The Osborns lived in a large two-story house, one of the finest in Dawson. It had been built by a man who had become rich in the gold rush, and it had cost him thirty thousand dollars. There were many expensive features, such as plate glass in the doors and real finished lumber on the porch floors. My room was at the head of the stairs and was sunny and pleasant.

I was really in the heart of town now, close to shops and the main street. Every day I did some shopping, mainly to get in a walk. Doug gave me the measurements of the windows in our house at the plant, and I bought material and made curtains. Then, with Mrs. Osborn's help, I made and tied an extra comforter to use in the summer instead of our very heavy blankets.

Dark, vivacious, filled with energy and warm, human sympathy, Mrs. Osborn was a tonic to everyone who came in contact with her, as well as being a superfine nurse. She had a way of commenting on people and things that was full of original humor. She would pull down the corners of her mouth, eyes twinkling, and utter the one word, "Shocking!" The Church of England was her church, and she was an active member of the Imperial Order of Daughters of the Empire, which occupied about the same place in their social regime that the D.A.R. occupies in the States.

As the Carnegie Library was very near Mrs. Osborn's house, I could get books regularly there. I was deep in the third volume of the *History of Architecture*.

There was continuous daylight now, and it seemed a pity to waste any of it in sleeping. Golden sunshine and the clean, crisp air gave one the feeling of floating in a new element after the long dark winter we had so recently left behind us. Sounds traveled far. There was a noise of hammering, of cheerful talk, of new activity, as Dawson emerged from her long hibernation and housewives brought their possessions into the sun to freshen them. Spring repairs were made, and the children scattered to the wide outdoors in their play. Voices sounded loud and cheerful as the men and women went about their daily work after the silence of the snow.

Now the earth was glad, turning green and beautiful under the never-ending sunlight, seemingly supercharged with life and vitality. Birds were coming north again; winter and darkness had receded to a dream in memory. What a beautiful time to be born!

8.   We Welcome John

ON ONE OF THOSE GOLDEN spring days there was much ado in the Osborn mansion. The Ferrys had an eight and one-half pound son, and his name was John Douglass—a beautiful baby, strong and perfectly formed.

Now I was kin to all the mother creatures of the earth and could understand them, possessing that secret knowledge which links together those who bring forth new living beings to keep the line unbroken. With the enveloping new mother love was born another racial emotion, fear. I, who had never been afraid of anything for myself, would now know fear for my offspring. As I gathered him close to me, I wondered why something so priceless had to be housed in so frail a container! Surprised, I realized that from that moment on I was another person—no longer myself alone, but John's mother, and John would be my first care, above everything else.

"I am the only mother he will ever have," I thought, "and I must never let him down."

Heavens, what a responsibility, with no second chance to make good! Since other women seemed to be doing it quite nonchalantly, I decided I could too.

Fortunately Doug was in town. He stayed a day or two and grew used to the marvel of being a father. How Mrs. Osborn did everything I do not understand, but I had perfect care and so did the baby. We came first, even if other things had to wait. She also took care of her family and her house, with part-time help.

The twenty-four hours of daylight were most convenient. There was no tiptoeing around with a night light trying to keep it out of the baby's eyes. The night feedings were taken care of in a perfectly light room.

Visitors said, "Talk about Doug Ferry!" when they saw John. John's nose was not quite up to the Ferry standards as yet, but his hands and his face were uncanny little replicas of his father's.

One day when the doctor came in I was sitting up in bed reading my *History of Architecture*. I did not see anything amusing in the situation as I peered out from behind the big book, wearing my devastating lace cap with a pink bow on top, and advised him to read it. He laughed and laughed. Probably few of his patients greeted him from behind such heavy reading matter. Failing to interest him in the history, I procured from the library a copy of Van Dyke's *The Three Wise Men* for him to read. That he liked very much indeed.

Mrs. Osborn was so good to me and to John that our debt to her could never be paid. She gave me Swedish massage every day and brought me eggnogs to drink. I, who knew nothing at all about liquor, developed a great fondness for the taste of brandy with which my eggnogs were flavored, partly, I suppose, because it killed the taste of the canned milk. I had them at all hours and used to look forward to their arrival on a tray, above which was Mrs. Osborn's cheerful face to add to my feeling of well-being.

John received many gifts from far and near. I had one too, a belated wedding gift from the Lake Forest Ferrys, which had been held up in the winter mails. They had asked us what we wanted, aand I had replied, "Something in table linen." Here were linens that simply covered the bed when we opened the package. Like Hannah in *Little Women*, I said, "Here is a set-out that will last me all my days." I put them away to await a more favorable time to hem the tablecloths and napkins and felt rich indeed to have such a supply.

It was almost time for the annual breakup of the winter's ice in the Yukon. Until I had spent a winter in the North and seen the ice go out, I was still a cheechako, so I would not for anything in the world have missed seeing this phenomenon. With the breakup of the Yukon's long winter imprisonment I would become a sourdough.

For weeks the bets had been coming in on the day, hour, and minute the ice would start going out. These first pools on the going of the ice, now instituted in other places also, originated in Dawson. Sometimes they would amount to several thousand dollars for the lucky winner. A responsible citizen took charge of the pool, and a whistle on the N.C. building was connected by cable to a stake in the middle of the river's ice. When the ice broke and started down the river, the tug on the cable blew the whistle, recording the exact second of time.

John was just a few weeks old when Mrs. Osborn and I heard that whistle. For a minute I did not know what it was. Mrs. Osborn hurried into the room, picked up John and put him into his buggy.

"Hurry, hurry," she admonished, "we have to get him down to the river to see the ice go out. This is his chance to be a sourdough right from the start."

I rushed into street dress and sweater and followed Mrs. Osborn out the door. A veritable stampede had started for the waterfront to see the spectacle. We trundled John's buggy along the rough plank sidewalks together with housewives, businessmen, and the mass of humanity making for the river. Right to the edge of the wharf we went, where the swift-moving current took the ice along in a fearsome race.

I had never seen any exhibition of the unleashed power of nature that approached this one. Crushing and rumbling, huge cakes of ice, some as big as a house, ground and smashed against each other with thunderous roar as the ice raced for the freedom of the lower river and the sea. The size of those cakes of ice, as they reared up and crashed down again, gave me some idea of the resistless surge of water that was behind them. Truly, this North country was a land of superlatives.

If an ice jam piled up, as it did sometimes, Dawson was in for a flood, as the river rose behind the ice and overflowed its banks. Occasionally whole sections of the docks along the waterfront were sheared off from their pilings and sent down the lordly Yukon with the flood.

In all it was a mighty and awesome sight. Mrs. Osborn lifted John in her arms and let him look, even though we knew his eyes were not yet in focus. Tiny child of the North, he was initiated. He was a sourdough, that much was certain.

For a cheechako I had done pretty well. By the time the ice went out I had produced a son.

When John was a month old, we moved to the plant. I had engaged a woman to help me with the housework and the baby for a week and then I would have a young girl to help me for the rest of the summer. Mrs. McClusky, my helper, kept things going smoothly until I could orient myself. I had been spoiled at Mrs. Osborn's and now would have to learn to take care of the baby at night and also run the house by myself.

The house we lived in was the largest at the plant, two stories, and fortunately for us, partly furnished. We bought a few things to fill out and I improvised shelves and cupboards from packing boxes and potato crates, which I painted and lined with paper.

There were three bedrooms upstairs, while the first floor consisted of a very large front room, kitchen, pantry, and back porch. There was also a porch across the front of the house. Like all the other buildings at the plant, the house was painted dark red. The inside was papered hideously. The floors were unfinished and bare except for a few small rugs.

I did my best to create a homelike appearance but never did succeed. The place was too big and too bare. The former occupants had left their piano, however, and that made up for a lot. Besides, any place that held Doug and John and me was home.

The young girl, Mary, who took Mrs. McClusky's place had to be taught almost everything, but she learned readily. We soon adopted a regular routine of work and baby care. Again we had to save water. All we used had to be carried from the cookhouse, easily two city blocks from our house. Mary and I used to say that first we bathed the baby, then we washed his clothes, then we mopped the floor and finally, not to waste any, we watered the flowers, all with the same water!

We had to buy a cookstove for the kitchen, which I used during the summers as long as I was in the North. It was so small that Doug's large bandana handkerchief would just about cover it. If the teakettle and the frying pan were being used at the same time, both would hang over the edge a little. To give the stove enough height, we put several bricks under each leg. The oven was so small that when we baked bread, one loaf at a time, the loaf would rise and stick to the top of the oven so that it could not be moved. Fortunately there was a door on each side of the oven, enabling us to open the door at the back and push the loaf out from the front. The firebox was so tiny that the wood had to be cut practically to kindling size before we could use it. This meant a constant vigil to keep the fire from going out. Every day, after his long hours of work, Doug would have to carry the water and chop the wood for the next day.

On baking day we set the sponge in the morning because bread set at night would become chilled. Our yeast was made with Magic Yeast cakes and potato water. By the time the last loaf was out of the oven, it would be 10 P.M. Mary would sit there in the kitchen keeping the fire going with the semi-kindling wood, perfectly happy with the equivalent of *True Love Stories* or whatever they had in those days, to keep her company. At 10 P.M. the sun was still shining.

We gave John his daily bath by the big heater in the front room, as the mornings were still chilly. Doug had made me a screen fitted with pockets to hold the bath necessities and this we placed behind the tub to keep off any draft, the little tin tub sitting on a wooden box. I held him in my lap to dress him, while Mary came in and carted away the tub. Our teamwork was perfect.

Mr. Schellinger—"Shelley"—was the head assayer for the company and did the retorting, melting, pouring, and assaying of the gold which came in from the nine dredges and all the hydraulic mines. The assay office was a very interesting place, completely equipped for handling the large amount of gold which was brought in. Each dredge was "cleaned up" of its gold, which, in the form of amalgam, was taken to the assay office in locked iron buckets. Here the weight was checked against the weight declared when it left the dredge, a mere formality, and then the amalgam was put into the retort to drive off the quicksilver, which was vaporized and distilled and used again and again. To avoid salivation the operators wore gas masks.

The gold was then melted in a crucible, set into a furnace capable of a temperature of 2500 degrees and when melted white-hot was lifted, crucible and all, with long iron tongs by an operator who wore an asbestos apron and asbestos gloves. The crucible was carried on a crane operated by a system of cables and pulleys to a spot directly above an iron table on which rested the iron molds, for all the world like huge bread pans. With precision and delicate maneuvering the crucible was tipped and the molten gold poured, a stream of sparkling liquid fire, into the molds. One mold would contain a bar varying according to the size of the mold from $20,000 to $50,000 in value. Each bar was stamped to show ownership and a sample was drilled from it which Shelley would assay to determine the fineness of the gold and the consequent total value. Gold from the different creeks would differ in fineness, color, and physical appearance, so that an expert could tell from just which place a gold and specimen had come. This was one reason that stolen gold was not easy to dispose of, if its appearance and quality did not tally with the story told by the thief.

When the cleanups came in from the different sources, there would be perhaps as much as $350,000 lying around the assay office in gold bars, and perfectly safe in that land of the Mounted Police. The gold was so heavy that it was hard to handle and almost impossible to lift. Mr. Thomas, known to all as C.A.T., used to have a stock joke for visitors.

"You may have that brick if you can carry it away," he would say. The guest would puff and tug but could not move the bar, while the bystanders looked amused. Carrying gold around the assay office was done by means of a little wagon made entirely of iron, wheels and all. The floor of the assay office was concrete, both for fire protection and because a wooden floor would not have held up under the heavy traffic of the gold bars. The concrete floor also averted the loss of gold dust and quicksilver in cracks between boards of a wooden floor.

Blond Shelley was a quiet-spoken, efficient young man with gentle manner and not much to say. He had great ability in his field and also in his hobbies, which were photography and furniture, and he took many pictures of us all. I think that we did not give him half the credit for all that he could accomplish.

Hoyt stopped in frequently for dinner. I would put John to sleep in his buggy and wheel him to a corner of the front room. After dinner Hoyt and Doug would shout many verses of many ribald songs while I played the piano and John peacefully slept, Mary grinning at the kitchen doorway, a dish towel in her hand. Sometimes the boys would dance together, singing,

> If *I* had minded *moth*–er,
> I'd *not* be here to*day*,

plus vigorous stampings, catcalls, and various pantomimes.

Hoyt would extract delicately a handkerchief from Doug's hip pocket, mop his face fastidiously and return the handkerchief, dancing all the time. Or Doug would pause and polish his boot daintily on the back of Hoyt's trouser leg, keeping time to the music, swaying and never missing a beat, always deadly serious.

When I was too busy to play for them, Doug would take the piano. A good dancer, he had a fine sense of rhythm and could play any tune by ear, but his wrong bass notes made a doleful accompanimeit to their raucous singing. Hoyt, as assistant superintendent of dredges, and Doug, as thawing superintendent, both had responsibilities beyond their years, and this was their way of blowing off steam. The performance might go on for hours, but it never disturbed Sourdough John.

I was learning to make soap. I decided to utilize the drippings from our breakfast bacon and ham, and Doug told me the cook at the mess house would be glad to get rid of some of his drippings. So I consulted my *Century Cookbook,* a wedding present, and started in. It was no trick at all, and I even beat air into my soap to make it float. Then I poured it into corset boxes which were exactly the right shape for the long slender bars. After they were cool and hardened, I cut the soap bars into cakes the right size to handle. The soap was better than anything I could buy, and I continued to make pounds of it every year.

Washing the laundry had been such an ordeal in the winter that I dreaded it from start to finish. First there was the heating of water, a long process. Getting the tubs in from the cache where they hung on nails and warming them up was another disagreeable duty. Then, after the job was done, the water had to be disposed of a bucket at a time, poured out on the snow, which meant sweater, mittens, arctics, and a lot of such bother. The clothes were wrung out by hand and hung indoors in the severest weather, making a steaming labyrinth of the kitchen, or when the weather was fairly mild, hung outdoors. Hanging clothes outside required another technique. One had to wear mittens to keep the hands from freezing, and when these became wet they must be removed and others substituted. Sometimes the day would be so cold that all I had to do was to bend the clothes over the line and they would freeze to it without the necessity of using clothespins. I had to be very careful not to tear them when I took them off again, all stiff and frozen and piled in the basket like sheets of cardboard.

Although frosted and beautifully bleached by the freezing, the clothes were not dry when I brought them in at the close of the day, so they would have to be dried in the house overnight. It was after wrestling with the washing on a very cold winter day that I stood in the middle of the kitchen floor and said loud enough for Fate, or whatever it is that listens and never replies to our human plaints, to hear, "Now I have had *e - n - u - f, with a capital F!"*

Sourdough

1912 — 1913

9. Visitors From Afar

By summertime I had completely forgotten all the trials of the winter, and I loved this north country with renewed devotion. Washing became really fun. I had my super-duper soap that I made myself; I could leave the tubs on the back porch all the time and wash out there while I soaked in the beauty of the Klondike River back of the house and the hills across and beyond the river. One hill especially I called my mountain, and I watched it every day, its color changing with the seasons, the play of light and cloud shadows on its slopes. Little breezes brought the scent of wild roses to me, and bees hummed in the blossoms. Summer verdure and baby robins grew equally fast in that eternal daylight and were wonderful to watch. The clear, sweet air made me thank my stars I was alive and right in that spot.

My fragrant wood fire crackled and snapped in the little stove as the water heated for the tubs. I could bury my arms to the elbows in the fluffy suds and swish the clothes into freshness and cleanness, producing a pleasant miracle. Hanging them up in the bright sunshine while the friendly birds sang nearby and the breeze blew them from the line in gay banners was a rare experience too, only to be heightened by going out to gather them in at the end of a long serene day, sweet-smelling from the sun and the breeze that fluttered them. I never wanted to iron the sheets and pillow slips, because ironing destroyed that delicious sun-drenched perfume. But the real uplift came from knowing I had done something fundamental and useful.

I liked to wash the windows too, seeing them emerge so clear that everything they framed looked brighter and cleaner. It was a little like having a good talk with Doug over something that I was unsure of. His engineering mind would brush away all the hazy obscurities of the question and produce the facts on which we could go to work, all clear-cut and exact and ready to frame!

So the pleasant days went by until one day a letter came that put Mary and me into a state of great excitement. Doug's parents were coming to pay us a visit, all the way from San Diego, to see their new grandson. I think Doug was equally excited, but he was so busy we had little time to note his reactions as we buzzed around getting ready for the guests.

The extra bedroom upstairs must be prepared for their use and we must have the house in good order, so Mary and I set to work. We made curtains for the window and manufactured a sort of dresser from potato crates, paint, and chintz. We made a washstand likewise and acquired a washbowl and pitcher of white enamel. The bed was a problem, but we finally borrowed one, a three-quarter size, from the warehouse. The mattress left something to be desired, but we could not help that. We made the bed up with the new comforter I had made at Mrs. Osborn's and a white spread, then stood back and surveyed our handiwork with much satisfaction. It was scarcely credible that we had created such marvels all by ourselves! We hardly stirred for fear of creating a little dust in this freshly scrubbed bower of beauty. At the very last minute, the merest split second ahead of time, we would add a bouquet of wildflowers in a water glass to the improvised dresser—just that perfect touch!

We expected *les parents* in the late afternoon. Doug kept phoning to Dawson every hour to find out when the boat was due. Mary and I had worn ourselves out completely but had the satisfaction which comes with the secret knowledge of clean cupboards, plenty of food in reserve, and the washing and ironing all done. John slept, unconscious of the family dither.

Finally we learned that the boat would not be in until six-thirty the following morning, so we all went to bed exhausted.

In great haste Doug dressed and was off to Dawson the next morning, while Mary and I made the beds and straightened up the house before we prepared the breakfast. Then here they came, in Doug's buckboard. Amid laughter, greetings, and much ado over baggage, they were taken into the house, which looked quite beautiful to us but must have looked as novel to them as Mother's smart traveling suit and furs looked to us, in contrast to our regulation clothes, Doug in khaki and high boots and I in a simple housedress.

After the parents were settled in their lovely new room, they unpacked and brought down many gifts, which we opened with as much excitement as if it were Christmas. We did nothing but talk the rest of the day. Father wanted to write postcards to his many friends, while Mother had to get acquainted with the new grandson. Hoyt came in to dinner, and we all visited until Father asked, "What time is it?"

"Ten to twelve," Doug answered, rather loudly, no doubt thinking of his rising hour the next morning.

It was broad daylight. Father looked at his watch, shook it and returned it to his pocket. "Oh, yes, midnight sun," he murmured. "Come, Clara, we were up pretty early this morning. This daylight certainly fools a person!"

At breakfast the next morning both Mother and Father appeared a bit distrait. It was disclosed later that for many years they had occupied separate rooms, and the joint occupancy of a bed not much wider than a couch had not brought about that settled slumber so much desired by the global travelers. As for the comforter, it was but a flimsy thing at best and did not provide the warmth necessary for San Diegans suddenly transported to the Yukon.

So during the day Father gathered many small boughs of spruce and spread them on the back porch of the vacant house next door. Over these he spread several of our heavy blankets and some bedding, declaring that now he had a bed just suited to him and reminiscent of his many camping trips in the mountains. Mother was provided with more warm covers, and now everybody was happy.

Father could not stand Doug's long trips and long hours, but when they did appear together they were taken for brothers. Finally Doug took a day off and drove the whole family up the famous El Dorado and Bonanza creeks to see the hydraulic mines and the dredges. Alas for plans which should have been happily fulfilled! It rained the entire day and John yelled all the way home from the Forks. It was a silent group that climbed down from the surrey when we reached home that evening and Doug went to put the horses away. The Californians were not used to a summer climate where it could rain any minute!

The Thomases gave us a grand dinner party soon after and that made up for it a little, as well it might, with the Thomas brand of hospitality.

Aside from these highlights the days were quiet ones, punctuated by the time Mother decided to bake some of her famous baking-powder biscuits for Doug's dinner at six. Doug appeared at nine. During the interim Mother sat poised and ready to pop those biscuits into the oven, a few at a time because the oven was so small. The three-hour suspense wore heavily upon her, but I was accustomed to such goings on and never expected my husband until I saw him.

Doug was working such long hours and so hard that when he came home late and tired he was not in the mood for much visiting. Mother told me afterward she missed his laughter, so spontaneous when he was a boy. His heavy responsibilities gave little impetus to laughter, but he could let down on occasion and be himself, as I knew.

Father mooned about with not much to do, sitting on the front porch reading until midnight almost every night, forgetting when it was time to go to bed. There was no outside diversion such as is found in a community and no opportunity to go hunting. He could not go with Doug on his trips every day. So it was not surprising that after two weeks they left for home. I wonder that they endured it as long as they did.

Father had had some experience with roughing it on his hunting trips, but to Mother it must have been a real ordeal. We hated to see them go but took them into town and waved goodbye as the steamer *Casca* pulled away from the dock at 11:30 P.M. For the first time in two weeks Father must have slept comfortably.

One of nine camps operated by the Thawing Department.

Sling dumping, with Doug and his 30,000-cord woodpile.

Notice sent to all camps.

Yukon Gold Co. Office, Dawson,
Feb.27, 1913.

NOTICE TO ALL Y.G.CO. FOREMEN:

PUT THE ENCLOSED POSTERS up on telegraph poles and other conspicu-
ous places along the main traveled road near your plant, and wherever
they will be most easily seen.

Insist upon night watchmen being armed. I have obtained special
permits from Judge Macauley to allow each night watchman to carry arms

No fires will be allowed on the dredge. The watchmen must patrol
around the dredge continuously, and vigilance must not be relaxed for
a moment.

(Signed) D.H.Perry.

$5000.00

REWARD

On or about February 22, 1913, Yukon
Gold Company's dredge No. 1, situate on
No. 95 Below Discovery on Bonanza Creek
was wrecked by dynamite. Yukon Gold
Company will pay $5000.00 reward to any
one that will furnish the Royal Northwest
Mounted Police with sufficient information
to convict the person or persons that caused the said explosion.

YUKON GOLD COMPANY

John and Eudora at Gold Bottom, winter of 1912.

Christina leaves Dawson at midnight, July, 1913. Left to right: Mrs. Ferry, Christina, Mrs. Schellinger, Mr. Schellinger.

Seeing Christina off. Left to right: Mr. Pretty, Christina, Mr. Powell, Mrs. Ferry, Mr. Ferry, Elsie Schellinger.

John with a quarter of a million in gold bricks. (Summer, 1914.)

Our red cabin on the hill.

The red cabin in winter, 1913.

Mrs. Ferry and John out for a stroll.

Another view of the cabin in 1913.

Left to right: Mrs. Ferry (with John), Miss Iredell (with Charlie Thomas), Mrs. Schellinger (with her cat), Mrs. MacFarland (with Bunny), Mrs. Costar (with Garrison Guntor).

On board the Princess May, *October, 1914.*

John and his leash on the Princess May.

"Soapy Smith" and the gang in Skagway, Alaska, 1898. Fourth and fifth from left; George M. Esterly and Mr. Jardine. Seventh from left to extreme right; Mr. Bartlett, Dougall McMurray, Major Z. G. Wood, F. F. Clark, "Soapy Smith," "Doc" Runnells, "Sam."

July drifted into August, and August into September. Mary and I were making jelly from some of the berries we picked during John's daily airings. Slender, dark-eyed Mary, left with responsibility for the jelly while I was feeding John, appeared with troubled face.

"The jelly don't boil, Mis' Ferry; it just flubbles."

"Your fire isn't hot enough," I suggested. "Put in more wood."

The popping and murmuring in the little stove soon told me that Mary had more fire and the jelly would turn out all right. Every glass we made, clear and jewel-like, was miraculous to me. I hoarded them all on my shelves, gloating over them like a miser and thinking about how much Doug would enjoy them in the winter.

Doug was always easy to feed. In fact, I used to say that he would eat creamed ten-penny nails and call them good. One Guggie wife, when urging her husband to have more appetite, said once, "Eat, Ralph, eat like Doug Ferry." My meals were never the problem that meals were to many a Klondike house-keeper.

Doug never knew what I was going to call him; it might be Snodgrass or Petunia Face, or whatever happened to come into my head at the moment. He would assume the new role instantly and reply in a meek petunia-face voice, "Yes, ma'am" to my salutation. On the other hand, I never knew when to ex-pect my serious hard-working husband to turn into a sophomore who would wheel around the room, waltzing by himself, arms outstretched and fingers snapping, singing in a burst of full baritone, "You are my ba-a-by, too-dle ooo-dle-oo."

No matter how rough his clothes were, his black hair was always brushed to a sealskin smoothness, the contents of his pockets arranged just so, even when he wore heavy muddy boots and a faded old khaki coat.

An old friend, one of the Stanford professors we knew, said, "Doug was really hatched a dude!"

That summer John grew, Doug worked, and I learned more

about housekeeping and a lot about babies. With John in his buggy I explored the whole area of the plant and with Doug sometimes took a drive, but not often. Occasionally Mrs. Osborn would pay us a visit, sometimes with little Harriett. The time was one of long days and followed routine, of teaching Mary and of learning myself. There was a deep and settled feeling of belonging as the months went on, and I had been in the North over a year.

John had outgrown all his first baby clothes, and I was busy making him a new outfit. At that very time Mrs. Coldrick came out to spend the day and brought John a little jacket. She had made it herself, and I thought it must be typically English, since it obviously was not American and practical. Already too small for John, it was made of pink velvet, lined with white silk. All the edges were ornamented with an elaborate decoration of fluted white ribbon. It was delectable to look at, must have taken hours to make, and was utterly impractical since it could never be laundered. I loved it because it was so like its giver.

Mary often went to Dawson to see her family getting rides by various means. There was a stage that went in every day from the creeks, and the company errand-teamster, Danny, also would oblige with transportation. She usually came back with some small luxury to add to our enjoyment of the day; often it was ice cream. She and I would make a party out of the ritual of eating it, setting a small table and consuming it slowly to make it last longer.

Other days she roamed the hills every afternoon in her time off. One day she astonished me by taking the little .22 rifle with her and coming back with two rabbits for dinner. As usual Doug was eating at one of the camps, so Mary and I feasted by ourselves.

Suddenly summer was no more, and we felt again the presentiment of the cold which was merely lurking back of beyond, ready to pounce upon us again with all its relentless ferocity. As the wild cranberry and blueberry and the kinnikkinnick felt the first touch of frost, the hills turned gold and red. We began to think of Dawson and a house for the winter. It was now time to begin negotiation for that little green house I liked up on Seventh Avenue. Mrs. Thompson had moved some weeks before. When I wrote to the owners, the answer was favorable.

Doug and I drove in one evening and paid the first month's rent. The house was ours for the winter, and I was well pleased. Mrs. Osborn would live just two blocks below us on Fifth; Mrs. Johnson on Sixth, just the next corner; and the Garrison Costars next door.

On September 22 we woke to find everything frozen solid. Mary and I worked faithfully to finish the sewing and keep the routine going at the same time. The owners took the piano out of the house and some of the other furniture, leaving us a living room that seemed even more bare and cold.

While I was busy one morning, Marian Gifford, a friend from Dawson, walked in. She sat down wearily in one of our hard rocking chairs. "Tired," she groaned. "I cleaned, and Liquid Veneered all the furniture, before I walked out here."

"Stay for lunch."

"No." She wore a silly expression, as if she were not quite sure whether to smile or to frown and had her mouth ready to go either way. "I should get back by noon. All I came for was to see if you were doing what you ought to be doing on your schedule." She went over and looked at it, where it hung on the wall.

"You ought to be dusting," she said accusingly, "according to this, and you're baking cookies. I smell them."

"All right, all right," I agreed, "you may have some." I liked Marian. Tall and dark, she was talented and gallant, making an effort to be contented in a world of older people and young marrieds, with no real companionship of her own, while she kept house for her father, a fine gentleman but rather austere.

Marian loved to tease me about my schedules. Experience taught me that unlike a school program, my routine must be elastic enough to allow for the unpredictable human element, like a baby, or a husband late for dinner, so that the interruption would not throw me into confusion. I was forever trying adjustments and changes to see if at last I could have a schedule that would work and was always coming a cropper over it. Marian was my amused and critical commentator.

No one used to shopping in large well-equipped stores can realize how much those who live in isolated areas depend on their mail-order catalogues. The arrival of the Fall and Winter catalogues from the big mail-order houses of eastern Canada was the formal announcement of the coming season as well as our encyclopedia for future wants. They became the objects of most careful research—the new hats, the fullness of sleeves, how many gores in the new skirts as well as their length, the disposition of pockets and other trimming features of coats. All these items were carefully checked over, giving us hours of glamour and inspiration.

That was not all. We browsed among the pages devoted to household wares, linens, drugs—such nuggets of value, enchantingly described. Some of them we had never even heard of or seen, but it did seem prudent to consider them as perhaps valuable in mitigating the rigors of a long Dawson winter.

So we sharpened our pencils and made out long lists of orders. Then, adding up the totals in the last column to the right, we were horrified to find to what lengths of extravagance our wishfulness had led us. Back over the order again, curtailing the fanciful gadgets with which we had livened our prosaic feast of necessities.

The bill would be enough, at best, and looked very formidable, causing a faintness at the pit of the stomach. I did not stop to consider that we never spent money by day in little driblets as most housewives do, and thus I was justified in spending more at one time.

The order was finally made out, the money order bought and the envelope sealed, with its printed warning, "*Have you enclosed the proper amount? Have you forgotten anything?*" That last was a bogey that could haunt one for days after the envelope had been dropped in the post-office slot and departed into the unknown. Especially could it haunt *me*, who surely was not one of those superhumans who never make mistakes and never forget anything. All I could do now was to shrug and leave the outcome to fate. The die was cast, the order mailed; now I could await the inevitable.

After weeks and weeks of waiting there would one day come to our door a bulky package, done up very stoutly in brown paper, with the name of the mail-order house on the label.

Now to relish to the full the realization of our dreams, to see in actuality those glamorous articles displayed so cunningly in the catalogues adorning smiling ladies and strong, silent men —on different pages, of course. Especially glamorous were they in the pages devoted to the heavy woolen underwear, as the residents of those pages chatted gaily and unconcernedly while clad in "short-stout" or "extra-tall," long or short sleeves, or 95 per cent wool!

The bundle opened at last—string saved, of course—a number of articles came to light, limp and shapeless from being tightly compressed in packing, each in its own envelope bearing the catalogue number and price. We laid them out for inspection and checking with our list. *Is this all?* Is it possible we spent all that money for this sparse array? How unglamorous as we shake them out and they hang droopily from our hands! Why in the world did we ever think we wanted *that* thing, which looked at us so seductively from the catalogue? We shall never be so foolish again.

By and by the various articles took on value and were absorbed usefully into our lives. We were grateful for them and could hardly wait for the Spring catalogues and another orgy of devouring their contents and making out our orders.

10. The Winter of Our Content

IT WAS PLANNED THAT MARY and I would move into town the first week in October and Doug would remain until the plant closed for the winter. On October 5 the much-loved hill across the river behind our house was covered with snow. Now I had seen it in every season. It was time to go. We said goodbye to the warehouse and the plant until next year, and I moved the following morning. As usual Denny took our things, and Doug brought Mary, John, and me to the town house.

As I walked up the steps to the porch I saw some late pansies, purple among their still-green leaves, blooming on the embankment around the house on the sheltered side. They were a sweet welcome, but what Mary exclaimed over, as we deposited various articles on the kitchen table, was the big kitchen stove.

"Look at that grand cookstove!" was her delighted comment. "I can't help thinking what lovely cakes and pies are going to come out of it!"

It did seem huge in comparison with our wee stove at the plant, and we promised ourselves to make the most of it.

Mary and I commenced happily to settle the house while the October sunshine flooded the front windows during the middle of the day. Doug had gone back immediately to the plant, and the old familiar loneliness was with me as I worked and our voluble kitchen clock industriously knitted up time into all the hours I would have to spend until he moved into town.

We were going to like this house. It faced in such a way that it caught all the sun and from its windows I could see the streets of Dawson winding down to the river and the town itself spread out beneath me. The Johnsons' house on the corner was a fine home with a fenced yard, big lawn, and lovely garden, since they had their own greenhouse and could start all their plants under glass early in the spring. The amazingly prolific characteristic of northern summers could be seen here in their setting of green lawns until the first frosts cut them down.

I could see Mrs. Osborn's roof and felt closer to her than I ever had been. As our friends found out that I was in town, the telephone began to ring and I saw that I would be given little time to be lonely.

Mary slept at home, coming to work for me during the day. Our house consisted of bedroom, living room, dining room, and kitchen, with the usual closets, a pantry, and a cache built around the back door. In the bedroom Doug had a large sheet-iron drum installed which was connected to the heater in the living room by stovepipes through which the smoke had to pass before it could be released up the chimney. The drum provided added heat for the bedroom but was a nuisance because it collected creosote and had to be cleaned out very frequently.

The furniture was nondescript but adequate and comfortable. In the dish cupboard were six majolica salad plates in grape-leaf design. I begged the owner to let me buy them, as I knew perfectly well that she did not value them at all and that they would be broken by subsequent tenants. She firmly refused to sell them, just to be perverse, I thought, but I tried to get all the use of them that I could while I lived there.

As soon as we were settled enough to find our things in the bureau drawers and had some groceries for a meal, I put on clean clothes and took John to call on Mrs. Osborn. It was good to see her again and to be enveloped in the warm, big-hearted friendship which she poured out so generously. She marveled at John's weight, seventeen pounds, and his growth in general.

Doug came to town for a few days, made arrangements for the winter's wood supply and for cases of canned goods from the plant. Wood and food—these were the first things to be thought of after our necessary warm clothing. These being provided for, we could face the winter with fortitude.

The old associations, interrupted by our summer at the plant, were now pleasantly revived. I went to call on Eileen and her baby, Margaret, just a few days younger than John, and saw other friends I had not seen all summer, as well as collecting from the library the last volume of the *History of Architecture*. Clara Costar ran in at all hours, and one day Mrs. Thomas came bringing Chesterlyn and Margery and stayed for tea. We had toasted muffins, to which Chesterlyn took a great fancy.

The storm doors and windows were put up for the winter, but this time there was no need to chink the logs and shiver in the process, because this house was well built and warm. As the last boat left for Whitehorse I settled back and had no qualms. We were braced for the cold weather and could pretend to be nonchalant about it.

Christmas presents were not going to be a problem that year. I had sent to Ireland for linens during the summer and was hemstitching and monogramming towels and pillow slips. For Mother Ferry there had to be something very special. I embroidered elaborately a wide petticoat flounce of fine nainsook and whipped to the scalloped edge some handmade linen lace I had sent for. So much embroidery was not good for the eyes, but the fine stitchery yielded an esthetic pleasure to the worker that was not found in other kinds of handwork. The even stitches, laid so precisely along the pattern on the fine white linen, gave an exquisite sense of delicacy and value to an otherwise prosaic undertaking.

Not satisfied with all the embroidery, I was dressing a doll. I had always adored making doll clothes, and when the ladies of the Catholic church asked me to dress a doll for their bazaar, I gladly agreed. With a very fine needle and 200 thread I made the underwear from fine nainsook, trimming it with narrow Cluny lace. The doll was about nine inches high with bisque head and real hair, pretty enough to warrant such fussing. I rolled the hems and whipped on the real lace and put the seams together with *entredeux*, using the tiniest of pearl buttons and buttonholes. There was a silk dress, a little blue velvet coat lined with white satin, and a white satin hat made from a pleated ornament I had discarded from a white felt of mine. Altogether the ensemble was quite dazzling. I loved the doll devotedly, and the church sold her for ten dollars.

Snow came with the last of October. It is fortunate for northern countries, deprived of winter sunlight, that snow is white and not, for instance, dark green! I was sewing and had the dining-room table covered with sewing materials and scraps of fur, while I was remodeling a fur hat to go with my coat and adding to it a bunch of satin berries in shades of bright red. Clara Costar came running in the back door, wearing her raccoon coat and on her head a frivolous little white lace cap, a style we all adopted for mornings. The incongruity between the coat and the cap was delightful.

"How do you cook a pot roast?" she wanted to know. "I am going to have one for dinner."

I explained, and she vanished. We went in and out of each other's houses without ceremony, borrowed recipes and eggs and traded ideas, while our boyfriends were away. When the winter season started, Garrison and Doug would both return to keep the home fires burning, so Clara and I would have less wood to tote and more meals to cook. Garrison was coming in that day, hence the pot roast.

Dawson society was already in full swing when I arrived in town. The new commissioner, George Black, had arrived that summer with his dynamic American-born wife, and they were inaugurating the winter season with card parties, luncheons, and dinners. The commissioner of Yukon Territory is appointed by the Dominion government and corresponds to the governor of one of our United States.

All of Dawson society turned about the axis of Government House and the Blacks. Once started, the round of bridge parties continued. Mrs. Osborn, as a very special friend of Mrs. Black's, was in the thick of the whirl. Mrs. Black had come to Dawson in the early days and had actually walked over the Chilkoot Trail. In the course of a colorful and eventful life in the Yukon she had made many friends, who were delighted to see her return as the First Lady of the Territory.

I did not play bridge very often, giving John as an excuse. Interested in so many other things besides bridge, I did not have the time to devote to becoming a really good player. One woman took me to task for refusing the parties, telling me I was staying at home too much.

"I can play bridge any time in my life," I answered her, "but I can enjoy this baby only now. I'll take the baby and let the bridge parties wait."

She shook her head over this incomprehensible attitude and left me as a hopeless case. To this day I have never been able to find much time for bridge and probably have missed a lot of fun. On the other hand, as long as there are books to read, music to hear, the outdoors to explore all over the world, and wonderful people to know, I am afraid I won't get around to bridge.

Mary had left me, and I was carrying on alone. What with the housework, the care of John, and his laundry, I was going to bed every night completely tired out. When Doug moved to town in November and realized this, he sent for Mary at once, and things began to go more smoothly so that I felt less like a wreck by dinnertime.

When Doug discovered what we had to contend with in drying John's daily laundry, he started to cope. As it was, if we hung the diapers outdoors they froze instantly and eventually had to be dried inside anyway. I had lines strung across the kitchen right-of-way for that purpose. Doug said that in after years, if anyone should ask him what the thing was that he remembered most vividly about the Klondike, he could answer "Being slapped in the face by drying diapers."

He devised a square frame, strung parallel clothes lines through it, and rigged it with pulleys and ropes to the ceiling, where the air was warmest and where the wet articles would be out of the way. After hanging it full, all Mary had to do was to hoist it to the ceiling, where it could remain as long as necessary. Then she could lower it to remove the washing. I really thought much more of this invention of Doug's than I did of the fancy sling that hoisted a carload of wood!

There was a certain maiden lady in Dawson we usually called Becky, who liked to spend a great deal of time at our house and who was one of the two or three women in the world Doug thoroughly disliked. One of her favorite plans was to come to see me in the afternoon, stay for dinner and spend the evening. Then Doug was expected to take her home, a long walk in the cold both ways for him. After she had done this several times, Doug came home one evening to find her there.

He had been away for dinner, and Becky had waited until he came home.

He spoke to us sweetly, so sweetly, in fact, that I suspected something right there. Then he went on to the kitchen. There was much rattling of stove lids and handling of wood. Then I heard the washtub being brought in from the cache and the wash boiler being put on the stove and filled with water—many, many buckets. I was in high bewilderment. This sounded like a bath, but I knew that Doug had stopped at Wholoomoloo for a shower and that was the reason he was later than usual. I tried to keep up a conversation with Becky while my ears were tuned to the sounds in the kitchen. It was getting late too, and time Becky was going home.

Doug was still pottering around. Once he appeared, went into the bedroom and came out again, his arms full of something all covered up with a bathrobe. More mystery. Any minute, though, he would come in, Becky would get around to saying good night, and off they would go, in the cold and the dark. Poor Doug! It is tough to be gallant at times. He looked tired too.

Suddenly a queer look came over Becky's face, and at the same instant I realized what was going on.

Loud splashings came from the kitchen, interspersed with bursts of "Wait till the sun shines, Nel---*lie*," at the top of Doug's voice, which was penetrating, if I ever heard one that was.

"*And this is the end of a per-r---fect day.*" His tones rang out clear and exultant. More splashings.

Doug was taking a bath!

There was nothing else to do. Becky just got up and went home alone. After that she hardly ever stayed to dinner.

Now that I had Mary again to stay with John, I could catch up with my social duties. Clara Costar and I went together to pay many calls. Taking our card cases and white gloves would give us a dressed-up feeling very salutary after a morning spent in housework. We went to Government House several times, a visit which never failed to thrill.

Mrs. Black, prematurely gray and smartly dressed, would

have given atmosphere to any house, but she had done even better with the mansion which housed the governors of the Yukon. Hitherto an ugly, rather run-down structure, the building sat in extensive grounds close to and overlooking the Yukon River. It was a large frame house, two stories and a half, with porches around three sides of the first floor and a recessed balcony on the second where the Blacks slept out under fur robes even in the coldest weather. Large, and built for entertaining, it had been neglected under previous administrations until it resembled a barracks.

Under the genius of Mrs. Black it became a spacious, charming mansion, the large drawing rooms filled with handsome furniture, luxurious carpets, and satisfying color and arrangements. Mrs. Black did not neglect the table service, ordering a complete set of china with the Canadian maple-leaf décor, and silver likewise, while the linens were woven to include the same design.

Now Dawson had something to be proud of with one of the most gifted and charming women in the country to act as chatelaine. A visit to Government House was a trip into another country so far as the rest of us were concerned and did much to keep up our morale. Since there was a steam-heated greenhouse on the property, Mrs. Black, herself a distinguished botanist, kept the rooms at Government House always lovely with flowers.

Mrs. Black and Mrs. Osborn spent the afternoon with me one day shortly before we had another interesting visitor. Both Doug and Hoyt had mentioned a timekeeper at one of the dredges who was out of the ordinary run of workmen. Originally from England, he had come here from the States—New York, to be exact—and taken any job he could get at the time. They spoke of him so often that I said to Hoyt, "Bring him over to call."

One evening they came. William Desmond Taylor, the timekeeper, proved to be a gentleman of the world who had at one time been an interior decorator in New York. He had imported old English wood carvings to serve as woodwork for such mansions as William K. Vanderbilt's. Vanderbilt sent him abroad on a special mission, to select and purchase an Oriental rug for a certain room, which cost thirty-five thousand dollars, Mr. Taylor told us in the course of the conversation and our questions.

Mr. Taylor conversed so readily on so many subjects, including art, and was so delightful a guest that I was very curious about him.

"More than one man has come in here to take up an entirely new life," Doug told me, "probably to make a clean break from something he wanted to forget. There is a chance that Taylor is one of them." More than that we did not know, but we could guess much despite his reticence regarding his past.

Mr. Taylor left the Yukon the following year, and we heard that he was in Hollywood. In time he became one of the best-known directors in silent pictures. Years later we heard of his murder, one of the unsolved mysteries of that era.

The days were growing shorter and shorter, and most of our waking hours were spent under artificial light. We gave a farewell dinner for Hoyt, and he left by stage for the Outside. Dawson seemed much emptier after this good friend departed.

Clara Costar came in one morning, the light of ambition in her eye.

"I want to make Garrison some warm pajamas," she told me. "He has always worn night shirts; I think pajamas would be warmer for winter. Do you happen to have a pattern?"

Doug's pajamas would be too big for Garrison, I decided, so we had better think of something else. My faithful cross-barred ones were big, heaven knew.

"I haven't any paper pattern," I told Clara, "but these pajamas are just about right, I should think. Can you use them as a guide?"

Clara carried home the pajamas and worked industriously for several days. The outcome was a beautifully made pajama suit, the buttonholes firm, a hard thing to achieve with Canton flannel, the seams all felled evenly. In short, Clara had turned out a professional job.

Clara was a good little housekeeper, neat and systematic. She had been raised by two maiden aunts who were school teachers, and her whole life had been lived on a fixed program. When she discovered that I, with poor success, was striving to pour my days into a scheduled mold, she begged me not to do it.

"You won't like it," she said with her doubting little smile, "I never did."

She was so earnest about it that I promised. I was pretty wobbly on the schedule business anyway.

Thanksgiving again. A whole year had rolled around since we attended the dinner given by "Mikkle" McCarthy, and now I was a seasoned northerner and what was more, I had a son. This year Mrs. Thomas was entertaining us, all the more generous of her since the company had given each of the office and engineering forces a turkey for Thanksgiving. These were cold-storage turkeys, and we would keep ours for Christmas, as we had done last year.

Frank was preparing three turkeys for the eight engineers and office men and their wives who were invited, making a table of eighteen covers with the Thomases themselves. We were told to bring John, who with other Guggie babies would be put into one of the upstairs rooms at the Thomases' to sleep during the evening.

It was quite mild when we left home for the dinner at seven. John had been undressed and put to sleep in his sleigh, where he would remain until we took him home for the night. The babies were taken upstairs by two of the men, sleighs and all, as their parents arrived and put into a cool bedroom to sleep, with an occasional check-up by Miss Iredell, the Thomas children's nurse.

The long table stretched from the Thomas dining room out into the living room. Every detail of the dinner was as perfect as Frank's talent in the kitchen and Mrs. Thomas's ability as hostess could make it. C. A. T. made us the target of his wit and the jokes he loved to play, while Mrs. Thomas's sure instinct kept the party going as it should. With the example of women

like Mrs. Black and Mrs. Thomas and others, social life in
Dawson was anything but provincial. In fact, as Mrs. Osborn
once said, "Many a little girl who thought she knew something
about society has come into Dawson and received her real social
training right here."

I had begun to notice that as the evening advanced the
room seemed to be a little chilly around the edges. When we
started home sometime around midnight, it was 37 below. We
hurried as fast as we could, so that John would not feel the
sudden cold. I realized again what I had so often heard, that
the thermometer could drop 50 degrees in five hours and that
one must always be prepared for these sudden changes.

Once in our house, we had a lot to do. On such cold nights
Doug would get up about 3 A.M. to refill the heater, which
meant bringing in extra wood. Canned milk, potatoes, eggs,
and other perishables must be put high off the floor. If they
were left in the pantry or at floor level, they would freeze. We
used the dining room table as our repository.

Then John's crib must be taken from the bedroom and the
mattress and blankets warmed by the heater before we put him
to bed. All this took time but was worth the trouble. By morning the kitchen, having no fire, would be almost as cold as the
outdoors. The first thing to do was to touch a match to the fire
already laid the night before.

Our babies were inured to the cold to some degree, as it
was the rule in Dawson to let them sleep outside on the porch
until it was 20 below. Below that, we took them in! They were
bundled in down comforters and their faces covered with several thicknesses of knitted shawl. Little columns of steamy
breath rose from the coverings as they slumbered on. John was
none the worse for such Spartan treatment and seemed to
thrive on it.

That cold spell continued for quite a while. It dropped to
53 below, but our house was so much warmer than that of the
last winter that we did not find it difficult to keep going. The
temperature in our bedroom went down to 16 below zero and
the water froze in the pitcher on the washstand. We had a

down comforter as well as our blankets, but I thought we should have had nightcaps. We wouldn't go outdoors at 16 above in the daytime without a hat! Instead we buried our heads under the covers, leaving just our noses out to breathe. I did put a little cap on John but did not tell my friends for fear they would think I was making a softie out of him.

11. Frappé and Fortitude

MR. MCCARTHY AND HOYT were both Outside for the winter and Doug was in charge of the winter field work, which consisted of dredge repairs, regular maintenance, and so on. He was away from home a great deal, checking on the nine far-flung camps. Many of the working crews stayed Inside in the winter, using up all the money they had saved during the summer's good wages and thus postponing for years the opportunity to go Outside. A few of these men could be used in the abbreviated winter crews. Doug had to make periodic inspections of the dredges and the work as well as direct all the fuel and wood-contract jobs.

While Doug was away, I sewed diligently to make ready all the Christmas packages and add that personal touch considered indispensable in those days. In the same way, women's clothes were seldom ready-made. In fact, "It just shouts 'ready-made'" was a derogatory remark about any garment. Consequently most of us made our own clothes, since dressmakers were scarce in Dawson. We did other naïve things too, such as sweeping our carpets with a broom and washing our clothes by hand, boiling all but the colored ones. All the water for dishes, laundry, and baths must be heated on top of the stove. We baked our bread and cakes, did our own cleaning, and still had time for reading and seeing our friends.

However, women had no civic duties, had few organizations

outside the church, and paid little attention to politics since they had no vote.

Some of our friends were living just for the moment. Although the salaries were large, expenses were high and they thought little about savings. Since Doug was buying some property in California, we had to save. I tried not to buy expensive things, however popular. For that reason I did not take advantage of the opportunity to pick up prime mink or marten pelts, the costliest and most beautiful fur of the North. Besides, I did not think that our position warranted my wearing such valuable furs. Even though the untanned skins were comparatively inexpensive, about thirty dollars per pelt, by the time they were tanned and made into a coat the cost had risen until, as I said to Doug, "We might just as well buy an oil well and let the poor little minks live!" Prime ermine, the tiny skins never dyed in those days, was another possibility in the North, the white ermine coats being suitable only for evening wear.

"You know what that ermine coat makes me think of?" Mrs. Osborn whispered to me once as the owner sailed into view." A thousand dollars' worth of milk tickets!"

There were some very beautiful sable and mink coats worn in Dawson by the wives of prominent men and by others not so prominent. When their wearers appeared, they believed themselves to be the ultimate of something or other, certainly of the sables and the mink! However, there was one good reason for wearing fur, valuable or otherwise, in Dawson. We wore furs for warmth and not entirely to advertise our solvency, as many furs are worn today.

So Doug and I were frugal and we saved, pushing our sights ahead of us into the future. Once I was taken to task for this by an acquaintance. "You'll miss many a nice trip and pretty thing to wear," she reproved me, "that you might just as well have enjoyed." She was probably right, but we had the habit and saved anyway—just a bread-and-butter complex, I suppose.

Christmas that year was exciting because of John, even though he was too young to know anything about it. Our tree gave us much fruit, and we had a very happy day although there was the darkness outside which presaged the further cold which always struck especially hard in January.

And so it did, while Doug must of necessity make a two-day trip to Bonanza. I had sent to Quebec, for one of his Christmas presents, a special sash for him to wear over his fur coat. Tied around the waist, it took the weight of the coat off his shoulders while driving as well as keeping him warmer by holding the coat closer to him. This sash, made by the French Canadians, was hand-woven by a traditional process now almost a lost art. It was about ten feet long, including the fringe, and about a foot wide, made of woolen yarns in red, yellow, blue, and green in a complicated weave. The Canadians called it *ceinture flèche*. Doug wore it whenever he drove and it helped a lot.

While he was away and the temperature dropped and dropped, it was up to me to keep the fires going and the house safe and warm, as Mary never came on those coldest days. Having various skills with which to occupy oneself was an advantage. Those of us who could knit, sew, crochet, or play a musical instrument were more fortunate than the others. Days like these were the test of our morale. No wonder that men having nothing to pass the time with but cards and their own thoughts took to drinking!

One evening I went out about six to close the front storm door, which had stood open during part of the afternoon. Warmth for the house had thawed some of the icicles hanging from the porch and these had dripped to the porch floor, making a little glacier just outside the door. I was unaware of this as I stepped out, leaving the door open behind me in order to take quick hold of the storm door, which lay back against the house.

My feet struck the glacier, and I fell flat on my back, knocked almost senseless by the impact of the floor against my shoulders. I did have enough energy left, however, to roll over, get to my feet, grab the door and swing it around. Then I shut both doors and sat down, weak-kneed, thankful that I was inside the house. Had I lost consciousness, both John and I might have frozen, since Doug was away for two days and

Clara Costar never came over in the evenings. On such a slender thread our lives might sometimes hang.

The evenings were busy times. First, protected by sweater, woolen cap, and mittens, I must bring in a great many chunks for the heater from the cache off the kitchen, enough to fill the heater when I went to bed and once during the night. My kitchen fire had been allowed to die down during the evening so that the stove would cool off, the last embers glowing redly through the open draft. After the stove was completely cold, just before I went to bed I laid a good fire all ready for my match in the morning, so as to lose no time in getting the kitchen warm for breakfast. Plenty of stove wood was kept in the woodbox behind the kitchen stove and it was my job too, while Doug was away, to keep it full. Then there was the aforementioned care of all the perishables, last of all the full teakettle and the flatirons on the heater lid.

During that cold spell the moisture from the air in the kitchen congealed in the form of ice along the floor by the back door, even though it was protected by the cache from the actual outside air. I had a glacier three feet into the kitchen at this spot, about half an inch thick, of ice on the floor, and had to be very careful not to fall there.

Everything done, I could undress by the heater and dash into bed, to curl up in a tight little ball until the area around me warmed up and I could uncurl.

Life was severe but simple. We battled continuously with the cold but we had no war, strikes, inflation, or competition. Our business was never with the public; there was always a demand for our product. It was clean new wealth, never taken from anyone else's necessity. Our social lives were uncomplicated, because we were all in the same boat, and it would have been utterly silly to try to impress each other. We did not collect things, since we could not take them with us when we left for the Outside, except such small things as would go in our trunks.

Our ancestors or family prestige did not act as levers for our social position in this new country. Just one thing counted—could we make good? Making good included two features:

doing our work well enough to make us valuable and taking the country in our stride.

As to that last, we did more than just taking it in our stride. I, for one, loved it, as did many others, so that as long as we live we shall never get over the pull of the North calling us back to her.

I had been baking bread and cake one day and thought of Mary's words about the stove. Those old cast-iron cookstoves with the hot-water reservoirs at the back—how homey and cozy they made our kitchens and how shining we kept them! Indeed, what pies and cakes came out of their capacious ovens, not to mention baked potatoes and pots of delicious baked beans. The grates glowed red and cheerful, the teakettle sang on top of the stove, and all it needed was a cat curled up before the oven door. We had no cat. Cats were too hard to care for in the winter and regularly froze their ears. We managed to be pretty cozy anyway.

Doug came home, and suddenly it was 40 below again, just like that. I had sensed that it was growing colder but was unprepared for this quick drop. Again, as in the winter before, the couch pillows froze to the wall. It was too cold for the water man to come every day, and we had to conserve. The next day it was 65 below. Mary was coming to stay with John, and I had a date with Doug for lunch downtown.

I walked down the hill, seeing with one eye at a time, breathing short, labored breaths. The air was full of frost. It had rushed into the house in billowy clouds as I opened the door to leave. Now it was all around me. I was so intent on keeping warm that I practically collided with Mrs. Osborn, who had been out on a necessary errand and was on her way home. We exchanged greetings from behind our fur collars.

"Isn't this a teaser?" Mrs. Osborn said from behind her collar. "A real teaser, I call it. Where are you going?"

"To meet Doug, for lunch at Pete's," came from behind my furry barricade, my one eye beaming with cordiality.

"Going to Mrs. Black's reception next Saturday?" the other fur collar asked.

"Of course," mine replied. "No mere weather could keep me away."

"This weather is not mere," the answer came back, "but I must be getting home. I set bread this morning and if I don't hurry it will be coming down the street to meet me."

"How do you keep it warm?" I asked, stamping my feet to keep up the circulation.

"Put it behind the heater and wrap it in two sweaters," the other collar called back gaily as Mrs. Osborn turned toward home. "See you Saturday."

I went on my way to meet Doug, my coat white with frost. I met men walking beside their sleighs, beating themselves with their arms to keep warm, their horses heavily blanketed and covered with frost; a few women; and oh, such pathetic dogs, cowering against buildings, anywhere, to escape the stab of the cold.

Pete's was our favorite restaurant in Dawson, and we often went there for lunch, occasionally for dinner. In Dawson there were other places to dine, principally the Regina Hotel, a four-story structure completely sheathed with corrugated iron for fire protection, and the pride of the town, and the Yukonia Hotel, owned and operated by Mr. and Mrs. Segbers, friends of the Osborns.

At Pete's the menu was varied according to the season. Prices seemed terrifically high then but would be considered normal today during postwar prices. Interesting items on the menu for Christmas of 1912 included the following:

3 Ranch Eggs—any style—$2.00
Mountain Sheep Chops, French peas—$1.25
Calf Moose Steak and Jelly—$1.00
Loin of Caribou, Pan Gravy—$1.00
Peel River Stuffed Crane, Currant Jelly—$2.00
"Over the Ice" Stuffed Turkey, Cranberry Sauce—$2.00

"Over the Ice" meant that the item was brought in by heated stages over the winter trail from Whitehorse.

We had our lunch and I hurried home, glad to return to John and the warm fire. When I started up the hill, I saw smoke in great clouds coming from what I supposed was the exact location of our house. I rushed ahead, my heart pounding, forgetting all about the difficulty I had in breathing when it was so cold. Not until I reached the corner by Mrs. Johnson's house could I see that the fire was just a block below us. I opened my own door thankfully and saw Mary standing by the front window trying to see the fire through the frosted panes.

We finally found a handy man who would come to the house for chores, chiefly connected with the woodpile these days. He kept the cache full of chunks and split the wood for the kitchen stove. Doug and I were becoming idle rich, it seemed, after all the hours he had put in on similar jobs. Poor Fred, the handy man, showed me his thumbs, cracked almost to the bone from hard work and the cold. He told me his thumbs would not heal until spring.

During those days it was too foggy to see clearly, but we knew it was time for the sun to appear just for a few seconds at noon. So we are lifted by hope because the sun was on its way back to us. Again there were rugs on the floor in front of all doors and a blanket, hung on nails, over the front door. The frost stood deep on the windows and appeared at the corners of the rooms, from the ceiling to the floor, where the cold had sought and found an entrance through the joints outside the house.

There were reports that it was 72 below zero. Few thermometers would record down to that figure, but the old-timers had a way of telling the temperature by the freezing of different liquors. When rum froze, it was supposed to be 85 below. To our knowledge we had never experienced such cold, but how could we be sure when we had no rum? There was practically no entertaining those days, and our chief concern was keeping the fire going and staying close to it.

It was practically impossible to keep the floors warm. Mrs. Osborn told me that her cat spent its time perched on top of the open door between two warm rooms, the only place in the house it could be comfortable. I tried various kinds of foot-gear and discovered that Doug's fleece-lined slippers over my own shoes were not bad at all for indoor wear. Fortunately John was at the stage known in the South as a "sitting-up baby" and had not yet reached the creeping age. In his buggy, by the stove, he could be kept warm.

When Doug was home we read aloud, close to the heater, and ate our meals there too. Since marketing was so difficult, we ate what there was in the house, subsisting on expensive canned tongue and whatever else we could find in the pantry. I made some blancmange for dessert and set is on a shelf to cool. It froze solid, and we had a sort of extemporaneous ice cream. There was so much laundry and it took so long to dry that Doug went up through the trap door in the ceiling to hang the extra clothes in the attic. We were as smug over this new device as if we had rustled something, as I guess we had.

The noise of the wood sawyer's engine and the whine of the saw were continuous all day, as he replenished the dwindling wood piles with his gasoline-driven saw. How cold that man's hands must have been by the end of the day!

The frost raised the floors, and the houses became more uneven than before. I heard the current gossip of the town as Doug related it to me after office hours, since I had no callers. One man had lost his memory and was selling out. His piano, a baby grand, was selling for four hundred dollars, much less than the probable freight to bring it into the country—such an unheard-of luxury for Dawson! One more contrast besides that of climate in this far-off country.

This cold snap was worse than anything we had encountered the previous winter. For two weeks it did not climb above 50 below; most of the time it was nearer 70. We were getting used to it; our house was so much better than our previous one that the cold was not so hard to endure. Suddenly, with no warning at all, it rose to 20 above. The streets swarmed with baby sleighs and women out for an airing. We felt stuffy and close in the house and there was much airing out in consequence.

Yukon Gold

Now that the cold and resultant frost-fog had abated, we could see that the sun was really appearing a few minutes in the middle of the day. Up to that time there had been no more than a hint, and no full rays in at the window. On January 31, I telephoned several friends that I had sunshine in my window; I saw it before they did because we lived on a hill. That day was memorable in another way: John had his first tooth. We could not celebrate together because Doug was away, but from this time on we could set our sights toward spring.

I took John out for his first ride in many days in the new and larger sleigh that Doug had bought from Bishop Stringer. Little boys were out with their dogs and sleds even after the brief daylight had changed to dark. They carried "bugs" for light. A bug was a lantern, homemade from a tin can, carried sideways with a bail for a handle. Through the bottom was thrust a candle, which, when lighted, heated the tin until it gave off an oily smell. Everybody in Dawson owned a bug and carried it for light on trips to and from home all during the winter.

While I had been hibernating, I was thankful for my sewing. There were no Christmas presents to make now, but from my trunk I took out some fine blue woolen material I had bought several years before and put away, as I had a habit of doing. This would make a lovely new dress. Clara Costar ventured over occasionally and we planned the details. She brought over her new copy of *Good Housekeeping* in great excitement and pointed to a page.

"*Do you see that?*"—dramatically.

"That" was *one extra pleat in the new skirts!*

What if I had overlooked it and cut my dress by last year's design! We both shuddered.

After the dress was finished, I ornamented it with *soutache* braid in a design I made myself. The result was so satisfactory that I could hardly wait to wear it. While the frosty fog outside seemed less real and the nails' popping and the wires' humming just an incident, I was dreaming of spring to come

My new dress would give me a fresh personality and mood with its wearing.

Milder weather came in due course. May Norton appeared one day with a present for John, a lovely white fur robe for his sleigh. The fur was long and soft, the lining white felt extending in an ornamental border beyond the fur. Now John could be as luxurious as anyone could wish when he went out for an airing. On that same day the stage brought in many belated Christmas presents, giving us a holiday all over again.

12. Trip and Trouble

THE TERM "ROADHOUSE" did not then have the connotation that it has today. Those roadhouses were really hotels, respectable overnight stopping places, where meals were served. There was a bar but no unseemly drinking and no implication of night spot as there is in the States.

While some of the roadhouses were rather free and easy, being operated by former dance-hall girls as they grew older and less attractive, others were operated by families and were as decorous as any hotel. One of the former type was located on upper Bonanza. During a spring flood the place was inundated. The owner was heard to remark in great disgust, "It's a damn fine thing! Lookit—a lady has to send in her swamper with rubber boots to get it for her when she wants a drink from *her own bar!*"

The roadhouses were the only stopping places on the creeks and were patronized alike by teamsters, miners, merchants, and travelers, as well as by the Mounted Police when they were after their men, whom they always got! While drinking was not frowned upon, it was kept within decent bounds.

At the Anderson concession on Hunker Creek was a roadhouse known as the Last Chance, which was operated by a French family much as they would have conducted a little inn in France. Their eldest daughter was to be married. The father sent out invitations to his friends and patrons. Doug was invited, since he had once lived there for a short time before I had come into the country. One of the men in the office, newly arrived from the New York office, was asked also, as he had been going around with a Dawson girl who was a friend of the bride.

After the wedding there was a dance in the rather small general room of the roadhouse. The New York man, thinking this was the kind of roadhouse he was used to in the States, started to dance wearing his derby hat and holding a large cigar in the corner of his mouth. He was stopped politely and told that he must get rid of the hat and the cigar or leave the floor.

Outsiders never crashed the parties of the Ping-pongs, but the Ping-pongs often attended the public dances in Dawson, usually keeping to their own groups. On one such occasion there had been a dance in progress at the Arctic Brotherhood and a Ping-pong group attended just for a lark. Among the party were some women who had recently come in from the Outside, where they had learned to dance the one-step. They were showing the others how to do it, in a sort of walk, when the floor manager asked them to get off the floor. The new dance, so popular in the States that season, was just a little too reminiscent of the "ragging" that had been done in the dance halls of early Dawson days and would not be tolerated at a decent dance. So the exclusive Ping-pongs had to be shown by hoi polloi how to behave.

One of the couples seen regularly at the Dawson public dances, who were noted for their beautiful waltzing on skates at the D-three-A's rink, were living together in a common-law marriage, as were some others in the town, unmolested but carefully ignored by the Ping-pongs. Such social incongruities, existing in the once-roaring gold camp, reminded one that Dawson, like an old dance-hall girl who had formerly lived in the midst of excitement and wild doings but had married into respectability, now had nothing in life to look forward to except spending money and acting refined!

When the cold snap ended, I asked Clara Costar, Eileen Morrison, and some others in for tea. Eileen brought Margaret with her, and I was amazed to see how much smaller she was than John, who now weighed twenty-four pounds. Eileen told us that she had discovered something stupendous. During the bitterest cold of the previous two weeks, not without great trepidation, she had omitted Margaret's daily bath and bathed her every other day.

"And," she concluded, "I found out that if you don't bathe a baby every day, it doesn't die."

We listened in fascinated enlightenment.

Doug would be away for several days, then home again. On the days he arrived things seemed to click into harmony and life to have meaning again. Finally he thought of a wonderful plan. It was then the later part of February and there was daily sunshine. Doug decided to take a vacation and at the same time check up on dredge repairs at Gold Bottom and look over the wood being hauled in near there. John and I could go with him. The Costars would drive us out and return the next day with the team. They would stay at the Gold Bottom Hotel, while we could use a little cabin back of the hotel which Doug knew was empty.

"You do sprout the nicest ideas," I enthused, as I started to rush over to tell Clara the news. She was as excited about it as I and we began to make plans immediately, to leave in safety all our perishables and assemble clothes for the trip.

Doug and Garrison had so much to do the day we left that it was five o'clock in the afternoon when we drove away from the house. The company sleigh we used was kept at Pickering's, a "bobs" with red runners and plenty of bearskin robes. The company grays were fairly fast and kept to a steady trot. Contrary to custom, Doug did not drive but sat in back with me to help hold John, who lay across our laps in cap, sweater, shawl, and a bag made from his down comforter. Garrison drove well and we made good time, singing Stanford songs

while we jingled along. The air was mild and the snow gave
us enough light to see the road, but the grays would have
carried us even if we could see nothing. We reached Gold
Bottom at seven-thirty, having covered the twenty miles in two
hours.

Ever since Honeymoon-on-Hunker, I had thought of the
Gold Bottom Hotel more or less as home. It welcomed us into
a barroom heated comfortably by the huge heater, the wavy
floor and dark linoleum looking strangely familiar, yet different
in the wintertime. Two canaries, singing in total disregard of
the frosted windows, and big hanging baskets of wandering
Jew gave hominess to the crude surroundings.

We ate a huge supper in the dining room, likewise warmed
by a big heater, then, full of drowsy comfort, went to our cabin
in the back after saying good night to the Costars. They would
have to sleep in a cold unventilated room in the hotel, where
all the windows as usual were nailed shut for the winter.

The cabin assigned to us belonged to the owners of the
hotel. It was furnished for the most part with homemade furniture. We put John to bed on the couch and barricaded it with
chairs for a railing. The cabin contained two rooms and a
kitchen, which we looked at shivering and closed up. The bed
consisted of a homemade frame on which were set the springs
and two mattresses, the top one only three-quarters size, making the edges of the bed sloping.

The water supply was melted snow. Water for the hotel
was brought from a spring nearby, the same one patronized by
Doug for us when we lived there. It was brought to the hotel
in barrels drawn on a sled by a fat pony.

After one night of trying to sleep two in a bed on the three-
quarter mattress, we decided that Doug would take the couch.
We made a bed for John in a homemade armchair, supple-
mented with two camp chairs, pillows, two fur coats, one big
blanket, and two smaller ones. We knew he would sleep beautifully!

The hotel itself was built of logs, as was the cabin. The
hotel strung out along the road for possibly fifty feet, the

spaces between the logs filled in with white plaster. The second story was low, the windows small and four-paned, the sashes about twenty inches square and impossible to open. Most of the walls were out of plumb, the floor as well. Muslin had been tacked over the logs on the inside of both hotel and cabin, and wallpaper pasted to the muslin, how long ago we could only guess.

Our cabin snuggled into the hill behind the hotel and was neat and orderly. The ceilings were only as high as the doors. Cotton portieres and couch cover, in red, as well as a tapestry table cover gave the color required for cheerfulness, while cheap lace curtains, hung on wooden rods with wooden rings, provided elegance. There were books of poetry in padded leather covers as well as ancient magazines on the table and gaudy cushions on the couch. A Brussels carpet covered the floor. One could see that this was a luxury cabin and money had been no object in its furnishing. The heater was burned through at the back and leaked creosote, while the green birchwood provided for our use smoked continually. Fortunately the weather was very mild, so it did not greatly matter.

Mrs. Lemaster, who owned the cabin, asked us to the hotel the next day to have cake and whipped cream, since they owned the only cow on the creek. Clara and Garrison joined us in the feast. They were going to stay until after lunch, take some pictures with Garrison's new Graflex camera, and then drive the team back to Dawson.

There were many things to see. The Lemasters had five big hairy pups they were raising for a dog team, promising us a ride the next time we came. Since the pups were very mischievous, carrying off moccasins and overshoes if not watched, we were told to bring ours inside the house instead of leaving them at the door. Mr. Lemaster was hydraulic-mining on the hill and would have made a lot of money, he said, with sufficient water, but there was no way to get it. It was one of those cases of "so near and yet so far" which often happened in that country.

We found that the little one-room schoolhouse also served

as a home for the teacher, her husband, and three children. The big barn for the hotel was built high up on the tailings left by the dredge, of necessity since there was so little land between the road and the hill.

Out in the bright sunshine we took pictures and forgot the snow, the day was so mild. We watched some miners at work. They had decided to tunnel under the road with a shaft and had found enough pay to warrant their going on. The ground had to be thawed ahead of them with wood fires. The smoke and fumes were carried off by a smokestack, emerging strangely from the ground at the side of the hotel, like the outlet from some hidden inferno.

We ate good and extremely jolly meals at tables filled with rough men in working clothes, miners, and teamsters hauling wood for a contractor who was putting in several thousand cords for the company. This was the place to see the real life of the Klondike; Dawson was too citified and fashionable. Children here were regarded as little less than angels and in no way as nuisances or brats.

The telephone at the hotel was used by all the inhabitants of the creek for miles around. The rent, Mrs. Lemaster told me, exclusive of the toll charges, was thirty dollars a month.

Lunch over and the pictures taken, Garrison tucked Clara in the sleigh, gathered up the reins, and drove the grays and the sleigh out of our sight. Now for that week of vacation which Doug needed so much and which would be a rest for me, with no meals to cook.

I went back to the cabin to put John to bed for his nap, expecting to see no more of Doug until nightfall. He had been called to the telephone just as I left the hotel, but I thought nothing of that. Not many minutes later I looked up and saw him in the doorway.

"Get packed up and ready to leave," he began with no preliminaries. "We have to go back to Dawson. I have phoned Pickering to come and get us."

And the Costars hardly an hour on their way! I blinked my eyes in astonished unbelief and gazed at him stupidly. We were to stay a week. What in the world—

"Dredge Number One has been dynamited," Doug went on, cramming things into his duffle bag, "and I have to get there as quickly as I can."

Dynamited! I felt as if the dynamite had gone off right there in the cabin. Nothing violent like that ever happened in the Yukon, because of the Mounted Police. I had heard that assurance myself, a hundred times. What could be back of all this?

By the time the Pickering sleigh jingled up to the hotel and came to a stop I had John and myself ready. Mr. Pickering drove the team. As we bundled ourselves into the fur robes there was a sense of frustration and unaccustomed foreboding. Foreboding because of some unknown menace, alien to the bright day and gleaming snow, the blue sky and sparkling, clean air. Frustration because we had to return to town, our errand unfulfilled, our plans cut off at their inception. Nobody said much on the way home.

Once we were in town, Doug took his own horse from Pickering's, where it was kept, and went at once to Dredge Number One, while Mr. Pickering took John and me home. The house seemed very empty and cold; I kept my wraps on until I had two good fires going and the house habitable again.

Then Clara Costar came over and we discussed the dreadful crime and wondered who could have done such a thing and why. We could hardly wait for Doug to come home and tell us all about it.

That night Clara and Garrison came over after dinner, and we had all the details as we four sat around the heater and discussed the situation.

The deed had been done at night. The dredge was frozen in its own pond, fairly close to the Bonanza road, not far from its junction with the road up Hunker Creek, a very accessible place for the culprit to reach. All around the dredge on the snow-covered ice was a network of ski tracks, but whether these were made by the dynamiter or somebody who came to view the damage, nobody knew.

The dredge had been blasted in the hull and lay over on one side, like a wounded duck, as Doug said. Nothing was known of method or motive, but the police were at work on the case and there was already a reward of five thousand dollars out for the criminal. Doug would be doing little else in the days to come but working for a speedy solution.

Mrs. Thomas came to call the next day and again we went over this new and baffling development, the most exciting thing that had happened since the company had started to operate. Doug had gone to the Forks to uncover some possible evidence and also to check up on the other dredges and install guards on all of them, a proceeding hitherto considered unnecessary in the well-policed country. He would be gone for several days, and I was living with the same old loneliness in spite of much to do, daytime callers, and sewing in the evening to fill up the time.

Next day Mrs. Thomas came for me, driving Jim, and we drove out to see the dredge. It did indeed look like a wounded duck. There was a repair crew already at work and certainly if there had been any clues they would long have been obliterated from our curious and amateur eyes.

By the time Doug returned he had a lot of information to satisfy my curiosity. The police had checked on all who owned skis in the Dawson area, an easy task because skis were not at all common. A small colony of Swedes lived in the north end of Dawson and they seemed to have in their possession all the skis in the vincinity and only a few pairs at that.

The dynamite had been obtained by breaking into one of the caches along the road leading from Dawson to Guggieville. In the side hill along that road, well out of town, several concerns stored their dynamite where it was unguarded but remote enough so that any explosion would not wreck Dawson buildings. Nobody ever dreamed of putting a guard over it, not in a country where people did not even own door keys!

The dynamite was frozen, of course, so in order to thaw it the thief had broken into an empty cabin on the hillside farther along the road. In the cabin were found the utensils he had used. He had built a fire in the long unused little stove, thawed the dynamite sticks in an old kettle, and then proceeded up Bonanza Creek to the dredge and set off the explosive.

Doug told me then of the day's trip which he had made just preceding our trip to Gold Bottom. He had inspected all the dredges and camps and interviewed the different foremen. While he was at Number Three and Number Six, which were very close together, he had turned suddenly to the foreman and asked, "Who is that fellow up there on the tailings?"

"Oh, that's just the Educated Swede," the foreman replied. "He's been skiing all around here. We never pay any attention to him. He's kinda crazy, sort of a socialist."

"He has no business here," Doug insisted, "I don't like it. Keep your eye on him."

Naturally, after the dynamiting Doug reported this incident to Mr. Thomas, who had the Educated Swede, actually a Norwegian, called in. The man gave a very plausible story, accounted for the ski tracks around Number One by saying he had heard an explosion and had gone out there on his skis before anyone else had arrived. Mr. Thomas was satisfied and let him go. Then the Swede offered his services to the police, saying he had been a detective in the old country and would like to work on the case.

Every time Doug would go up the creek thereafter he would meet the Swede somewhere along the way, skiing along, doing his detecting, remote and always very busy. Doug could not help having a queer feeling about him.

The Mounties always got their man, it is true, but in Dawson things had been so quiet and orderly ever since the early days that they had no equipment for detective work and very little experience in that line. There had been so little lawlessness in the Yukon that they were out of practice, to say the least. Week after week went by and nothing was done; the criminal was still at large and no doubt having a good laugh at the impressive redcoats with their Stetsons and their guns at their belts. In the meantime he might wreck another dredge. Doug, with others, was growing impatient.

In the ranks of the company engineers were some mighty keen fellows and they wanted action. Finally, after almost a month had gone by, they decided to begin a little investigation of their own. One of these men was R. E. Franklin, head of the electrical department, a whiz in his field and a dynamo for energy.

At no time had Doug been satisfied with the plausible Swede. He and Franklin had talked the matter over many times. The police were bogged down and getting nowhere. All the ingredients of a mystery thriller were present, in fact. Doug and Franklin decided to do something about it. They tracked the Swede to a certain cabin where every day the little colony of Scandinavians gathered during the winter for conviviality along their own lines. Finally Franklin rigged up an ingenious contrivance and took it along with him on a day when he made sure nobody was at home in the little cabin.

Working at top speed, Franklin installed what was the equivalent of a dictaphone and concealed it in the cabin. He knew by his days of observation just when to expect the gathering of the Scandinavians, so he hid outside the cabin in the early dark of the winter night and waited. Soon they arrived and went inside. He listened through his device.

They settled themselves and started to talk things over. Franklin was enraged at the good laughs they had over the stupidity of the police and the Guggies, fat capitalists that they were! The boys working around the dredges were no capitalists, Franklin thought, as he crouched there in the cold; they weren't sitting back smoking cigars that evening. At least one of them was hiding out in the dark and cold, trying to track down a skunk.

The Swede told how he had planned at first to dynamite Three and Six, the very day Doug had seen him snooping around there on his skis and warned his foreman. But the Swede decided, he said, that Number One was more accessible, and being nearer to town, would be more easily quitted after the dynamite was laid ready. Besides, his alibi about getting out there before anyone else would sound more plausible. He had to explain those ski tracks some way! So he finally picked on Number One.

They talked and talked, and Franklin took it all down in his notebook. When he had all that he could get and the

Swedes started in on something else, Franklin, half frozen, got up and left.

This information gained through the dictaphone brought about the arrest of the Swede. At the trial he confessed and was given twenty years in the penitentiary at Ottawa. He had no personal grudge against the company, but his socialist ideas, plus the long winter in the Arctic, had brewed a state of mind which told him it would be a good idea to injure a rich concern just on general principles. What he apparently failed to see was that in risking so much capital in this gigantic mining enterprise, the company had benefited the whole area and given work to thousands of men who must otherwise have been forced to go Outside or starve. Until he was in a position to duplicate the benefits accruing to a region through an enterprise made possible by capital, he should not have been in such haste to tear down what he could not possibly have replaced by himself.

As a matter of fact, there was no socialistic talk in Dawson and this man was considered to be a crackpot. Everyone knew that if it were not for the Guggies and others like them, the country would have lapsed into its former status of inactivity before the gold rush. I had noticed that the attitude of "You are wrong because you are rich" changes quickly enough when the former workman becomes a boss! I really believed that if all malcontents could themselves become capitalists, there would be an end to socialist ideas.

Right in the midst of all this excitement, on March 3, the Thomases' son was born, Charles Field Thomas, named after the famous Charlie Field of early Stanford days, a close friend of the Thomases. I took a walk to the hospital a few days later. All the Thomas children were beautiful, and this new baby would be no exception, I decided.

On March 9, John was christened by Bishop Stringer at the little church. Hoyt and Mrs. Osborn were the godparents. John was an armful and biffed the bishop in the nose so heftily that he almost upset the ceremony. That was not all that threatened to break up the occasion. Doug was called out right in the middle of things and told that Dredge Number Five was sinking! He left immediately, and we finished the christening without him. Later I heard the details.

During the winter the dredges were frozen in their ponds. An ingenious method of making a natural cofferdam, called "freezing down a hole," had been developed. After the ice had frozen about eight inches thick on the surface, four inches of this thickness next to the hull was carefully chipped away, leaving four inches of ice to hold the water down. Care must be used to prevent its breaking through to the surface again. After days or weeks, depending on the intensity of the cold, when the four-inch thickness had frozen deeper, a few more inches of ice were carefully chipped away. This process was repeated very cautiously week after week. It usually took all winter to freeze down a hole and make a narrow space next to the hull where ship carpenters could remove and replace a worn plank, when such repairs were made in the spring.

By this means a hole eight feet deep had been frozen down alongside Dredge Number Five. The carpenters had removed a worn plank, leaving the hull open. One carpenter, fresh from the Outside, decided he needed more space to swing his sledge. He began chipping into the side wall of the ice-enclosed cofferdam, not realizing that pond water was just beyond that thin wall.

The water rushed in, the stupid carpenter climbed out, the hull began to fill, and Dredge Number Five started to sink.

The dredge pumps were fifteen miles away being overhauled at the machine shops; there was no power at the dredge, as the power line was being rebuilt. It seemed hopeless. They sent for Doug, locating him at the church, since he always left word where he could be found.

The next few hours were hectic ones for him. He got together a power crew to string a temporary power line, while a crew at the machine shop put together pumps and motors and rushed them up the creek on a sleigh. The dredge was saved. There were few dull moments for Doug that winter!

Incidentally Dredge Number One was not expected to be

ready to operate until late summer. Yet in May, when the other dredges started digging, there was Number One, raised from the bottom of the pond, entirely repaired and starting the season along with the rest. Doug had hit on something new, designing a false bottom to close off the blasted hole inside the hull. The capable ship carpenter Oscar Wicks built the false bottom in a much shorter time than it would have taken to build a new hull or repair a large portion of the old hull on the outside.

During the investigation of the Swede, I had been sewing. Mrs. McClusky, my nurse when John was a new baby and we had just moved out to the plant, was helping me. All of us gave her work whenever we could, as she was trying to save her little home, which had been half paid for when her husband died. Mrs. McClusky was a good milliner and was remodeling one of my hats. I went to the local millinery shop to see if I could get some flowers to replace the old ones on the hat. The milliner looked over her small supply doubtfully.

"I hardly have any flowers at all," she apologized, thimble on finger and needle in hand as she poked among the flowers in a big box. "You see, there have been so many funerals in Dawson this winter. . . ."

I was stunned. Up to that moment I had given no thought to there having been funerals in Dawson, let alone the obvious need for flowers. There were no fresh flowers to be had, so people sent artificial ones to funerals. And there were none for my hat.

I went home sobered and all out of the notion for flowers. We trimmed the hat with silk ribbon.

Mrs. McClusky helped me make some things for John, who had outgrown all his clothes and also in a small way to get myself ready for spring. While we sewed, the main topic of conversation was the dynamiting. Both she and I had agreed long ago that the Swede was guilty and we said, "I told you so," to each other when he was convicted. We really felt competent enough to be engaged on the detective force ourselves. I think the men who really felt the most jubilant over the outcome were the guards, who used to have to walk the ice around the dredges at night and simply could not keep warm. What a relief to them to have the Swede locked up!

Our needles traveled along the seams, the sewing machine hummed under our active fingers in my sunny little dining room, as the hours went by, and I heard all about the loneliness of widows and how Mrs. McClusky still had a little romance left in her makeup. With the scarcity of women in the Klondike, there was no reason why she should not have married again and I hope she did. She was a real homemaker and a good cook, and she knew enough gossip to enliven the evenings of any man for years.

About this time in the year the men were coming in "over the ice" to prepare for the start of the summer season. Ruth and Warren McFarland had returned, so Clara and I went down to see Ruth. She looked very well indeed and had a lot of lovely new clothes with which to refresh our eyes. We had looked at our own things so many times! Ruth was wearing a new suit, but the really tricky thing she had brought back was a front-lacing corset! That was something none of us had ever seen or heard of. She also had a new expression, the "movies." Saying it made us feel sophisticated and blasé. We had always said "moving pictures." The abbreviation was new and jaunty.

By the last of March the gang were pretty much together again, and that was fortunate for me, as I planned to give a surprise party for Doug's birthday. I would have six couples, all the house would hold comfortably, and it was easy to keep the plan a secret from Doug, for he was away so much of the time.

I ordered a large cake and the supper—chicken salad, hot rolls, salted almonds, relishes, ice cream, cake, and coffee— from the cateress, who would come in for the evening, serve, and clean up afterward.

For days I was busy cleaning the house, preparing the table decorations and improvising the games we would play. The

Thomases could not come, but I was assured that the Morrisons, Costars, Osborns, Nortons and the "F.A.'s" would be there.

During the party John stayed at the Costars' with a baby sitter so that we could use the bedroom for the guests' wraps. Doug was completely surprised, and I was also surprised to think that he was! The games gave us a good opportunity to make jokes on him, which nobody overlooked. Thanks to the cateress, the supper was just right. We all toasted Doug and made him give a speech.

This was our last good time for the winter. On April first the summer schedule went into effect and Doug moved to the plant, leaving me alone again.

Action was the thing. Get out and forget how quiet the house was. I took John for walks, I made calls, I had afternoon parties for my friends. Miss Iredell, Anna Harken, a girl who was keeping house for her brother that winter, and I started a German Club, meeting once a week for reading a conversation, another way to keep busy.

One by one the days passed. The hours of sunlight grew longer, the snow melted, the warm breezes came to drive away the last vestiges of winter. We cautiously left off our fur coats, substituting woolen ones. Once more the sun had triumphed and the memory of the cold receded into a dim background.

The board walks were clear, the sleighs put away and baby buggies again put into use. Soon I would have spent my second winter in the North and be starting on my third summer. Heigh-ho and yoicks for the plant and Guggieville!

13. A New House

PLANS FOR OUR SUMMER HOUSE at the plant were already started. We were not to have the big house again, for which I was thankful, but a smaller one next to it which had stood vacant the summer before and on the porch of which Father Ferry had made his bed of spruce boughs.

Two years before, the Klondike River had flooded all the flat surrounding the plant and twisted Ogilvie Bridge out of line. During the ice jam this little house had floated off its foundation and been forced a block down the road. After the flood had subsided, the house was put back again where it belonged, but its floors were still covered with silt. We decided that a thorough cleaning would make it habitable.

This was going to be stimulating. Next to playing the piano and sewing, I loved to plan houses. I would have the privilege of selecting the wallpaper, paint, and floor coverings, all to be *new*. I would not have to suffer the depression I always felt in the company of hideous wallpaper, varnish, and old carpets. At least, I could have my way about color, although no extravagances were to be tolerated.

The house was boxlike, with a porch across the front and another across the back. The living room took up the front half, the other half being divided lengthwise into two rooms. Of these the bedroom was just seven feet wide, the kitchen about eight, and each was twelve feet long.

We did the front room in light oatmeal paper with white woodwork. China matting went down on that floor and in the bedroom, since I was fortunate and found a roll of it in Dawson. The bedroom walls were pale green; the kitchen, yellow with tan linoleum. We repainted the white iron bed, left from last summer and bought new springs and mattress.

I had hung fresh scrim curtains in all the rooms and ordered from Toronto the material for chintz side curtains in the front room and a couch cover of golden-brown monk's cloth in wool. Humble and inexpensive as it was, the house gave off something of ourselves. We were so entranced with the results that we would stand and look at everything, thinking how wonderful it was that we had such a beautiful place to live.

Given the simplest necessities for living, we could express our individualities freely in making cupboards from packing cases and painting them sky-blue or sea-green besides having all the fun of creating something. One of the greatest satisfactions of living in the North lay in our freedom from a hankering after possessions and pinch-hitting with homemade substitutes.

I stained the homemade furniture a light brown, hung up my baskets of wandering Jew and placed runners of heavy Russian linen on the table and bookshelf. The result was restful, homelike, and clean.

Our tiny kitchen stove was to be put near the back door for convenience in handling wood and also for an efficient working pattern. The stovepipe must traverse the entire length of the kitchen to the safety outlet at the front end of the room, where one chimney served both stoves. Since it was so long, the stovepipe had to be suspended from the ceiling by several sets of wires. The tiny cookstove looked ludicrous at the end of that long pipe, and the draft that was created threatened to carry stove and all right up the chimney.

John was sitting in his high chair one morning, near the kitchen table and almost directly under the stovepipe. Doug had finished his breakfast and was in a hurry to go to the office.

Suddenly and without any warning, the whole stovepipe fell down, missing John by just a hair. My nice clean kitchen was a mass of soot. Doug had to put that pipe together again, piece by piece, and hang it to the wires while he thought about the work waiting at the office!

I thought I had heard language on the occasion of the collapsing bed, but what I heard after the stovepipe fell down surpassed even my most fertile imaginings! The pipe would fall apart in a new place just after Doug had one place joined together. Finally it all held; Doug got off the stepladder, washed his face and hands, and went to the telephone. Then I cleaned up the kitchen. The only one who had any fun out of it was John. He was vastly amused by the whole performance and seemed to think it had been staged just for his entertainment.

The only closet in the house was off the kitchen. We hung all our clothes there and put our boxes and trunks in the attic, accessible through a trap door. Among other things I put there was a lovely little steamer trunk I had bought in Rome. I forgot to take it down when we left, and I suppose it is still there!

We extravaganted that summer. I bought an electric flat-iron, one of the few to be had in the Dawson stores, and felt that ironing would be simply nothing in my life after that. Doug, who never spent anything on himself, sent to his college tailor in Palo Alto and had a corduroy suit made, the coat lined with wool flannel. It was exactly right for his work during the summer. With his Stetson sombrero and high laced boots it made a very good-looking outfit.

All the laundry was done on the back porch, Doug still carrying water from the cookhouse two blocks away. In the corner of the kitchen was a washstand made from two canned fruit boxes, one set on top of the other and covered with white oilcloth, the front curtained off. Beside it stood a white enamel bucket to receive the waste water, which Doug emptied at night. After these simple arrangements were complete, Doug decided to make a gesture of real elegance and provide me with an icebox. It was not very difficult.

First he found a fair-sized wooden packing case and joined the boards of the cover together to make a lid. This he fastened to the box with leather hinges. The case and the lid were then lined with zinc at the machine shop, Doug working late at night to do it. Now my icebox was ready to be installed. On the northeast side of the house he dug a pit close to the wall, going down about eighteen inches. By that time he had reached the perpetually frozen ground.

The zinc-lined box was fitted neatly into this pit and the extra dirt packed around it. The lid was left just a little below the surface of the ground and over it was an insulation of several thicknesses of old woolen blanket. Our food kept ice cold there on the warmest summer days.

Again the sound of the dredges formed the background of our days. There was one dredge just down the road from us, at that time the largest in the world, which operated continuously. If for any reason it stopped during the night, the cessation of sound woke us up and the silence seemed frightening.

Also, as a background of sound, there was the din and clatter of boiler flues being cleaned at the machine shop, a racket beside which the noise of trains or traffic would be mild. Each of the nine thawing plants had a battery of steam boilers, whose flues would become crusted with solids from the water they heated. Cleaning these flues had been a problem never completely solved until Doug thought out a fiendish scheme. The crusted flues were removed and clean ones substituted. Then the dirty flues were brought to the machine shop in large numbers and cleaned. Suspended by two endless revolving chains, one at each end of the bundle of pipes, they were revolved over and over, hitting against each other and loosening the crust which lined them.

The constant din from those flues was with us twenty-four hours a day. It was deafening, maddening. We finally became used to all the various sounds and lived unconcernedly beside them. The air was sweet and tangy, the wild roses and bluebells were opening along the roadside, and the wildflowers colored the hills. Life was wonderful and good.

That summer the company decided to grow a garden. In the continuous daylight these grew so rapidly that it was not long until there were lettuce, radishes, and root vegetables, not only for the camps but for us as well, and they kept fresh and crisp in our icebox. Mr. Pretty, the man in charge of the commissary and warehouse, often brought us presents of fresh salad vegetables or young onions which were a real treat after the long diet of canned goods in the winter. Mr. Pretty, a kind, very correct, and prosaic soul, was known confidentially to Doug and me as "Old Platitudes." Nevertheless, he did his best to make the summer pleasant for us all.

One day Doug brought me a queer-looking object and told me I could use it as a doorstop. About the size of my head, it wasn't stone, it wasn't bone; I couldn't decide what it could be. It was gray and brown, ridged on top and rough on the surface.

"What is it?" I asked, lifting the heavy thing in my hands.

"A mastodon tooth," Doug answered, "and a fossil reminder of the days when this climate was tropical." I had heard stories of the finding of the mastodons, imbedded in the icy muck, and that sometimes even the hide and the meat had been preserved. I never believed those stories, but here was evidence that the mastodons had existed. Such fossil bones, teeth, and mammoth tusks were to be seen here and there as curios in many a cabin in the North.

We were so pleased with our bright clean little house that every day seemed complete and full. The final good fortune came with Doug's decision to buy a new horse to replace the old gray one he had driven for so long. Besides, Doug liked to have his horse just for himself, and Mr. McCarthy had said that if the electricians needed to go to a breakdown at night they could borrow any horse that happened to be in the company stable.

"This time," Doug announced to me, standing in the living room wearing his hobnailed boots, whether the matting liked it or not, "I have my eye on a horse that will be driven by nobody but myself."

"How can you be so sure of that?" I asked, taking the hot biscuits out of the oven for our lunch.

"Wait and see." He grinned.

The very next day he went to Dawson and bought the horse, leaving it at Pickering's and walking out to the plant until a stall could be arranged for at the Guggieville stables. From his description I knew the horse must be handsome, but I was not prepared for the high-stepping chestnut with arched neck and impatient pawing hoofs which Doug drove up to the door the day after that for me to see.

Doug drove the horse proudly and exclusively from that time on; exclusively, because it had the bad habit of trying to climb the nearest tree whenever it met anything it feared, especially one of the few automobiles in the country. The other men called it Doug's Devil and not only would not drive it but even refused to ride behind it when Doug was driving!

To Doug it was the perfect horse and it took him over the country in half the time that it used to take with old King.

Fortunately the few times I went riding with Doug, holding John in my arms, we met nothing frightening. One day we were driving along the road close to Number One Dredge, the one which had been dynamited. It was so close that its pond came right to the roadside. We rolled along in Doug's high-wheeled buckboard, the wheels so high that they had to be sharply cramped for me to get in or out using the small step midway between the bed of the buckboard and the ground. In my descent I always had to grasp the edge of the seat too, in order to keep my balance. As I say, here we were, I holding the heavy baby, Doug with his hands full, driving the fractious horse. Suddenly Doug said casually, "Be ready to jump any minute. We may meet an automobile along here."

Just how I was to jump over the wheels with the baby in my arms I wasn't sure. Fortunately I never had to put it to the test. Finally the pleasure of driving with Doug was not so great as the uncertainties and the hazards, so I went very seldom.

Whatever happened, John had his daily walk in which we explored the retort house, the greenhouse, the machine shops, and the cookhouse, where the Swedish cook would give me a starter of "jeest" for my next day's bread baking, or some ice cream, with which I must rush home so that John and I could eat in before it melted.

Our quiet Shelley was in as much of a dither as he ever permitted himself. He had been Outside the previous winter and had married his schoolday sweetheart, Elsie, and she was coming in by boat with Mrs. Hardy, the wife of the machine-shop superintendent, in just a few days.

They would live in the house next to ours, upstream, and Shelley had equipped it with furniture he had made himself and a fine new cookstove. It was twice as big as ours and had a real oven. The whole house was fresh and clean and ready for Elsie long before she arrived.

All our houses were more or less playhouses, with furniture made to serve just for the present. The motions of house-keeping routine were there, but all were impermanent and we knew it. The outdoors called us, the day had no night, we lived in the charm of fairyland every summer, while the wicked ogre Winter was forced to hide in his distant cavern at the back of creation. We pretended to forget that he could ever come again and lived just for the moment in the midst of the color and perfume and humming activity of the endless daylight.

There were wild roses for pink and bluebells for blue, and on the distant clearings the rosy shafts of fireweed. I knew where the wild berries grew and would gather them later in the summer. One thing I had surely learned: to take the beauty of the moment where I found it. Formerly I had been addicted to the cut-and-dried variety of beauty, in which nature is assisted by art in clipped lawns, massed vegetation, and all the contrived vistas of landscape architects. Now I could sit on Doug's chopping block, my feet resting on the mat of chips fallen from his axe, and contemplate the beloved mountain across the Klondike River, quite oblivious of the unfinished and uncouth aspects of the camp spread about me. How sweet the air and how glorious the freedom of that arctic summer, when nature worked overtime and life was doubly good because we knew that one day winter would come again!

The boat was in! Mrs. Hardy had arrived with Elsie and Shelley was off to Dawson to get her and bring her with him out to Guggieville. We were in almost as much of a dither as Shelley was!

Elsie was young and very pretty with creamy skin, dark hair, and dark eyes. Traces of a Boston accent, carried over from early childhood, gave her slow speech and soft voice definite charm. She was always saying things unintentionally that were screamingly funny, and we all fell in love with her at once. She had brought a lot of pretty clothes with her and many things to provide touches of luxury in the cabin Shelley had started so well.

I invited the Schellingers to dinner that evening, the first
of many, many dinners we were to have together. We usually
divided up the courses, each taking part. To Elsie usually fell
the preparation of whatever was to be baked or roasted, since
her oven was so much larger than mine. The boys would bring
wild ducks or rabbits for those combination dinners and we
used our ingenuity to find new recipes or new ways to serve
old standbys. The fresh green things Mr. Pretty would send us
or the ice cream the cookhouse found time to make and send
over were a big help and made those occasions very special.

Elsie now joined in the daily walks with John, and we explored all the area for berry patches and flowers for our houses.
Elsie liked to sew too—in fact, she was much cleverer at it
than I—so we had much in common. We never had a fuss,
never grew tired of each other, which was fortunate. Whenever Clara Costar could get away, she came out for the day
and made a threesome, bringing her sewing and all the latest
news from town.

So the days passed, and it was June 21 again and the longest
day, when from the Dome back of Dawson the midnight sun
could be seen. It was a very warm day too, so we packed a
lunch and when the men came home we had a picnic supper
down by the river and were just like any picnickers anywhere
in other latitudes. That evening, as we often did, we took a
walk to the huge dredge that would eventually mine out the
ground upon which our houses now stood. They would be
moved upstream at the end of that very summer to leave the
ground clear for the dredge.

The dredge machinery created the symphonic illusion against
the deep background rumbling of rocks tumbling in the interior mechanism and the lighter rattling of those same rocks
as, cleaned of their gold content, they came off the stacker
belt and fell upon the tailings piles in a delicate pattering.
By that time I was fully accustomed to a dredge, yet there
remained a certain fascination which would keep me standing
there minute upon minute, watching it as if I could not bear
to leave. There was an endless, soothing monotony about the

rising bucket line and the steady sound of the ponderous
mechanism that was almost mesmeric; and others besides me
had commented upon it.

The house was light all night, but we were used to that
and it did not interfere with our sleep. When we drew down
our window shades, the light coming through them, combining
with the pale green walls, was as soft and restful as if we had
been immersed in the pale waters of the sea, and we dropped
to sleep as easily as we did when it was completely dark.

One morning I was washing on the back porch, and Elsie
had called over from her house, "If I went at my washing as
hard as you do, I'd fall dead in the tub!" I liked to put a little
energy into whatever I was doing and washing was no exception. The clothes, rinsed and clean, were ready to hang out
when Doug came around the corner of the house from the field
office where he was working that day. He had some mail in his
hand.

"The mail has just come," he said, "and there is a letter
from Christina Rose. Thought you would want to read it right
away."

I dried my hands and slit the envelope with my finger.
"She's coming to visit us," I announced eagerly, "and will be
here in ten days, to stay a month." I was almost too excited
to finish and hang out the washing.

14. Christina's Visit

CHRISTINA WAS ONE OF MY very best friends. Several years
older than I, she excelled me in many things. A talented musi-
cian, she cultivated also her fine and inquiring mind, dressed
well in clothes made mostly by herself or her mother and demanded of herself a high development of personal and social
grace. I could hardly imagine my beautiful Christina in the

setting of Guggieville, but if she was willing to come, I was only too eager to have her.

Luckily the material had come from Toronto, and I could make the hangings before she arrived. Rodin's thinker would have been needed for the next problem that occurred to me. *Where would we put her?* Doug had gone back to the office, and I stewed over this question while I finished the washing and cleaned the house.

At lunch Doug settled the matter instantly. It was always such an effort for me to make up my mind about things, while Doug could make a decision quickly and be right nine times out of nine.

"We'll put her on the living-room couch," he said, "and I'll bunk next door."

In the empty Kelton house, where we had lived the summer before, there was plenty of room and the place was reasonably clean. Doug requisitioned a bed from the warehouse and in no time at all I had cleaned a room for his bedroom.

Marian Gifford came out that day with Miss Iredell and the Thomas children. We all began to make plans for entertaining Christina, Elsie helping.

I had to be very careful when I cut the draperies as I was pretty sure to cut at least one length with the wrong dimensions, in spite of measuring carefully, not having the mathematical exactness of an engineer. Elsie came over to help. We spread the material carefully out on the kitchen table, measured, put in pins, measured again. Finally, with trepidation, I set the shears to the selvedge and plunged in.

We really worked that day, turning hems, basting and stitching. The results were perfect and the curtains all hung the same length. In a small way this was a major triumph, while the room took on a simply glamorous appearance, to us at least.

Everything was ready. Christina's bed was made up under the couch cover with a beautiful satin puff Elsie insisted on bringing over since I did not own one. The day arrived. Doug had gone to town the night before to stock up on groceries, and Mr. Pretty had brought over some fresh green vegetables which were in our icebox outside. Elsie had baked one of her wonderful cakes. The scene was set.

Christina's boat would dock about five in the afternoon. Elsie and I could think of no more to do. While Doug and his Devil went after the guest, she and I eased the strain of waiting by taking John and going for a long walk, returning just before Doug pranced the Devil to a standstill before the front porch.

He helped Christina out of the buckboard and together they came up the steps, Christina tall and handsome in a gray traveling coat trimmed with black Persian lamb which suited her brunette coloring. We greeted each other in the good old traditional Stanford DeeGee manner of that time, much high soprano and crescendo with ejaculations and osculations.

John objected strenuously to all this, both because he disliked noise and demonstrations and also because here was competition of a sort he had never seen. He set up a yell that was pacified with much difficulty, and he was very aloof to Christina for several days. Eventually he was won over, just as Christina won everyone she encountered on that visit.

We were in the house and John was quieted. Christina looked about her. "What an attractive room!" she exclaimed.

That was reward enough for all my labors. "I thought you might be living in an igloo or something," she went on, as we settled her possessions, "but this is really charming."

Apparently, between the mail-order catalogues and Elsie, I had accomplished something.

Christina soon became adjusted to the primitive life, the lack of running water, the constant daylight, and the noise of the dredge working so close to the house. She and I talked all hours of the day and into the night and went for walks with Elsie and John. Christina had recently completed two years of piano study in Paris with Moritz Moszkowski and was full of music and French phrases which she used unconsciously half the time. I could see that she missed her piano very much, but there were no pianos in Guggieville.

To be sure that her education in mining would not be

neglected, Doug took her on one of his trips to the Anderson Concession, where all the men immediately fell under her spell.

"She has such lovely manners," one of the men explained to Doug later.

The moment anyone heard the timbre of her voice and that delicate articulation of ordinary words that we just tossed around, he realized that here was a Somebody and a highly cultivated Somebody at that.

It was this quality of voice which brought her the instant homage of those men—her voice, so different from the casual, careless voices of ordinary individuals. They could not analyze this quality, so they called it her manners. Actually it was Manner, which Christina had in a superlative degree, and the *oo-là-là* atmosphere she had brought back with her from Paris.

The next day they went up Bonanza Creek to the Forks, famous old mining center of the days of '98. Here Christina met E. E. "Mikkle" McCarthy, who was there on one of his inspections trips as superintendent of dredges.

Mr. McCarthy was known as a man who never looked at a woman. It was by his order that no woman was ever allowed on a dredge. "Damned dangerous," he used to say. "They might get caught in the machinery. Besides, we lose five dollars a minute while the dredge is shut down to let 'em on." "Useless creatures anyway," he might have added. We all understood his attitude and that he believed also that a woman on the dredge would bring bad luck.

So it was with surprise amounting to stupefaction that the entire creek learned the next day that Mr. McCarthy had invited Christina to spend the day with him, touring the creeks in his car and visiting the dredges and hydraulic mines.

That was not all. They had lunch together at the cookhouse at the Forks—and then *he took her on the dredge!*

The crew were so stunned that they could hardly go ahead with their work, stealing furtive glances at Christina as McCarthy explained every detail of the operation to her, from the top of the winch house to the hull. The men could easily see that Christina had a way with her—but *McCarthy!* They shook their heads and stored up this dazzling bit of news to tell their wives and after that anyone who would listen, for the next six months.

Christina had a very good time, she told us when she came home. Doug relished the occasion especially and could hardly wait to see some of his cronies and take the whole thing apart with them.

Every evening we went walking in the still-bright sunlight. Shelley often took pictures of us. "Now, Christina," Elsie said once, with the unexpected naïveté we always found so delightful, "you practically spoil every picture you are in. You should stand *this* way." Christina, sophistication and all, obediently allowed engaging young Elsie to move her around like a prop on a stage play while Shelley snapped away.

Christina always carried the sheerest of white handkerchiefs. Her shoes were delicate and of materials unsuited to our rough gravelly walks. Her clothes were built for city wear and looked very dressy in contrast to the simple cotton dresses worn by Elsie and me in our close association with housework, a baby, and the great outdoors as it existed at the plant.

Here were very few trees, some old fences, wild berries, and other small bushes. Underfoot was the gravelly Klondike alluvium, which led to the river behind the house and the mountains just across it. Although to Christina the crudities must have been disconcerting indeed, the vegetation was so green and fresh, the skies so vastly blue, life so gay and independent, that we ourselves did not miss the refinements of civilized life.

Fortunately Christina had brought walking shoes, a washable hat for the boat coming in, and a long knitted coat. These, with crisp white blouses and linen skirts, were her salvation. The dressy clothes were hung away until her return to California.

Mr. Pretty haunted our door. Any hour of the day he might be standing there with fresh greenstuff in his hands, waiting to be admitted so that he could get another look at Christina and be enchanted afresh by her "manners," of which he spoke feelingly to Doug. Doug and I watched with amusement his complete subjugation, since we knew of a certain young lady in Dawson who had up to this time been really hopeful. Christina's dazzling invasion of the Klondike was putting a terrible strain on that little romance, which was really too bad, because it had meant a lot to the girl. There was nothing we could do, so we let matters ride and Mr. Pretty continued to present himself, with gifts, at our door.

I decided to give a dinner party for our guest, inviting the Schellingers, Mr. Pretty, Mr. McCarthy, and Mr. Powell, handsome assistant to Mr. Pretty at the warehouse.

The dinner was cooked entirely on the little cookstove and we omitted none of the frills. Entertaining after dinner was no problem at all because Christina could have kept many more than that number at ease and interested. Mr. Pretty was put entirely in the shade by the surprisingly genial and urbane Mr. McCarthy, who, when he put his mind to it, could be really delightful. Everybody stayed late and nobody cared about tomorrow.

Several times we went in to Dawson. Mrs. Osborn gave a luncheon for Christina and that same evening Mr. Pretty entertained us with a dinner at the Hotel Yukonia. Afterward we went to a show and a dance, ending the evening with a midnight supper, while John stayed at the Osborns.' This was simply a killing pace for us Guggies, although to Christina it was more or less daily fare. Doug was so busy he moved through those days like a wraith. Sometimes he appeared at meals, but I seldom saw him at any other time. It was an extra-special treat when he could accompany us on the trips to town and our evening adventures.

One afternoon Mrs. Johnson came out with some friends, and Elsie appeared just in time with ice cream from the cookhouse. That evening we all had dinner at Elsie's and we came home singing and dancing a new ragtime step Christina was teaching us, which would probably have horrified the floor managers of Dawson dances.

It was evident that Christina missed her piano, and I think I missed it as much as she did, thinking of the many hours I had spent in her Berkeley home sitting by the fireplace listening while she played.

"How would you and Christina like to go into town today?" Doug asked at breakfast one morning.

Surprised, I answered, "That would be easy. Anything special?"

"Somebody has left a nice little piano at the furniture store to be sold. The owner went Outside. If Christina says it's all right, I'll get it for you." He buttered a piece of toast as he talked.

Buy a piano? No Guggie ever did such a thing! Doug was always taking my breath away like that by getting me something he knew I wanted very much.

"Well, how about it?" He looked at the two of us, sitting there just blinking with incredulity.

We both jumped up and hugged him. "We're practically on our way this minute," I declared, "although I can't believe it. How did you ever find out about the piano?"

"Fellow told me at one of the camps. Says it's a nice piano." Doug was preparing to leave for the day. "Have a good time, children," he called back as he went out the door.

We were so excited we hurried through the morning work, dressed John in his best and took the stage into town. The piano was really lovely, a light mahogany case and in perfect condition. Christina's test of its quality satisfied her and left the furniture man gazing after her like someone who has just had a glimpse of realms beyond imagination.

Denny brought the piano out the next day.

The rest of Christina's visit was made even more perfect by hours of playing, morning, afternoon, and evening, to the delectation of everyone about the plant.

At Government House in Dawson there was to be quite a celebration in honor of the Seattle Chamber of Commerce, which had sent a delegation on a trip to the Yukon. Incidentally the Fourth of July would coincide with the visit of the delegates to Dawson. Mrs. Black sent out invitations for a garden party the evening of July 3, and since there was continuous daylight, the party was expected to last well into the Fourth. We all knew the visitors would be entertained in true Commissioner Black tradition.

The men would wear their business suits, since this was a garden party, but Elsie and I brought out our very best for the occasion. This was a rose-colored dress for her, and for me the blue with the train. Mrs. Hammell, the Dawson furrier and milliner, had made me a hat from some of the blue material left over from the dress and trimmed it with a stick-up feather of cerise which earned me the name of Robin Hood.

Christina wore a cream-colored broadcloth of softest texture, trimmed with handsome heavy handmade lace she had brought from Europe. It was frightfully daring, being made with an opening at least six inches long in one of the seams at the hem. This showed a portion of Christina's satin evening slipper! Elsie and I could not keep our eyes from furtively straying.

Doug and Mr. Pretty arranged with Pickering's for a team and three-seated carriage to call for us. The Schellingers, Christina, and Mr. Pretty, and the Ferrys, set out at 9 P.M. in broad daylight, intending to leave John at Mrs. Osborn's for the evening. Christina wore an innovation—evening makeup. In the bright light of day it looked garish to our unsophisticated eyes, but Christina had lived in Paris and undoubtedly knew what she was doing. Thus, elegantly, and so far as Mr. Pretty was concerned, refinedly, we drove into Dawson.

We arrived at Government House, to find the grounds already crowded with guests and many forms of games and entertainment in progress. After paying our respects to the commissioner and Mrs. Black, we were free to find our own entertainment. Christina was presented to all and was immediately taken over and monopolized by different groups for the rest of the evening. We hardly saw her except as she flitted from house to garden for refreshments and back again, always the center of a laughing, animated group of satellites.

At half past one in the morning we were all called together

and grouped about the porch railings and steps for a large photograph to be taken so that the visitors could carry it back to Seattle. In honor of the group Government House was flying the United States flag as well as that of Canada.

"Probably the only time in history," Mrs. Black murmured to me, "that the United States flag has been flown in Canada on the Fourth of July."

It was all of 2:30 A.M. before Christina could be induced to depart, she was having such a good time. But I, mindful of John at the Osborns' and 7 A.M. on the job for Doug and the rest of the men, insisted, despite Christina's teasing me for being so domestic and prosaic. I was almost ashamed to face Mrs. Osborn at that hour, but she was a grand sport about it and told me it was all right.

We drove home, still in daylight, and tumbled into bed. John, who hadn't celebrated, would want his breakfast as usual. Elsie and Christina slept until almost noon. How John stood the gadding about that we did, I just can't see. He never minded in the least and was always affable and good. He was a personality from the moment he was born, and I think he liked people as much as I did.

Christina was such a rare bird for those parts and one of such brilliant plumage that everyone had to look twice. So we had many callers at our little house at the plant and many invitations to town, up to and even including the day of her departure. The boat was to sail at midnight and we left for Dawson in the morning by stage: Elsie, John, Christina, and I. Christina's luggage would be brought in at dinnertime by the men, as Doug, Shelley, and of course Mr. Pretty would all be at the boat to see her off. Mr. Powell trailed along as not too serious a rival.

It was raining, but we all wore our best because there were parties coming up and we must do honor to our hostesses.

First there was luncheon given by Mrs. Thomas. That really was an affair, with all the formality and elegance that Mrs. Thomas knew so well how to achieve. She even served our favorite dessert, a huge melon mold of ice cream, the center of which was grape sherbet. This was served on a large silver platter and carved at the table, a triumph her chef never tired of producing.

It was our custom after a meal for Elsie and me to go out to the kitchen and compliment Frank on his artistic and delicious dishes. This never failed to please him and his appreciative grins would let us know how much he liked our little stunt. This time we had a lot to say, for it was evident that he had outdone himself in honor of Christina.

Later in the afternoon there was Mrs. McCauley's tea. Mrs. McCauley, wife of the chief justice (whose proper title was Senior Judge of the Territorial Court), was entertaining that day, with Christina and me, as her hostess, the featured guests. All the Ping-pongs were to be there. As a great favor Christina was persuaded to play the piano for the other guests. Her acquiescence meant more than mere courtesy, so far as she was concerned, for she seldom did such a thing.

The music, added to Christina's sparkling personality, must have given those women something to think about for a long time. It was apparent in their faces that some of them had never before heard such music. Like a brilliant comet across our Dawson social skies, Christina really left a cloud of glory trailing behind her and it was almost as an anticlimax that we all stood in the drizzling rain on the upper deck of the steamer *Dawson* that midnight after a dinner party given by Mr. Pretty and said our goodbyes while Shelley snapped our pictures.

We watched Christina, waving, as the boat rounded the bend and swept her from our sight and from our lives. Mr. Pretty's gaze followed the boat. Christina was forever beyond his reach, but her coming had spoiled the chances of the little romance we had all been watching. No wonder he looked serious as we turned toward home and the more drab aspects of our daily life.

Now there would be the familiar threads to pick up again. The next day I washed and ironed, and cleaned the house, and then Elsie and I took John and went to pick berries. Doug moved back into the house, and the former routine was resumed just as if there had never been the vivid and brilliant interval of Christina. The poignant reminder was the pretty little piano in our living room and the memory of her slender fingers scampering across the keys as we sat withdrawn and spellbound by her music, each one lost in his own dreams.

Old-Timer

1913 — 1914

15. Our Very Own Cabin

Doug took John and me to the Forks for two days. We were to stay at his little cabin two miles above the Forks on El Dorado Creek and would have our meals at the cookhouse after the crew had eaten and gone. I wanted to learn more about the Forks—Grand Forks, it was called in the gold-rush days when it was a large settlement, second only to Dawson in size. Dredge Number Eight was mining right in the old town, now little more than a collection of dilapidated buildings, where once miners thronged to spend their rich findings and seek recreation in the noisy dance halls.

The walls of the cookhouse were of bare unpainted lumber, as were the floors. There were long tables, three planks wide, covered with white oilcloth. We sat on long benches. The dishes were of Swedish white enamelware with blue rims. Large pitchers of water stood on the table as well as the big, comforting coffeepots and pots of tea as black as the coffee. For breakfast we were served canned fruit, cereal, hot cakes with syrup, platters of bacon and eggs, toast, jam or marmalade in large tins, and coffee. If the way to a man's heart is through his stomach, how those men's hearts must have fluttered for the Yukon Gold Company!

None of the camps had any bathing facilities, so Doug had rigged up showers at all the thawing plants, there being plenty of water, steam for heating it, and men capable of installing the showers. This made a big difference in the men's comfort, and all used them except the Scandinavians, who would have nothing but bathtubs. A few were put in for their use.

The foreman of the thawing crew on El Dorado above the Forks, Al Brostrom, was a fine example of the Nordic type, strong, clean, and dependable. I listened to Al and Doug talking. Complacently I heard about pups, draws, and gulches and knew the difference between them.

All around the cabin there were men working day and night, hammering down the thawing points. One fact struck me as significant. I said to Doug. "Never once have I heard a man here sing or whistle at his work."

"Al Brostrom likes his own kind," Doug answered, "and most of these men are Scandinavians. They are a dour lot. Seldom relax enough to sing."

I had sometimes compared the music of Scandinavian countries with that of Italy and noticed the great difference. Perhaps the business of living in a northern country is too grim for much gaiety, musical or otherwise.

"I know why the Scandianavians don't sing," I decided. "They have never learned to sing in the shower!"

Doug considered this flippancy unworthy of a reply.

Although the hills blazed pink with fireweed and the days were sweet with the ripeness of deep summer, I had a sense that just behind the wall of mountains to the north the cold was waiting and that, implacable and deadly, before long it would be upon us. Perhaps these non-whistling men felt it too.

There was much to be done before winter. John would need new clothes, and I was beginning to feel the urge to see the fall catalogues. Most of all, we must get a house.

We had decided that in order to have warm floors for John, who would be creeping, we would buy a house and install a furnace. It was unheard of for a Guggie to buy a house, since we all knew we were more or less transient, and equally exceptional to find a furnace in Dawson houses. Fewer houses were for sale than were for rent too, so it looked as if we had a problem to solve. Mrs. Osborn and others were on the lookout for us, so far without result.

At every opportunity now, Elsie and I picked blueberries to freeze for winter. They froze better than the raspberries, which were apt to become mushy when thawed. The blueberries, tiny frozen pellets like bullets, could be put in dishes at night and left in the dining room. By morning they were thawed and just as good as fresh berries. We kept a little wooden keg of them in our caches as a necessary part of our winter provisions.

Doug was away so much that I had a great deal of time

to myself, and the piano was a good companion while John slept and the evenings faded into late dusk, for the sun was well on its way south and there was some darkness now at night. The big dredge slowly and majestically made its way down the fields, like a three-story apartment house on a journey.

It was our anniversary again. Doug happened to be at the field office that day and could be home fairly early for dinner. I wanted to do something a little unusual in order to have a special memory for the day. Elsie and I decided to have a picnic. We would take John and Elsie's new pet, her fuzzy little Malemute pup, Quigley.

We packed baskets of lunch. When Doug and Shelley came home, we took John and the baskets and Quigley and crossed the Klondike on foot logs to the base of the mountain. Then we climbed a very steep trail, following it to a deserted cabin, hidden in the trees and roofless to the weather. Elsie and I prowled about, hoping to find something useful, but there was nothing within those walls except an old pineapple crate from Hawaii which Shelley said was made of mahogany.

How much human effort had gone into felling and hewing the logs for this cabin, how much hope and ambition into hunting for a mining claim—long, cold winters endured and endless summer days of toil—to sum up to this, a deserted, roofless cabin! We ate our picnic supper out in the open, feeling very far away from everything and stayed until it was time to take sleepy John home and put him to bed. This involved climbing down the steep hillside, a much harder task than climbing up.

Since my trips to town were apt to be strenuous, Elsie often took care of John for me. On one such trip I was told that there might be a possibility of getting a house owned by Dr. Catto, a Dawson physician whose antecedents went back to London. Dr. Catto was known as an excellent doctor, but he was also noted for his Great Danes, one of which, called Catto, he had sold to Gus Johnson. They were big brutes that terrorized all who approached the Catto house, where the doctor lived alone with the exception of a housekeeper.

I decided to go to the Catto house to see about this possibility. As I approached the fenced yard three Great Danes started toward me, all barking. Since I have never had the slightest fear of dogs, I kept coming, talking to them in a friendly tone as I came through the gate and up the front steps to the door. The dogs by this time were close around me.

When the housekeeper opened the door, she seemed very much surprised to see me there with my cordon of Great Danes. She asked me inside and told me that shortly before a man had approached the house, been frightened by the dogs and made the mistake of starting to run. The dogs pursued him, and he had to climb the high board fence to get away. He managed to elude them, with the loss of part of one trouser leg.

My visit did not turn out very well; the house had been withdrawn from the market. When I left, the dogs were all my friends and escorted me to the corner of the yard, where I said goodbye to them and went on my way.

Years afterward Dr. Catto went Outside, taking three of the dogs with him. While the steamer was passing some islands in the Inside Passage, all three dogs jumped overboard and swam to one of the islands. I always secretly suspected that the crew or someone on board had a hand in it, because it was hardly possible that the dogs would do such a thing of their own volition. When Dr. Catto, up on deck, saw his dogs in the water, he offered the captain any amount of money if he would turn the steamer back and rescue them, the story went. But the captain refused. It is interesting to speculate on the sort of life those dogs lived on that island—whether there was any game on it, fresh water, or shelter in winter. Nobody ever knew.

Apparently there were no houses in Dawson, and we were getting a bit panicky. The days were growing shorter and colder. Mrs. Thomas stopped in often, with the children, sometimes taking Elsie, John, and me with them in the car for a picnic along the river. Neither she nor Mrs. Osborn nor anybody else knew of a house, those bright, crisp autumn days. Our houses at the plant were definitely summer houses, and we felt the chilly mornings and evenings, especially one day in late August when it snowed.

At last, one day a man in the Dawson office decided to go Outside for good and told Doug he would sell his cabin. We bought it, *just like that.* On a rainy and cold afternoon, we drove to Dawson and closed the deal. The title was in my name, and consequently I felt very important. This was the first time I had ever owned a house.

It was a little log cabin, painted red, snuggled to the hillside on two sides. On the other two it stood high off the ground, overlooking the town and river, like the deck of a ship. The steeply pitched hill at the front left room underneath the house and porch for storing wood, storm windows, and so on. There were porches on two sides and from them we could see all of Dawson and the river to the south and west. I loved it from the minute I saw it.

There were four rooms—living room, two bedrooms, and kitchen. The living room and kitchen had the sun all day; the bedrooms were back against the hill. We could use one bedroom for ourselves; the other would be John's room and my place to sew and keep extra equipment. As in all the houses in Dawson, the floors were uneven, the walls out of plumb. The furnishings and the wallpaper were dark and ugly, but we decided at once to follow out the color scheme we had used so successfully in our summer house at the plant.

We found a pretty Brussels carpet at the furniture store in tones of green and brown; we had a long window cut in the east wall and a ventilator in the bedroom. The window was cut level, and was out of line with the ceiling, but nobody minded a little thing like that.

There were several rocking chairs and a small library table in the cabin, as well as a kitchen stove, beds, and straight chairs. I would add the little sewing cabinet Doug had made for me to make the living room look furnished, but the piano would dress it up anyway and make it look very elegant. Of course, there would be the hanging basket of wandering Jew! But best of all, there was the furnace.

That was the thing for which we had bought a house, so that we might have assurance of warm floors for John. This was to be the crowning glory, even though the crown was underneath instead of on top.

The furnace had to be made by the local tinsmith and consisted of a large heater placed horizontally instead of vertically, surrounded by an outer casing with a hot-air space between the two, from which furnace pipes led to all four rooms. The furnace lid was thus at the front instead of on top and would admit chunks twelve inches across by three feet in length. The floor above the furnace and around the smokestack was protected by asbestos. The furnace was set under the kitchen in a little room we excavated, just big enough to hold it and leave room for the operator to move around and put in the wood. A few days' wood supply could be stored there also. Probably our second-best luxury was the cabinet which was connected to the furnace smokestack for ventilation and was secluded behind the furnace.

We protected all floors from cold on the outside and cut a trap door in the kitchen floor which led to the furnace room via a little ladder. Now let the winter winds blow and the thermometer drop! We were snug and ready, our house sealed and chinked, our double doors and windows in place. Winter would present no problems *this* year.

Nothing I had ever experienced equaled the feeling of security that filled me those days. Warmth, light, harmonious surroundings of my own choosing, a well-stocked woodpile and supply cupboard, my own little house set against the hill, with Dawson and the Yukon for my front yard—all these sources of repeated joy were mine, such untold wealth that no millionaire could surpass it. I knew absolute contentment and the impulse to reach up and pull down a star for Doug to light his cigarette!

I quickly made new scrim curtains for the windows and sent to Toronto for a new down comforter for our bed. All the time these preparations were going on, I was shuttling back and forth between the plant and Dawson, making all in readiness before we moved. Sometimes I took John with me, but often Elsie took care of him.

At the plant men were already busy working on our houses,

putting skids under them so that they could be moved upstream as soon as we were out. The big dredge was eating its way closer and closer, and soon would be ready to dig out the very ground on which our houses stood. Doug would have to stay at the plant after I left and would be housed at the bunkhouse for a few weeks.

Another beautiful Klondike summer had passed. With the turning toward town came that familiar premonition, like a faint twinge presaging toothache, that the cold had headed in our direction.

The birds had gone south, the days were shortening fast, the smell of frost was in the air. Covering the hills was a medley of bright colors—rich reds and blazing yellows. There was no end of comfort in the thought that struck across all this. . . . We had a lovely warm little cabin for the winter.

On the morning of September, 24, John and I moved. Denny took our goods and the piano, while Doug took John and me with his Devil. Since I had done so much settling ahead of time, it did not take me long to put things in operating order. Luckily too, for I had company for dinner—Miss Iredell, from the Thomases. We ate sketchily, from the dishes I had on hand, and spent our time admiring everything about the place. Fortunately the fire in the kitchen stove was sufficient to warm the house, as the men had a few finishing touches still to add to the furnace.

John could play on the sunny porches almost all day, while I hung the curtains and finished settling. I was so full of rejoicing over this little place that there seemed to be no room in my being for any additional joy. I missed Doug, but I knew that he would be moving into town before long and meanwhile there were the contacts with all my Dawson friends to renew and daily walks with John during the sunny afternoons.

I called on Clara Costar, the Thomases, Mrs. Johnson, and Mrs. Osborn, as well as the Coldricks. The nicest part of every walk was coming home. I loved every inch of that cabin just as much as if I had created it all by myself.

Elsie moved in October, and just about that time the Costars began to think about going Outside. Garrison would say dreamily, "The first thing I am going to have is some whipped cream and banana cake." Bananas were almost as unheard of in Dawson as was cream. We heard that remark at least fifty times while they were talking about leaving.

Doug moved into town and the winter office hours began. Why should we care if winter was almost here? We had a furnace. Over and around and below all our days, making up for isolation, discomfort or primitive living, was one compensating thought that blanketed us with its comfort. That thought was *security*. So long as the cold winds could be kept on the outside, of both our house and ourselves, we could live happily, free from strain and at a tempo pretty much of our own choosing.

Our dinners, for instance, were affairs of creative thought. Each one of us took the greatest interest in acquiring a new recipe or inventing a new dish. On our little stoves we often cooked a dinner of several courses for six to ten people, and those dinners were served just as carefully and artistically as our resources would allow. We did this, I am sure, purely for the pleasure it afforded us and our guests rather than for effect. There was no need for that. None of us was called upon to strut: we all knew each other and each other's affairs entirely too well.

It was important for me to have things about me that I liked. Shut in as we were all winter, the objects in the house became as familiar as friends. Ordinarily one would leave the house often enough to receive new layers of impressions over those made by the familiar household surroundings, but in winter those impressions would go very deep, depressing or satisfying as they might be. For me, then, who was most sensitive to surroundings, it was very important to like what I had around me.

There were two seasons in the year when I would be seized with the idea that I wanted a new dress. In the spring the crisp, gay cottons intrigued me into a sewing bee; in the fall the mood was for rich colors and soft woolen textures. I loved to design and create new clothes. Generally this urge to sew would result in a careful survey of the new fashion magazines and a canvass of what was left in my big trunks of the materials I had brought in with me.

This time I found enough material for a new skirt, which together with the silk for a blouse Christina had sent me, would make one new costume. I would buy a new hat at Mrs. Hammel's and remodel my fur one once more. There was another real find in the trunk—a length of blue satin, the shade known as electric blue, that would be my dressy outfit.

How stimulating to the morale! Mr. Pretty and Mr. Powell had asked us and the Shelleys to a show, and I was to have them at our house later for refreshments. Now I would have something new to wear!

One of the foolish but fascinating things for which I had sent Outside that summer was several yards of fluffy brown marabou trimming, about two inches wide. I decided to use it on the new blue satin dress, trimming the neck, cuffs, all the way down the front and around the bottom of the skirt. Our dresses that year were made coat style with the lower corners rounded off. The marabou was an easy way to finish the hem as well as being attractive.

I cut and fitted and craned my neck around to look at the hem in a mirror standing on the floor against the wall. The sewing machine whirred in the bedroom while John played on a blanket, spread out on the floor, over which were strewn my scraps of material and threads.

In the kitchen the pale October sun shone in at the windows with their crisp curtains, while the fire exclaimed and chuckled in the stove, glowing red through the grates. There was freshly baked bread cooling on the table, and the teakettle sang its little song as I sewed. I was very, very rich and best of all, I knew it. Soon those dresses over which I had worked furiously for days would be hanging in the closet. I would take many glances at them during the day, seeing them as a magic cloak to give me a new entity and a fresh personality. Life was so full and so rich that there could be simply nothing left in the world to ask for!

That fall we organized a Stanford Club—the Costars, Schellingers, Thomases, and Ferrys. We met once a month at each other's houses for an evening of fun and refreshments. When it was our turn to entertain, Doug and I made up a little game to be played with pencil and paper like a questionnaire, about Stanford, with prizes for the winners.

It turned very cold that night and snowed heavily. As our guests stamped the snow from their arctics, we opened the door to let them in with a steamy cloud of frost which rushed into the room like billows of fog. Our furnace-heated house was very comfortable as we passed pencils and papers, after singing a few Stanford songs, and started to play the game. C. A. T. (Mr. Thomas) grumbled good-naturedly, "I might have known that if we went to the Ferrys' we'd have to use our heads!"

I asked Elsie to help with the refreshments. Her soft voice answered, "I would be charmed to do it, Eudora," in that New England accent we all found so pleasing in contrast to our flat A's. It was easy for me to serve our favorite sherbet, since Doug and I had extravaganted with a two-quart ice-cream freezer. I had a recipe which called for a can of the wonderful Puyallup (canned) loganberries or raspberries, gelatin, and the whites of eggs. The sherbet had texture and body as well as marvelous flavor.

When I needed ice, I stepped out on the porch and broke off enough icicles hanging around the eaves to make the quantity desired. Doug would pound it fine in a gunny sack, fill the freezer, and in no time at all have the sherbet made. Our problem was keeping it warm enough to serve. If we were not careful, it would turn solid and hard as a rock. Sometimes we kept the packed freezer standing on the hot-air register in the kitchen until we were ready to serve the refreshments. With the sherbet we served our favorite spiced prune cake topped with white icing.

Elsie helping, we heaped the sherbet dishes and cut the

cake, while the boys passed the plates and napkins. The sherbet tasted good despite the cold outside, and again we blessed our furnace. Then it was time for the guests to put on their wraps and furs and brace themselves against the cold and the long walk home. We stood at the door and said goodbye.

This time, for us, there would be no coming home to a chilly house and chores to do. We were already in and warm. But there would always be a next time when we too must crunch shivering through the snow, late at night.

16. A Dog Sled Adventure

IT WAS MID-NOVEMBER. Doug having returned to town for the winter, all our routine was arranged in harmonious pattern in that little red cabin snuggled against the hill. Doug went to the office at nine and was ready to come home at four. The days were very short now, and the thermometer often dropped to 25 or 35 below. Life went on just as usual. Nobody would call off a tea party or stop a church supper for a little thing like the weather. We had a baby-sitter now, Faithful Rufino.

So it was that we held our Church of England bazaar on such a bitter evening. The crowd inside was intent on having a good time, with never a thought to the cold outside. They bought out the booths recklessly. It was all for a good cause, wasn't it, and how could we spend all our money anyway?

Doug and I spent the evening making silhouettes. Doug drew the profiles life-size on large sheets of paper and I cut them out. We did a big business.

It was 45 below, and the church cleared $1,300.

For Doug there would again be the peaceful routine of late breakfasts, seven hours of office work, home at four, and, after dinner and the chores, a long evening for playing the piano, reading aloud, and visiting.

Instead of starting this pleasant change at once, Doug was

slated for a trip into the wilderness. We were up owlishly in time for his early breakfast and then he was gone. After I had finished my work, I simply took John and went out for the day! Mrs. Johnson invited me to stay all night, giving me warmth and company, as I listened to her soft Virginia drawl and watched Mr. Johnson's pleasure in John, of whom he was very fond.

The next morning I returned to the cold house, built a fire in the furnace and in the afternoon was off again, this time to Ruth McFarland's. I found her contentedly baking bread and taking care of Bunny, her baby girl, nicknamed for John Bunny, a popular movie actor of that day whom the baby was thought to resemble. Ruth was perfectly adjusted to her life and environment and was a lesson to us all in the unruffled way she performed every detail of her various duties.

Doug came home the next evening, in high spirits as usual and in fine condition in spite of the cold trip. Those trips were a horror to me, but to him just a part of the day's business.

Soon it was December. We sent off all our Christmas presents for the Outside on the eighth of the month and after that I prepared gifts for our Dawson friends. Doug was away again, and once more I was taking John out for his airings, keeping myself busy during the day. The evenings were the hardest. I found that playing the piano was one of the best ways to put in the time. A little piano music to dress up the end of the long day put me in a good frame of mind until I could stoke up the furnace for the night and lose myself in the forgetfulness of sleep.

It was quite a process to get John ready for his daily walks. First there was the sleigh to bring in from the porch, where it stood tilted against the wall of the house out of the weather. Into the sleigh went a feather pillow, then a blanket and John's little head pillow. Fortunately we had been able to buy that larger sleigh from Bishop Stringer so that I could pad it well to keep out the cold.

John himself must wear his warm leggings, extra moccasins over his little shoes, a sweater, then his coat, cap, and mittens. Swathed thus, he was laid in his sleigh and over him was tucked the end of the blanket which went under him, then his down comforter, and on top of that the lovely white fur robe given him by Mrs. Norton. Now we were ready except for the soft loosely knitted shawl that I kept to go over his face in the coldest weather. All of this weight had to be dragged out the door and down the steps to the path. Then I went back and locked the door and we were ready to skim lightly down the hill. The sleigh, on its steel runners, glided along so easily that there was no effort on my part beyond steering it. Both John and I loved these excursions and we never missed them if it was humanly possible for me to take him out.

Just below us, on the next street down the hill, if it could be called a street, lived a man and his dog team, as one happy family. He was an old-timer who had come in with the earliest gold seekers, determined to make a fortune and then go back Outside to be the pride of his family and his community. He told us all this during the occasions when we met and talked, as neighbors, while all the dogs milled about the porch, in his house, and under his house.

Mr. Stansfield had not found the fortune he sought with such hazard. Luck had not come his way. Unwilling to go back empty-handed, he lingered on in the Klondike, still hoping to make a rich strike. A man of education and breeding, he carried in his face and demeanor unmistakable signs of being a gentleman, however rough his clothes and uncouth his surroundings. As his children grew up in his absence his wife had made a name for herself in her own field of endeavor, quite without his help or companionship, and given their children the background and surroundings they were by birth entitled to.

All this he told us in scattered fragments of conversation while he stood outside his house among the unruly dogs. We were never asked inside and indeed had no desire to go in. We knew already what to expect. As he showed us the pictures of his family, into his eyes came a look of silent pleading that we would not judge him too harshly.

He talked glibly of going Outside soon. We looked at his

family pictures and talked politely of their coming reunion. But he knew and we knew that it was too late. He had lost the necessary initiative. The inertia of habit held him too firmly. He would never go, and was as lost to his people as if he had perished years before in the perils of the Chilkoot. Just another well-born Outsider who had gone to pot, a shell of a man, living with his memories and feeding his pack of dogs on frozen salmon and tallow.

However, the present is the present, and it was arranged with much gusto and élan that Mr. Stansfield, with his dog team and sleigh, would take John and me for a ride, mushing like real sourdoughs.

One evening he came to dinner. He seemed perfectly familiar with all the conventions and conversed easily on many subjects. Instead of the heavy outdoor clothing and moccasins in which he was usually dressed, he wore a neat gray suit and regular leather shoes. Doug and I used to puzzle over him and what had broken the connection between his ambitions and his energies and left him marooned, an aging, lonely man, too proud to face defeat and go back empty-handed to those who loved him.

One morning, not too long after that, I walked and carried John the few steps down the hill to Mr. Stansfield's, where the dog team waited, harnessed to a light toboggan. John and I were seated on the sled, well wrapped in blankets. Mr. Stansfield ran behind, guiding the dogs.

It was very exhilarating to be flying along over the snow, the dogs' feet padding swiftly down the trail, until we turned a corner too sharply and the toboggan upset, throwing us into the snow, startled but unhurt. We were loaded in again by an apologetic Mr. Stansfield, but that ride did not last much longer, as the toboggan proved too difficult to manage. We went back home, and Mr. Stansfield unhooked the toboggan and substituted a regular Yukon sled.

A Yukon sled is the generally accepted carrier for freight and passengers in the North. A pair of long runners is provided with a platform like a bobsled on which can be placed the load. From the front ends of the runners are side pieces, slanting upwards and back to the height of a man's waist, ending in curved handles for steering. These are supported at the back end of the sled by a cross-barred square of light wood. Behind this is a low step on which the driver can stand if he wishes to ride and steer the sled by the handles. A lashing of interlaced ropes of rawhide or rattan, or wooden uprights at the sides, keep the load from falling out.

On the floor of the sleigh Mr. Stanfield had laid a pad of folded blankets for our comfort. Holding John in my lap, well wrapped in robes, I felt that this was something I would not have missed for the world, a ride in a real Yukon sled.

Another time Mr. Stansfield asked if Doug would like to mush the dogs instead of his doing so himself. This time we left John at home with Faithful Rufino. Doug was dressed warmly but lightly so that he would not be too warm while running alongside the sleigh, as perspiration is a sure precursor of freezing. If he had possessed one, this would have been the time to wear a parka, the lightweight, wind-repellent garment worn by all mushers.

We started off. The dogs swung into the trail leading to the river. We were going to mush on the ice of the Yukon down to Moosehide, the Indian village several miles below Dawson.

Out on the icy expanse of the broad Yukon we found ourselves surrounded by hummocks of rough-surfaced ice thinly covered by a layer of snow, so that it was necessary to keep to a definite trail broken and maintained by the many dog teams going to and from Moosehide on the Dawson trail. The river does not freeze over in one smooth surface of ice such as I used to see in the Middle West where skating and iceboating could be enjoyed.

For weeks before it freezes, the Yukon is running bankful of floating ice in great chunks that have been disgorged by its tributaries as well as formed along its own banks and in certain spots where the current is not so swift as it is in midstream. The open water is often mushy and half frozen. Consequently, when the temperature drops so low that the final freeze-up comes, all this conglomerate of huge chunks and mush ice is stopped and frozen together by connecting ice into a surface that is so rough and uneven that progress over it is extremely difficult except where a trail is made.

We swung down the trail back of our cabin of the first winter and out over the river, the dogs trotting briskly as Doug ran alongside shouting commands. The cold air stung our faces as it rushed past us; the sled runners sang over the ice. The dogs were pulling splendidly, when something went wrong. Instantly they were all piled up, tangled in their harnesses, snapping and barking.

Many times Doug and I had been outraged by what we considered the cruelty of drivers to their dogs. We had seen them kicking and cursing the poor animals until it required all the restraint we had to keep from interfering. Now a great light dawned upon us. After straightening the dogs out at least ten times on that trip, unbuckling and rearranging their harnesses and getting them started again, our sympathies were from that time on with the drivers.

I marveled at the new impetus and blossoming out of Doug's vocabulary, which had never seemed limited. That day he out-did himself. Epithets and insults rolled from his hoarsely shouting throat, past the dogs and into the eternal icy silence, like hissing hot sparks vanishing into a cold and sullen sea. It was a revelation to me of hitherto unknown resources of my husband's fighting spirit. While all I had to do was ride, he was battling the cold, the ice, and the dogs, running almost every step of the way as he spun out the most magnificent barrage of vituperation I had ever heard.

We swung through Moosehide, in and out between cabins, avoiding Indians and their dogs. The Yukon Indians were known generally as Siwashes. We did not have a very high opinion of these Indians, in their segregated town of Moosehide. How much the coming of the whites had to do with their laziness and disease I do not know, but they were both shiftless and unprepossessing.

Moosehide was a sordid, depressing habitation, and I was

not sorry when we left it and turned toward home and Dawson. Now the dogs were going really well, for they knew they were headed toward home and food. The way home is always shorter than the way to anywhere else. So in no time at all, it seemed to me, we were back at Mr. Stansfield's, the dogs panting and grinning, thinking no doubt of their reward of frozen salmon. Doug lifted me out of the sleigh, a little stiff but not at all cold, and we walked up the hill.

Some people travel by that means for thousands of miles, sleeping out at night with no shelter but a windbreak and no food except what they carry with them. After I had made that short trip with dogs I realized what fortitude and what courage it requires for these travelers to start out with their dogs across the icy wilderness, and such slight resources between themselves and death.

Clara Costar was going to have a baby. I had guessed it, by intuition, I think, and then she told us. Elsie and I began to work on presents for the little Costar at once. I decided to make a knitted shawl and bought white wool and large wooden needles. The knitted shawl I had owned was so indispensable for John that I knew no present I could think of would be more useful for Clara.

John was not walking yet. He was very heavy and seemed unwilling to make the attempt. I did not urge him to try, as I was definitely opposed to forcing a child to do something he seemed not ready to do. In spite of the scoldings of my friends and the good-natured teasing, I toted John around and let him creep when he wanted to. Finally he walked of his own volition, and then I knew it was right for him.

Just down the hill lived a little girl, Annie Churchward, who often came to play with John. She was a serious child, quite a little older than John, but she played with him as an equal, was never cross or selfish with him and undoubtedly did a great deal for his development, as he wanted to do everything she did.

They played in the south bay window in the living room, where any sun that existed found its way, serving tea with a tiny table, a little tin stove, and a set of dishes. While they were playing with imaginary tea or real milk and cookies, I could oversee what they were doing and yet have time for any task I wanted to finish. John had a pair of felt boots, lacing up almost to his knees and would wear them proudly with the additional ornament of a long string of colored wooden beads around his neck.

From the bay window I could look down upon the porch of Mr. Stansfield's house and see his dogs lying about as their owner was busy about his chores. Mr. Stansfield's eyes held that surprised, hurt look that one so often sees in people who seem to have come unawares into old age without being adjusted to it. Like the man who ordered to be written on his tombstone, "I expected this, but not so soon."

Just before Christmas, Doug had to go over the divide on a sixty-mile trip to Gold Run to check up on the wood contractors' progress in preparing the next season's wood. I thought of these trips Doug would take just in his stride and how soon we grow accustomed and adjusted even to the strangest environment and situations. All of us, busy little mites engrossed in our own affairs, lived on the very rim of the great arctic emptiness, much more engrossed with whether to have canned beans or canned corn for dinner than with the eternal enigma of the North.

Mr. Stansfield took his dogs and departed into the wilderness on one of those trips based on glimmering hope which he had made so many times before. Perhaps this time. . . . It seemed lonely to look at the empty house, no smoke coming out of the chimney and no sign of the dogs, and to think of them out in nowhere enduring discomforts and cold.

Already it was time to prepare for Christmas. We decided to give a dinner party and that took extra planning. Doug helped me, while I finished the presents for our Dawson friends, by taking care of John whenever he was home. A few days before Christmas we found a tree in the hills and trimmed it in a corner of the living room, leaving space for the dinner table and our guests—the Schellingers, the Costars, and Mr.

Franklin, who had done such clever detective work the winter before in the case of the Educated Swede. In order to seat this number, we put two tables together in the living room, and I decorated them with red candles, Christmas greens, and place cards.

As usual the dinner required much thought and time. There was the big turkey to thaw for several hours, then prepare and stuff. I gave it plenty of time to thaw, mindful of the story of the cheechakos who had served a leg of moose at a dinner party. The host carved it, after his wife had cooked it for hours, and after the first few slices he was into raw meat. Going deeper, he came to the center, frozen solid.

So I let the turkey take its time. The rest of our menu was to be oyster cocktails, celery, olives, pickles, cream-of-mushroom soup, mashed potatoes, creamed onions, cranberry and ginger sherbet served with the turkey, hot rolls, tomato aspic salad, frozen pudding, coffee, and mints. Luckily my stove was a shade larger than the one I used during the summers.

The guests arrived full of Christmas gaiety, each man bringing me a box of candy, which we opened after dinner while we sat around the table discussing the momentous things in our lives and the men smoked. These discussions were referred to as directors' meetings and usually were concerned with the mechanics of working for the men and with the different creative efforts in cooking and sewing for the women. There was very little gossip and less discussion of world affairs, books, or plays, not because we were clods but because those things touched our lives so remotely while the business of survival was always uppermost.

Shelley took some pictures and so did Garrison Costar, who, besides his Graflex, had a panoramic camera which Clara called his "pamoranic." John furnished us a lot of amusement as he reacted to his presents. He enjoyed the party just as much as we did and wanted to stay up until everyone left.

Another year had gone. The sun was no longer visible even at noon from our bay window and the little city below us lay shrouded in the frosty mist that came with the below 40 weather. Home fires burned steadily. This was the season for hiding from the intense and clawing cold wherever one could. Inside our cabin we were casual and lighthearted. Rugs went down before the doorsills as a matter of course; the ventilator was closed tightly save for a brief airing each day. The world was wrapped in mystery and silence, punctuated by the mournful howling of the Malemutes in the darkness.

17. The Granville Trip

JANUARY OF 1914 WAS JUST about like other Januarys except that now we lived high enough on the hill to see the sun for its first, momentary gleam on January 9, when it appeared at our window and almost instantly was gone again below the horizon. Jubilant, I telephoned all our friends. This was *the* news of the week. We were over the top. Even if bitter weeks were to follow, we could begin to think that spring was on the way.

As the tiny moments of sunlight grew longer we began to look for that inevitable cold spell in January. "When the days begin to lengthen, the cold begins to strengthen," was no idle jingle.

I was invited to a tea party at Mrs. Johnson's, way across the town, and would take John as a matter of course. That morning the thermometer hit 48 below. I was enough of a sourdough by that time not to let the weather make the slightest difference in my plans. We started the mile-long walk to Mrs. Johnson's, I battling the searing cold and trying to keep my hands warm as I pushed the sleigh. A little plume of steam arose from the shawl over John's face while he crooned and sang to himself beneath it.

Once at Mrs. Johnson's, I left the sleigh for a moment while I lifted John out and took him up into the house. Before I could turn back to get the sleigh up the steps, some wandering

Malemutes came by, and whisking the white fur robe off the sleigh, carried it across the street to a vacant lot, where they began to toss it about.

I started after them, knowing very well that they would tear it to pieces unless I interfered but at a loss to know how to get it away from them with my bare hands. ("Bare hands" is figurative, of course, as I was well gloved on that cold day). Luckily, just at that moment a wood skinner drove down the street with an enormous load of logs and going quite slowly on account of the cold. Man and team were white with frost as he beat his arms against his body to help the circulation.

At a glance he took in the situation of the dogs and my fur robe. He was wrapped snugly on the high seat of his sleigh and it meant great inconvenience to him to do what he did, but everyone in the North is a neighbor and a friend. So this perfect stranger stopped his team, unwound himself from the heavy robes, climbed off his load and took after the dogs with his horsewhip. After much beating and shouting he made them drop the robe. Then he picked it up and returned it to me as casually as if this were a common occurrence in his life. I thanked him, deeply grateful, and hurried back to Mrs. Johnson's house, the robe unharmed in my hands. I resolved never to take my eyes off that sleigh even for a minute whenever I took it out on the streets again.

Back at the house I had quite a tale to tell the women of the party. They had been wondering where I was, but the frost on the window panes prevented their looking out and it was too cold to investigate by opening the door. So they had taken off John's wraps and trusted that I would return.

After hearing what I had just experienced, they recalled stories of babies being left outside by mothers who went into stores and when they returned, the Malemutes had been there! I could not believe such tales, as I did not think any mother would be so careless. But it did make me glad that John was not in the sleigh along with the robe. The tea party progressed on schedule, and the incident of the robe was forgotten by all but me. I never forgot it.

Over at Government House, Mrs. Black was giving a series of luncheons. Covers were set for fourteen the day I was invited. It was bitter cold, 55 below, and Government House was at least a mile and a half away. I was certainly grateful when Mrs. Thomas sent her sleigh for me. The fine team drew up at our door with her sleigh fitted with soft lynx robes instead of the harsher bearskin robes provided by Pickering. The robe across the back was fringed with a row of fluffy tails, probably fox, which swung behind us. I felt like a fairy princess, and no pun intended.

That day John would stay with Faithful Rufino until Doug should arrive from the office. Each time I left him it was a minor tragedy, just a little scrap of John's life that I would not share. His unknowing baby stare followed me about the room, expecting to be dressed and taken along in due time. I knew he would be bitterly disappointed at being left behind, but his tears would be over in just a few moments. I kissed him and hurried away.

This was a real party, so I carried my best slippers and hat, as well as white gloves, in my bag, such as all of us owned for this purpose, while I wore the heavy felt shoes, tights, and stocking cap the weather demanded.

Once at Government House, I, with others, was shown to an upstairs bedroom. There we removed our cold-weather outfits, put on silk hose and slippers, smoothed our hair, donned our dressy hats and our white gloves and were ready to go down to luncheon.

Mrs. Black's table was what Doug would have called a knockout. Most of us were used to eating at very small tables, our lunch cloths being often of bridge-table size. Here in the large dining room of Government House we were seated at a table for fourteen, the lace cloth over blue satin and centered by a big bowl of pink roses. We blinked and decided that they seemed real. Oh, yes, we reminded ourselves, Government House had its own greenhouses. But still we were not certain. The entire lunch was equally surprising and delightful.

I sometimes wondered if Mrs. Black really knew what she did for us in the matter of morale. It was not absolutely necessary for her to entertain us as she did. Many of us were Americans and not her husband's constituents. Out of her generous, great nature she gave and gave to us as well as to the native Canadians, putting bits of glamor and delight into our days that none of us ever forgot.

The newly decorated drawing rooms as well as the table service installed by Mrs. Black were reflections of her perfect taste and originality and gave to her parties an elegance and dignity worthy of the Yukon. We, her guests, were enjoying the results of all the interest and work Mrs. Black had spent upon Government House. Handsome, perfectly gowned, and a consummate hostess, she kept the table conversation on precisely the right note. Since there were representatives there of several different groups of Dawson society, it took skill to make us all feel congenial and interested.

After luncheon there was bridge in the drawing room. It was exactly like the parties one might attend in any city in the world and hard to reconcile with the weather outside or the fact that we were at the top of creation.

When it was time to go, we had to face the realities again. We took off our party finery and put on our heavy outer clothing. There was a lot of joking among the women as they dressed. A certain Dawson matron had vainly neglected to draw woolens on over her silk stockings when she went out recently and had frozen both her legs in consequence.

Again in Mrs. Thomas's fur-caparisoned sleigh I was returned to my little red cabin.

I went directly to the kitchen, warm and cozy in the late afternoon. Here I found John and Doug, who had returned from the office and dismissed Faithful Rufino. My two boys, so much alike, looked at me gravely. They had had no magical day with pink roses and steam-heated rooms, no exotic food. I realized that I really had little desire to have something not shared by them, even if it was only a party.

I whisked into my housedress, prepared John for bed and finished getting our dinner, feeling a little sorry for people who could not have what I did, though there might be pink roses for them and not for me.

Doug had to make another trip into the wilderness in connection with the processing of fuel wood for the thawing plants. For many years the individual miners had been cutting the more accessible wood to thaw the frozen gravels with wood fires built in their tunnels underground, and later to make steam with small boilers. Also, thousands of cords had been cut to keep the home fires burning in Dawson and along the creeks through the long winters.

Then, when the company required such enormous quantities of wood for thawing to enable the dredges to dig the ground, the supply receded farther and farther. Finally it was exhausted on the slopes where wood could be sledded downhill to its destination, and Doug had to devise methods for tapping the hitherto inaccessible timber on the opposite sides of the slopes.

All such wood was hauled in winter over the snow, with horses and large sleds heavily loaded. Summer hauling was prohibitive except for the wood delivered to certain thawing plants by the narrow-gauge railroad running up Bonanza Creek from Klondike City, popularly known as Louse Town. Some of this wood had been floated long distances down the Klondike River, but most of it came down the Yukon River in large rafts, the long logs chained together and guided by a steamboat for about a hundred miles. These logs were sawed at the river's edge at Louse Town, and the four-foot lengths loaded on flatcars in cable slings to be unloaded at the thawing plants by electric derricks. This wood lost much of its heating value from long immersion in water. Doug had proved by tests that the dry wood hauled in winter was better in every way.

In order to make available this hitherto inaccessible timber, an ingenious procedure had been worked out. Doug lent one of the big boilers from the nearest thawing plant to the wood contractor; its steam powered a steam engine and hoist which hauled trains of loaded sleds to the top of the hill up a steep incline one to two miles long. From this crest of the divide teams were able to take the heavy sledloads downhill easily to whatever plant they were destined for over special roads constructed for the purpose.

Of all the various wood contractors, Charlie Stone was Doug's favorite, principally because he was fair and square. Certain other wood merchants would try to bribe, or cheat in their measurements, or slip in some wood not up the strict specifications. They had to be watched and checked constantly; Doug had to be pretty hard-boiled with some of them.

Doug and Charlie Stone got along famously. Stone gave good quality and full measurement. Tall and lanky, tobacco-chewing, hard-drinking, and hard-riding, a lover of spirited saddle horses, with an ever-ready laugh and joke when things were going against him, Charlie Stone seemed happy-go-lucky and easygoing, but he got results for the company from his men and equipment. He had come up from the ranks of the common teamsters by native initiative and a willingness to take long chances. He delivered the goods, win or lose.

Stone would go into a distant wilderness where ordinary contractors feared to tread; by utilizing new ideas and some company equipment, he broke precedents and sometimes his shoestring bankroll, but he was always ready to tackle another tough job. In the long run he made money, acquired a big stable, good horses, sleds, and other equipment.

In the winter of 1909 and '10, Charlie Stone made his headquarters at Gold Bottom and brought large amounts of wood to the various plants on Hunker Creek from beyond that divide. In 1912 and '13 he used company boilers and hoists to deliver wood to El Dorado and Upper Bonanza from the opposite side of those slopes. Wherever he set up operations it was known as Stone's Wood. This was a rather general term, however; when Doug announced that he was going to Stone's Wood for a few days, I knew it might include riding over thousands of acres of standing or partly felled timber; sizing up the great piles of wood where it had been "yarded" at the bottom of the mile-long incline, the boiler and hoist silhouetted distantly at the top of the divide; eating and sleeping in Stone's log camp-building, and finally driving home alone forty to sixty miles in bitter cold out of that crude wilderness to the comparative comforts of Dawson.

Tomorrow's trip was to Gold Run and Granville, which territory Charlie Stone did not invade until the fall of 1914. That is another story—and a good one.

Dredge Number Six had been dismantled on Lower Bonanza and was being hauled across the divide to Gold Run Creek near its confluence with Dominion Creek, the company's first operation in that distant field. Doug had prospected there during the early summer of 1911 before we were married; later, Fred Morris came in and took over that examination and Doug returned to the Dawson side of the divide. Now, two years later, actual mining was to start. That meant thawing in advance of the dredge and thawing meant wood. Fortunately a considerable supply of fuel had been cut and stored for the previous claim owners in past years. Now Doug was having it sorted and assembled at the new Gold Run thawing plant, with some other odd lots.

The night before his trip we had grouse for dinner, just for a touch of luxury. Then there was the usual hurried morning departure and the lonely days for me when I took John out, made calls and returned to the empty, but this time not cold, house. On one of those calls I took the finished shawl to Clara Costar.

Doug returned on schedule, bringing four ptarmigan, and we had another feast. We thought they were not quite so good as the grouse but a very welcome change from the frozen meat of the butcher shops.

By February 14, Doug had decided to take that trip again. He always spent the nights at Granville on Dominion Creek, which was nothing more or less than a roadhouse set in the middle of nowhere. The wood was now ready for Doug's final checking and accurate measurement before it was accepted and paid for. But this trip was to be just a little different from any that had preceded it.

The roadhouse at Granville was owned and operated by a Frenchman who lived there with his wife and little daughter and mother-in-law. Doug had found the place clean and the meals good. So a perfectly dazzling idea occurred to him. Why not take John and me with him?

This was no season to take a baby on a trip of sixty miles each way with practically unbroken wilderness the whole distance. It meant an overnight stop each way at a roadhouse, preferably at Gold Bottom, and many hours out in the cold. Should we do it? To Doug the plan seemed simple enough because he was doing it all the time, but what about John and me?

We had done some pretty unusual things before and gotten away with them, so we decided to do this one. A friend, Mrs. Hulme, heard of our plan and came to see if I would consider letting her keep John. She begged me to let her. However, Doug and I felt that John would like the trip. After all, wasn't he a sourdough? What real sourdough would hesitate over a little thing like winter and snow? So we thanked her and decided that John would go along, even if he was not quite two years old and was utterly unused to such an experience.

The road led up Hunker to Gold Bottom, then on up Hunker Creek over quite a divide and into the headwaters of Gold Run Creek and Dominion Creek, which flowed into the Indian River to the east and south of Dawson. This was an area drained by many creeks, all stemming from the highest peak thereabouts, known as the Dome, and not to be confused with the Dome back of Dawson. These streams were all bearers of auriferous gravels and figured in the early gold-rush days. Except for a few roadhouses, very far apart, there would be nothing in all this region between us and the unbroken expanse of snow, silence, and cold.

I packed carefully, including all the things we could possibly need for the trip. At two-thirty in the afternoon of a clear, cold day we started off, leaving our house as safe as we knew how to, with nothing in the way of food to freeze and spoil in our absence.

The cutter was light and well provisioned with bearskin robes over the back of the seat, under us, and down to the floor beneath our feet, and over our laps, tucked in all around so that not a breath of wind could seep in. We had hot coffee in the thermos in case we grew chilled on the way. John sat between us, arranged so that he was comfortable and warm. I could shield his face from the wind with a shawl if necessary. We all wore extra clothing for warmth and felt clumsy in consequence.

The team consisted of Doug's Devil and his teammate. When harnessed double, Doug's horse acted very differently and was perfectly safe. The team was both fast and in wonderful condition as off we went in a clear jingle of bells, skimming effortlessly over the smooth snow. The cutter was so light that the team pulled it just with their bits, the tugs often hanging slack at their sides.

We raced along, exhilarated by the motion and speed, into a landscape both snowy and deserted. The cabins we passed were closed tightly against the cold with few, perhaps no, signs of life around them. Only a thread of blue wood smoke from the chimneys gave us a hint as to which ones were inhabited. Those which were not were snowed in all around, their roofs, window sills, and doorsteps topped by mounds of snow, their eaves hung with icicles. The surrounding yards were a smooth expanse of white save for here and there little trails of snow patterns where some small wild creatures hunted or were hunted for food.

The road to Gold Bottom that we had traveled so many times in summer seemed unfamiliar now. There were no dusty hedgerows, no drooping canes of wild berries along the road, no clumps of wild roses or patches of pink fireweed in the fields, no green trees or blue sky. Instead there was white, white, white, ending only at the horizon, where the pale-green sky began. The sun had disappeared some time before as we swept up to the hotel at Gold Bottom, stiff and a little cold despite all our furs and wraps.

Mr. Lemaster, the hotel proprietor, came out to help us unload. Doug carried John, quite a bundle in all his wrappings, into the hotel and I followed into the big room with its red-hot stove, wavy floor, and dusky corners. Thankfully we took off our outer wraps. Later on, when we were warmed, we went upstairs to our icy-cold little bedroom, left our suitcase and outer wraps and returned to the warm lower rooms. I retained my heavy sweater. Since water left in our room would freeze, we took warm water upstairs from the kitchen to wash after we had made the necessary trip outside to the bitterly cold out-house back of the hotel.

After we had sat by the stove for awhile, dinner was announced. There was fried chicken and it was delicious. The hotel was filled with wood skinners, a rough, good-natured lot of men who worked hard, ate heartily and went off very early to sleep soundly in their little cold, air-tight rooms. Ours was air-tight too, but there was nothing we could do about it because the double windows, thick with frost, were all nailed on for the winter. Stale air always seems colder than fresh air.

It took all the fortitude we possessed to undress and climb into the icy bed. We kept John between us so that he would be warm, but the outer rims of the bed were as cold as Greenland at its reputed worst. All three of us slept huddled together for warmth. Once in a while, tired of being curled up, I would stretch out an exploring foot in order to straighten out and change my position. Then I would encounter hostile, frigid corners outside our little circle of warmth and quickly draw the foot back again. Needless to say, I was wearing those cross-barred pajamas so noted for warmth!

We slept because we were tired, but I doubt whether we really rested much. Getting up was another severe test of will power, but we had to do it. We finally braced ourselves to meet the cold and leaped out, hurrying into our clothes, our hands stiff. Not much time was spent by me in making myself beautiful. My hair was combed, my face powdered in record time. With blue lips and slightly red nose, I was ready.

We bundled John into a blanket and carried him downstairs to dress him by the warm heater. The wood skinners had breakfasted and gone, and we had the place to ourselves. After a hot breakfast with plenty of coffee (of horrid flavor from having been boiled), we felt better.

Doug went out to see about his team, and I accompanied Mr. Lemaster to the barn to see a litter of pigs born that night. We couldn't stay long, though, because I had to go back and get John ready by the time the team was driven up to the front door for our start on the second and longest part of the drive. We would go forty miles straight into the wilderness, over the divide and along Gold Run Creek, until we landed at Granville on Dominion Creek.

Again we went through the careful tucking and settling ourselves in the cutter which meant the difference between comfort and distress. The team were feeling restive and eager to start, shaking themselves and jingling the sleigh bells. At last we were ready and away, off into the shining and mysterious nowhere that was Dominion Creek, somewhere over there beyond the horizon. Doug made these trips often, but this time I was to realize what they involved and what stamina it required to undertake them.

Our team took us along apparently with no effort. John sat snugly between us while we sang songs to him, speeding over the frozen waste, our voices trailing out behind the sleigh into empty space. We sang:

> The gentle cow all red and white
> I love with all my heart.
> She gives us milk with all her might,
> To eat on apple tart.

and

> A birdie with a yellow bill
> Hopped upon the window sill,
> Cocked his shining eye and said,
> "Ain't you 'shamed, you sleepy head?"

with other verses from R.L.S., Doug roaring out the verses

while John took them in very gravely, his eyes on the horses trotting so rhythmically mile after mile. We were now climbing up the long grade to the top of the divide.

We stopped for a few moments' rest at the roadhouse on the summit and to ease the horses. Hunker Creek lay behind us, Gold Run Creek ahead. Then we went on again, flying down the slopes of the mountains into the vast and empty valleys of Gold Run and Dominion creeks, which eventually would become the Indian River and empty into the Yukon River above Dawson. There was such a lot of country lying around there that we decided it would take thousands of years to make use of all the land lying squarely under the North Star. It certainly would never happen in our day.

By noon we had reached the roadhouse where we were to stay for lunch. This was Murray's, a solid log building built to withstand the weather and not for beauty. Yet it had a most reassuring look of solidarity and comfort. It stood alone. Nothing else but snow and stunted trees was to be seen as far as our vision carried. This one outpost was all that wandering prospectors and trappers or teamsters hauling wood, machinery, or supplies had to depend on. If they could not make it, they had nowhere else to go. Snow was drifted against the log walls; icicles hung from the roof. The small six-paned windows were crusted deep with frost. There was a little storm shed over the front door. In back were sheds and a barn for travelers' horses.

We ate a substantial lunch in the dining room off the main room: meat, potatoes, canned tomatoes, homemade bread and butter, and canned fruit. The dishes were the same as those to be found in every camp in the North: white ironstone china, thick, heavy, and battered from hard use. Knives and forks were steel.

While the horses were being fed and rested, we looked around and amused ourselves in the big general room with the bar across one end. Some of the men were playing the phonograph and finally a record was put on—a woman singing an operatic aria, colorful and rich. If there is any sound in the world more lonely than such operatic singing heard in the midst of an arctic wilderness, I do not know what it can be. It reminded me that at that very moment there were people far away on the other side of the world, laughing, singing, living in surroundings of color, warmth, and beauty in a serene civilization with others of their own kind.

"That music is too rich for my blood," a big man in heavy mackinaw coat and trousers and snow pacs said, as he walked over to the phonograph and shut it off. He found another record and started it. This one was Harry Lauder. The other men laughed and relaxed comfortably. They liked Harry Lauder. He did not make them feel out of place by reminding them of things they knew nothing about.

The horses ready, once again we packed ourselves into the cutter and were off, the team as lively as before. It was as if they were running free over those miles of snow, the weight of the cutter hampered them so little. We sped on toward Dominion and the early darkness which came on while we still had many miles to go.

John slept in his nest of robes during this most interesting and mysterious part of the trip. We could see nothing, but we knew we were in the center of a vast, uninhabited area covered by a waste of snow which obliterated any features of the landscape. We were traveling at about ten miles an hour over those last twenty miles, in the dark and isolation, three little human beings in utter solitude.

Just as I was beginning to wonder if we had gone over the top of the world in the dark and started down the other side, we saw lights ahead.

"There's the Granville roadhouse," Doug said, and the words were as welcome as any I had ever heard in my life. As we came closer the bulk of the building began to take shape around the lighted windows and we pulled up before the door.

The proprietor and his wife greeted us and introduced us to their little girl, Ramona. We alighted, chilly and stiff. It was good to go inside, carrying John, who was blinking awake from his long nap and looking around him wonderingly.

Then we met the grandmother who lived with the owners.

The women were French and voluble, delighted to see new-comers, most hospitable, and eager that we be comfortable. We were shown to a room on the first floor, not such a long dash this time from the big living room, the one heated room in the house except the kitchen.

In the room we found a comfortable bed, a dresser, and a washstand with bowl and pitcher. I was amazed to find on the washstand a brand-new cake of Roger and Gallet's Violet soap for my use! I had long been a user of Roger and Gallet's Violet toilet water and their soap also. The Violet soap I had considered a great luxury, as even in the States it was forty cents a cake. To find it in this remote place, costing an outrageous price, I had no doubt, seemed to me simply incredible. There were many other evidences about the room of these French-women's desire to retain the small refinements that would make of this lonely place a home for them and for the little girl.

Living at this roadhouse was also the foreman for the thaw-ing plant serving Dredge Number Six, located on Gold Run Creek, Alec "Scotty" Gordon. He was there to meet us, a huge, powerfully built man with the strength and endurance needed for such a job.

It was so late that we were more than glad to sit right down to a hot dinner, eating alone since the other occupants of the roadhouse had already dined some time before. After a talk with Alec and the owners, all seated around the hot stove in the main room, we were sleepy and ready for bed soon after nine o'clock. Our long drive in the cold and then the heated room had made us drowsy, especially after the hearty meal we had eaten.

Alec asked us to dinner the following evening as his guests. He had already ordered the dinner with all his favorite dishes and bragged about what good cooks those two Frenchwomen were, promising us something very special.

During the next day, which was reasonably mild, Doug was gone with the team over at Gold Run Creek, inspecting wood and measuring the thousands of cords which had been hauled, then visiting Scotty Gordon and looking at the work the winter repair crew was doing. Meantime, after his day of inaction in the sleigh, John wanted to walk. He went around the hotel opening doors into cold rooms, with me after him shutting them to keep out the cold air. We had ourselves a very busy and active morning, but it did give us exercise.

In the afternoon I decided that an outdoor walk would be good for both of us. There was a little sleigh on the porch belonging to Ramona. She was a well-behaved, dark-eyed little girl who was very happy to let John use her sleigh. So we put on our many wraps and went out. The air was stinging cold, but the sun was shining over the white world. I kept John out about an hour, following the road in one direction and then in the other until we were both pretty chilly. After the first exhilaration of the clear, sparkling air had worn off, the idea of returning to the warm rom seemed attractive and compelling.

The dinner that night was an event in the lives of these people, that was easy to see. Both women had worked in the kitchen a good part of the day, preparing those favorite dishes of Alec's which he wanted us to have. One of them was pork pie made with the crispest, most ephemeral crust I had ever eaten. There was soup, several kinds of vegetables, hot rolls, a salad, and for dessert, a custard with fruit. All was splendidly done. Scotty was a proud host and pleased by our praise and enjoyment of his friends' ability.

Both women had dressed especially for the occasion. Little Ramona was wearing her prettiest frock, and her papa beamed as he served us with just that extra flourish that the French can summon when the occasion demands. We sat late at the table, satisfied and forgetful of the outside world and where we were.

The next day there were more good meals and a bath for John in Ramona's little tin tub. Then I made what preparations were necessary for the return as we were to start very early the next morning.

On the way back we had lunch at Murray's again. The proprietors greeted us like old friends and played with John. After lunch there was the same careful routine of preparation against the cold when we started on again, enlivened by the intake of cold air into our lungs and the swift pace of the horses. We could easily have imagined ourselves to be on the Russian steppes as our sleigh bells jangled musically over the horses' backs and our eyes took in the blue-white distances. I pulled the fur robes closer about John and me until I was conscious of the dry, acrid smell of the fur in sharp contrast to the clear purity of the air.

At six-thirty we pulled up at the Gold Bottom Hotel, tired, cold, and hungry. As we came to the door we were greeted like long-lost wanderers. It was wonderful to take off the heavy furs and outer wrappings and to thaw out beside the glowing heater before we went in to a dinner which tasted like a banquet, we were so hungry.

After dinner most of the log skinners and other men gathered around just for the privilege of seeing John and being near him. Doug set him up on the bar, and he entertained them all with his smiles and attempts at conversation. These men had seen no children for months, and they went crazy over John, who was as jolly and responsive as if he enjoyed them just as they did him.

When we went to bed, the room was as icy as it was before. Our rest was no better. We welcomed the summons to get up and dress for breakfast, heroic as we had to be to do it.

The trip to Dawson from there took only three hours. How good it was to see our little red cabin waiting for us and better still, to start a big fire in the furnace and unpack in a comfortable warm house! John found his toys and was immediately engaged, while I rushed around getting the house and ourselves back to normal. Meanwhile Doug took the team back to Pickering's. As ever, the greatest fun of the trip was coming home.

We arrived home at one o'clock, and at two Mrs. Johnson and Virginia came to spend the afternoon and hear all about our trip.

That very day Clara and Garrison Costar became the parents of a nine-pound son, Garrison junior.

The next day I cleaned the house, baked bread and cake, then took John down to the office to meet Doug and walk home with him—just the good, homey routine we were so used to and so content in doing. The wintry trip to Granville, over those miles of wilderness, receded into a memory, so unusual it hardly seemed real as we went about our accustomed living.

18.   A Hazardous Journey for Doug

RUTH McFARLAND AND I WENT to the hospital to see Clara and little Garrison junior and to commiserate with each other over the latest news. Doug was being sent to the Sixty Mile to inspect a new gold strike and to decide whether the ground would be favorable for dredging. A courier had come in secretly to the company with the information that a strike had been made by some Frenchmen, and Doug was elected to go over and look into it. Speed was the main idea, before anyone else could interfere.

The trip would take at least two weeks and Doug could take with him anyone he wanted to. He had decided on Warren McFarland.

They would take a team and a sleigh with a deep bed, big enough to carry all their supplies as well as hay and grain for the horses, about two tons in all. The trip involved the most careful planning and preparation since the men must carry their sampling outfit, extra clothes, and proper garb for going down in shafts to sample the ore. They would use the fur robes in the sleigh for their bedding. Doug would have to be ready to leave by the first of the week.

They left early in the morning on March 3. The Sixty Mile is a tributary of the Yukon River, entering it some miles above Dawson. The boys would drive on the ice of the Yukon to the Sixty Mile and then over a snow road to the camp, the courier guiding them, an extra passenger.

My thoughts were with them all day. Their sleigh would be so heavily loaded that it would take them all of one day and most of the next to make the trip.

Ruth and I had decided to join forces and stay together nights at her house, since the furnace at my cabin could be trusted to hold fire all night without watching better than her heater would.

Ruth's heater frequently blew up at night, so we filled the teakettle and set it on the lid of the stove. Everyone was asleep when, *boomph,* the stove lid blew off and tipped the teakettle perilously close to sliding into the interior of the heater. Ruth and I both jumped out of bed and sleepily replaced the lid, added all the flatirons to hold it down, and slept the rest of the night peacefully. Ruth was always calm, always adequate, and always good to look at, with her dark hair and eyes and rose-petal skin. Whether she was baking bread, bathing the baby, or calling on the Ping-pongs, she was always the same Ruth, and I do not think she ever realized how lovely she was.

One day I hurried through my work and started away from the cabin early, as I intended to stop and see Mrs. Johnson on my way to Ruth's. We had a good visit and I was again on my way, thinking about Doug and wishing that there could be some way I might hear from him. I walked along, pushing John's sleigh and turning these things over in my mind, when I came to an intersection of two streets. I could look up the hill and see our house from this street corner, but I seldom did. Something impelled me to turn my head and look back over my shoulder when I was nearly across the street.

My glance went past the array of cabin roofs and snowy yards up and up until it came to the long low roof lines of the red cabin. There it stood, serene and very fair, its windows overlooking the town.

But something was wrong. I looked and looked, trying to decide what appeared different and out of the ordinary. Then I realized what it was.

There was no smoke coming from the chimney!

From all the other cabins a thin column of wood smoke

rose straight and plumy. From mine there was nothing. I turned the sleigh around and started up the hill as fast as I could go. As I came closer, I could see what I had dreaded. Instead of smoke, what was coming from my chimney was a series of heat waves, dancing in irregular motion against the sky. Something had happened, and the furnace was overheating terrifically. If only I could get there in time!

Pushing John's heavy sleigh uphill was a task I usually took my time about. This time there was no limit to my speed. When at last I reached the house, quite breathless, I left John in the sleigh and ran up the steps to the front door alone in case the house was already on fire and needed only the draft from the opened door to set the whole thing ablaze.

When I opened the door, there was no smoke, but the air was as hot as that from an oven. A queer, gassy smell filled the house. I ran to the kitchen and opened the trap door to the cellar, again risking starting a blaze, but I must see what was going on down there.

I saw soon enough. On the cellar floor lay the door to the furnace, which had blown off. The furnace was red-hot and the floor beams above were almost too hot for my hand to touch in spite of the asbestos, while the gassy smell in the air was almost unendurable. The wood inside the furnace was a mass of red-hot coals and flame, created by the immense draft of the open door.

Instinctively I picked up the door and replaced it on the furnace opening. Then I investigated every inch of the woodwork in the basement. It was hot but not yet smoking.

I rushed back upstairs, mindful of John, leaving the cellar and front doors open to clear out the gas. I found John quiet and contented in his sleigh, brought him inside and then closed the door and sat down, suddenly weak and tired.

What if I had not happened to glance around and look up at the cabin when I did? If I had not, we might not even have a cabin by this time, since it took only a few minutes for a cabin, dry as timber, to burn up once a fire started. But I did look, and everything was safe. The furnace quieted down; I took off John's wraps and settled him among his toys. I felt too unnerved to go away and leave the cabin again that night, so I telephoned Ruth that I would not be down.

Then I telephoned the tinsmith who had made the furnace, telling him what had happened. He promised to come the first thing in the morning to fasten clamps on the door.

During that night I wakened several times to look down the cellar and make sure that the door was in its proper place.

The tinsmith spent all the next morning putting on the clamps with an interlocking device. By giving the door a half turn, I could engage it into the clamps, making it so firm that it could never blow off again. Now I could leave the cabin with confidence.

As there was no heat in the rest of the cabin while the tinsmith worked, John and I remained in the kitchen and kept warm by the cookstove. After the man had left, I rebuilt the furnace fire and heaved in a couple of big logs.

"Now blow off," I dared the door.

When the house was warm again, I felt as secure as I would have if I had suddenly been given a trust fund. That evening the Schellingers took me to a movie, while Faithful Rufino stayed with John. I had no fears about the place, and when we all came home for a Welsh rarebit and coffee, the house was warm and cozy and I went to bed without a qualm.

A week had gone by since Doug and the other boys had left that cold morning. I went back to Ruth's the next night and found there letters from them that had come through by a courier. We each read our letters and wrote replies to go back by the same courier in a couple of days. I carefully omitted all reference to the furnace in order not to worry Doug.

It was 30 below. Ruth and I had social engagements which took no account of the weather. There was a reception at Government House and a card party at Mrs. MacPherson's which functioned no matter what the thermometer said. Twice Ruth and I went to a picture show and left the babies in good hands. Thus, even if we were widows, we were not without some diversion.

Almost two weeks had gone by. Mr. and Mrs. Thomas took a trip to the Sixty Mile so that Doug could show Mr. Thomas the ground they were examining and give him the results of the investigation. Mr. Thomas was very eager to get some action on the strike, as it was rumored that another company was showing interest and he wanted to get the ten miles of claims safely optioned.

Miss Iredell asked me to spend the night with her and the Thomas children. The Thomas cutter called for me and I crossed the town in ease and luxury, arriving in time for dinner. We sat up late, visiting, Miss Iredell and I, and did not hurry down to breakfast the next morning. It was about eleven when we were finishing our coffee, idly discussing this and that. The pleasant table, with Frank's smiling service, tempted us to linger on; it was such a contrast to the bleak vista just outside the dining-room windows, a gray sky with drifts of snow and no color to relieve the scene. The children had been fed and were playing near us.

With no warning at all, Doug walked into the room and stood behind my chair. He leaned down and kissed me from that safe vantage ground and then came around my chair and sat down to have some coffee with us. I was too surprised to notice this somewhat strange manner of greeting.

Cautiously, bit by bit, Doug unfolded the history of the past two weeks, the reason why he had returned without the others, and most significant of all, why he had stood behind my chair when he kissed me.

In short, he was all taped up with three broken ribs and did not want to be hugged!

This was the story: Doug and Warren had been on their way to town with the same courier who had guided them out to the new strike, when they met the Thomases going out to Sixty Mile. The two sleighs stopped. Doug told Mr. Thomas that he had been injured and was going into town, but Mr. Thomas wanted him to go right back with them, nevertheless.

Mrs. Thomas called C.A.T.'s attention to the way Doug was shaking while he stood there conferring, and finally Mr.

Thomas told him to go on in with the guide and Warren could go back with them. He told Doug to go to the Thomases' and go to bed there until they returned.

It all sounded pretty mixed up to me. One thing was sure: Doug was to go to bed at once, by doctor's orders, and at the Thomases', since those were the orders of C.A.T. By strange coincidence, John and I were already there!

Bit by bit I had the whole story, as Doug lay in comparative comfort in the Thomases' guest room.

On the trip out to the Sixty Mile, two weeks before, Doug had driven almost all the way, when finally Warren took the reins to give him a rest. Then they came to a glacier over the road, hidden by snow. These glaciers formed when water collected in the road from an overflowing spring or during a thaw and subsequently froze. This ice, when covered with snow, was deceptively harmless-looking until one struck the glacier underneath.

The sleigh slid on the ice and tipped over. Doug, being on the left and downhill side, went out and against a tree. The frightened and unmanageable horses pulled the heavy sleigh until it came up against the same tree. Unfortunately Doug stopped the sleigh too, since he was in front of the tree and was caught between it and the sleigh. He was smashed flat!

By the time the team was quieted and the sleigh unloaded and lifted away from Doug, he fell unconscious to the ground. The others thought he was dead. They began to turn the team around to take him back to Dawson. During the time consumed for this operation Doug's flattened lungs were painfully filling with air again as he regained consciousness. When they told him what they were doing, he ordered them to continue on to the Sixty Mile as planned. They demurred, but Doug was still in charge.

"Company first." Doug was in constant pain and realized that something was definitely wrong. But in full recognition that there was a job to do, he climbed ladders and went down the forty to sixty feet into shafts, several times a day, as well as crawling on hands and knees through drifts and tunnels in the various prospects. Both Frenchmen and Americans were there, each group not too trustful of the other. Doug was the only man the Frenchmen would deal with; consequently he had to look at all of their ground, leaving the others to take care of the Americans.

At night they slept where they could. On floors made of small poles, with nothing under them but a fur robe, Doug really suffered. Occasionally there would be an extra bunk for him in one of the Frenchmen's cabins, with a bed slightly more comfortable. They would rise for an early breakfast and more crawling around through prospect holes. Doug, ever mindful of being salted, did his own sampling and panning in every case.

After this had gone on for two weeks, Doug was really in bad shape, but he would not go back to Dawson until all the work was completed. The handling of a pick in frozen ground, traveling from cabin to cabin with dog teams, and little sleep, combined with constant pain, had worn him out. They started at five in the morning to return to Dawson and halfway there met the Thomases. Had Mrs. Thomas not realized Doug's condition, he would have been obliged to turn back.

Once in Dawson, Doug went directly to the company doctor, who was leaving his office just at that moment to take care of a woman with a broken leg. After looking at Doug, he decided that he was the worse off of the two and returned to his office, letting the broken leg wait. He found three ribs broken and internal injuries, strapped Doug up and ordered him to bed for three weeks at least. On C.A.T.'s order Doug went to the Thomases', finding John and me already there!

After I had heard all about the trip to the Sixty Mile, I told Doug about the near fire I had fortunately averted.

"I, carefully keeping from you the news that I was hurt, and you, keeping from me the news about the fire." He grinned. "We certainly don't like to worry each other!"

Doug spent that day, which was Sunday, and Monday in bed, while I kept John in the playroom with the Thomas children and Miss Iredell. Phone messages and inquiries for Doug came in continually and the invalid received plenty of attention.

On Tuesday the Thomases returned in time for lunch. Mr. Thomas went at once to Doug's room and found out just what was the matter with him. Then he said, "I'll have to send you right back there, Doug."

Doug mentioned the doctor's order of three weeks in bed. "They won't deal with anyone but you," C.A.T. protested, "and we've got to option that ground before some other company beats us to it. The Frenchmen say, 'Nobody but that fellow Ferry.'"

Doug went to see the doctor that afternoon, and John and I went home. That was the last of the three weeks in bed. Doug spent every afternoon or the whole day in the office, making up option forms for all the claims they were interested in on the Sixty Mile and also prepared an elaborate report to be telegraphed to the New York office for authorization to start prospecting as soon as the ground was optioned.

COMPANY FIRST.

On a cold morning, just a week after he had returned, Doug, stiff in his heavy reinforcement of doctor's tape, dressed slowly and awkwardly and departed again for the Sixty Mile at six-thirty, with my derogatory remarks about the company in his ears.

The doctor was indignant, I was indignant, but *Company First.* How true it is that women think in terms of life, men think in terms of property! There was a tough job to do and Doug had to do it, and I might as well have sung my opinions down a well.

I tried to fill my days with sewing, calls on my friends, and John's airings. I went through my whole library of music during the evenings, especially some new things Christina had sent me. Then I decided to have some pictures of John and me taken for Doug's birthday. So I went to see Mr. Jerry Doody, the well-known photographer of the North, and arranged to have him take them in our living room. There would be plenty of light in the bay window during the middle of the day, as there was now abundant sunshine. He promised to come, although he was much more used to taking outdoor views and had no special equipment for interiors.

By doing something I thought would make Doug happy, I managed to compensate to some extent for his being away.

Doug had been gone almost a week, when Mr. Pretty decided to give a dinner and theater party for the widows. He invited Ruth, Mrs. Thomas, Elsie, and me. Right in the middle of the dinner party, Mr. Pretty at the head of the table looking important and full of responsibility, like a masculine hen with chicks, in walked Mr. Thomas with Doug!

Some people are born to have their best plans frustrated, and Mr. Pretty seemed to be one of them.

The thawing plants were a month behind schedule, due to Doug's trips to the Sixty Mile, so now he was busier than ever. He spent his birthday in his office, but we celebrated that evening with a roast saddle of mountain sheep which he had brought back with him. I made sherbet and a cake with thick frosting and was right in the midst of these preparations when Ruth and Elsie came to call.

Carefully wrapped and tied with gift ribbon was Doug's present, the pictures Jerry Doody had made. There were six five-by-eight prints in soft finish and all were good, each a different pose. I had hoped that Doug would like them, and he certainly did.

As the spring season advanced and the start of work along the creeks grew near, many things were happening. Mr. Thomas went back to the Sixty Mile and Mr. McCarthy came in over the ice to start the summer work. Garrison Costar was sent to superintend the prospecting on the Sixty Mile, which meant that Clara would be alone in town for several months with the little baby.

John and Annie Churchward could now play out on the sunny porch for a little while each afternoon. I began to think about materials and spring sewing.

During the winter I had sent to Liberty's in London for samples of materials shown in their catalogue. The descriptions had made them sound so enchanting that I ordered samples of cottons, silks, and elaborate brocades. From advertisements in the London *Graphic* and other periodicals I had obtained the names of other firms. Catalogues had come from Robinson and Cleaver's of Belfast, Ireland; from Egerton Burnett, of Wellington, Somerset; and from the White House, Laces and Linens, of Portrush, Ireland.

In these catalogues Elsie and I had discovered not only what was being worn, presumably by ladies and duchesses in the best London mode but also the kind of embroidered sheets and towels they used, how much it would cost to embroider one's coronet above one's monogram, and the type of aprons and uniforms worn by their maids. A liberal education, in fact, hard to come by in any other way by a remote Colonial American.

There were pages and pages of descriptions of English and Irish woolens of every kind, from the heavy steamer rugs and tweeds to the finest of baby wear. Looking through those catalogues was almost as good as taking a trip to the shops themselves. Liberty's was probably the most entrancing of all because one could find so many exotic things mentioned. These catalogues served not only us but the entire British colonial empire with its demands for many differing climates and people.

I ordered samples lavishly. There was a double purpose in this—things for ourselves and gifts for friends. Absorbed, I pored over descriptions of silks, velvets, laces, and brocades, trying to decide whether to resist this allure and succumb to that or just to be reckless and send for samples of both. Then I sent the letters off and forgot them, only to remember suddenly and apropos of nothing that oh, yes, samples would be coming along some months from now.

I watched for them to come just as eagerly as if they were bright little patches of heaven sent on ahead so that we could try them for color and texture. As a matter of fact, I would think them all perfect and my only embarrassment would be in having to reject any when I wanted them all.

One day, early in April, when there was just enough of

winter left to give me a real stimulus in seeing something gay
and beautiful, the samples arrived. I spread them all out, bright
jewels of color, on the couch in the living room, and there
they would remain until Clara and Elsie could see them too.
Again and again I would walk through the room just to catch
a glimpse of them, my thoughts spinning and creating them
into lovely finished things. It was not enough that I simply
make the things I required. By dolling them up a little, adding an ornament or a flower, a bit of gracefulness, I could
make of life much more than a dull routine and at the same
time create from these fabrics something worthy of their beauty.

Materials. Texture, weave and color, design, weight. I loved
to look at them, to appraise them with my fingertips, to work
with them and fashion things from them with careful cut, true
seams, and exquisite finishing. One of my never-failing joys
was using materials.

So I worked hard one day to finish a dress from material
out of that magic trunk of mine to wear to an evening party
given by Mrs. Thomas. Alas, Doug had a bad cold and did not
feel well enough to go. So we went to bed instead.

Those days John was walking very well. When we went to
town, he often walked home and I would push his empty buggy
up the hill while he held onto the handle. Sleighing was over
for that year, and all the sidewalks were clean and dry, so
walking was pleasant again.

Then, just as if to show us how freakish the weather could
be, one day when Doug had gone to Gold Bottom in the buckboard, the temperature dropped to zero and a blizzard was
raging. Annie had come to play with John, but when the sky
darkened over and the snow began to fly before the windows
in sudden blinding gusts, I bundled her up and sent her quickly
down the hill the half block to her home. I knew Doug would
be all right but hated to think of him out unprotected in all
that storm. He was the one who bore the brunt and came home
the unsung hero. All I ever did was to stand at the window
looking out and shiver to think about it.

He came home wet and cold but in no way harmed. The blizzard whipped and tore around the corners of the cabin all the next day. It was Easter Sunday! The porch lay drifted deep in white and there were no more nice dry sidewalks for John to practice walking. That day Doug worked on his reports and late in the afternoon he moved out to the plant for the summer, which, considering the state of the weather, seemed an entirely fictitious season.

Again I was plodding through soft snow as John and I took our daily walk. This little cosmic joke just served to remind us where we were geographically. I went downtown, John again in his sleigh, and mailed an order to Liberty's. Months later the materials would arrive. It was like planting seeds, knowing that through unseen forces there would be beauty in our lives later on.

Pure unadulterated joy comes to us in just such small portions—a jovial occasion, a bit of color, a look of happiness we have brought into a child's eyes, a sense of perfect rightness in a situation—the more precious because so small. Thus the opening of that future package from across the Atlantic was going to be such a bit of joy!

It was 30 below, absurd for mid-April. We would enjoy the spring all the more when it came. Again I decided that those who had endured the hardships of a long winter were doubly entitled to the rapture of the first bird's song, the initial breath of warmth crossing the chill air, the sound of running water in an ice-bound creek, the exultation of finding the first crocus blossoming on the hillside almost under the snow. Then the appreciation is so much keener, just as one who has fasted detects hidden flavors in the simplest slice of bread, which those who have feasted entirely miss.

Not that it mattered in the least what I thought, as I walked along the streets of Dawson or carried out my small routine of housework at home. I was merely entertaining myself by thinking, because there was no radio in those days to entertain me with the thoughts of someone else!

19. Idyllic Summer

THERE WAS A VERY EXCITING plan afoot in the Ferry house that spring. Every year the company office and engineering force were entitled to a month's vacation with pay. Furthermore, if they should decide to spend this vacation in the States, their expenses would be paid both ways provided they returned. If the vacations were not taken, they became cumulative so that at the end of three years there were three months coming, which gave plenty of time for a winter Outside, with pay.

By the winter of 1914, Doug would be entitled to his three months of vacation. So we were making plans to spend that winter in California. I flew my wishes before me like a little flock of colored balloons, each one airy and fragile, full of color and buoyance, tethered to me by a tiny thread of hope.

Harvey Parmelee, one of the new engineers in the company, expected his bride to come in that spring on one of the first boats and was looking for a house. As soon as it could be done, I would move out to the plant for the summer and resume the pleasant neighborliness with Elsie and Shelley, who would move out at about the same time.

Elsie called me one morning on the phone. "Harvey Parmelee asked me yesterday if I thought you would rent your house to them for the summer. I said I'd ask you."

"That's not a bad idea," I replied. "Tell you what we'll do. You and Shelley bring Harvey over to tea this afternoon and then he can see the house for himself and decide whether it suits him."

I Liquid Veneered all the furniture and made everything just as attractive as possible before they arrived. As yet, Doug and I had said very little about our plans for the winter. I know that we would much prefer to have someone in the cabin rather than allow it to stand vacant. If the Parmelees had it for the summer, they would surely want it for the winter too, since ours was one of the very best cabins in Dawson. Doug agreed with me and we decided on the rent, twenty-five dollars a month, completely furnished. We would leave our good company blankets, two pairs worth twenty dollars a pair, enough linen and silver to get along with, our down comforter and many other necessary and valuable things, including a dozen or so linen-damask hand towels I had gotten from Toronto.

After seeing the place, Mr. Parmelee decided to rent it and it was arranged that they would move in just as soon as I went out to the plant for the summer. Since the property was in my name, the rent checks would be made out to me. I felt very important and capitalistic.

Suddenly spring came in earnest. Mr. Pierce bought John's buggy for their baby, Dorothy Jane, and I spent the money for a gocart which would be smaller and easier to handle. This spring weather brought the same urge that regularly came with the lengthening days, the urge for new clothes. Since I must make practically all the clothes for myself and John, that meant some planning. For John, I ran up a number of little wash suits. It was the fashion then for little boys to wear knickers and long belted blouses over them. John had them in every color.

For myself this spring was to see a new venture. I was going to try a tailored suit and was much excited over the idea. I found a fine wool in a small shepherd's check and a good pattern. The coat was to be lined elegantly with white satin and there were three buttonholes, a test of good tailoring.

I worked hard and very carefully. The results were better than I had hoped for, even to the professional way I put in the lining. The suit was what today would be called a dressmaker suit, therefore was not so hard to do as a strictly man-tailored suit would have been.

With the suit I needed a fur to wear around by neck for cooler days. I could have bought one from Mrs. Hammel, but first, could I rustle one? I could and did. Among the useless possessions in my trunk I found a lovely wide light-blue silk ribbon sash, about three yards long and twelve inches wide. I also had several yards of the brown marabou trimming left over from making my blue satin dress.

Some consideration of these materials resulted in a scarf of blue, edged with the marabou and with a third row of it down the center. The sash, doubled over lengthwise, provided a lining. The ends were drawn together to a point and finished off with brown silk tassels and frogs, ten inches long, which I found at Mrs. Hammel's. I loved that scarf devotedly because I had rustled it, even more than had it been made of marten skins at fifty dollars per skin!

Then I bought a new hat at Scugale's dry goods store and was partially satisfied in my zeal for new clothes.

The streets were now free from snow for the second time, the days long and sunny. Every time I took John out I noticed how much more easily the new gocart was handled than did the old buggy. John sat up and looked about him with the greatest interest at everything on the way.

On one of those matchless afternoons I put on all my new finery and took John out. I was roving along, when I met Miss Iredell, out with Charlie Thomas.

"Let's walk up the hill to see Elsie," she suggested. We wheeled around the corner and started up the hill.

"Look just ahead," I prompted. There were Ruth McFarland with little Bunny and Clara Costar with Garrison junior.

"Whither bound?" I called, as we hurried to overtake them.

"Oh, just out for a walk," Clara said, smiling absently as she adjusted the sunshade on the buggy.

"Come along with us as far as Elsie's." They agreed.

When all of us arrived at the Schellingers', we made such a splendid array of Guggie mamas with their babies that Shelley, who happened to be home, decided to take our pictures.

We all lined up in a row with our baby carriages in front of us. Elsie stood in the center of the group, but the best she could manage was to hold up with one hand her little gray cat. Elsie, much cleverer than I was at making her own clothes, wore her new plaid skirt and a very pretty blouse she had just finished. She balanced the cat on her upheld hand, while John and Charlie Thomas looked on with absorbed attention.

After the picture was taken, it was time to stop frivoling and hurry home to get dinner. We parted and went our several ways.

John could walk alone very easily now and required more watching. He was alert and learning all the time.

On the first of May we had another snowstorm, but I took John downtown anyway. Although the daylight was practically continuous, those freak storms roared out of nowhere, hurled at us by the Ogre who lived in icy hauteur beyond the mountains. With the melting of all the extra snow came a big flood at the plant. The surplus water and ice jams reached the lower flats of the Klondike River just before it flowed into the Yukon.

May Norton phoned and asked me if I would like to see the flood from the top of the hill. I left John with Faithful Rufino and collected Elsie, Miss Iredell, and Chesterlyn. All of us walked over the Acklen Trail on the hills above Dawson. The trail led around the bluff to the old, now idle, Acklen hydraulic mine. We stopped before reaching the mine, at the edge of the bluff which hid the settlement at the plant from Dawson, and around the foot of which the Klondike River swirled before it reached the Yukon.

We looked down into the yellow, boiling waters, spreading across the flat, full of grinding floe ice and very dangerous, not at all like the peaceful stream that flowed behind our houses in the summertime. All the rush of extra water and ice into the Yukon might cause the ice in the larger river to break at any moment.

I did not know it then, but at that very time Doug was battling the flood which threatened Dredge Number One. For seventy-two hours he did not have his clothes off as he commandeered all the thawing-plant men, company horses, and teamsters, sending them into the woods to cut logs and haul them to the river where he was building a dam to hold back Bonanza Creek from the dredge. He was out on the dam directing the men, when McCarthy came by.

"It's risky for you to be out there, Doug," called Mikkle. "You'd better get back here."

The roar of the water, the shouts of the men to their horses, and the rumble of the logs almost drowned out the sound of McCarthy's voice. Doug turned and shouted back, "*I* am building this dam and I know it will hold. To hell with the danger."

It did hold, and Dredge Number One was out of peril. But smarty-pants Doug was so exhausted by the time it was finished that he fell into the water, clothes and all. He made his way to the bank and was hauled out, whereupon he went to the bunk house and fell into bed, sleeping the rest of the day!

As in every other year, there were pools of several thousand dollars each waiting in Dawson for the lucky winners who would guess the time the ice would break in the Yukon. There was a feeling of tension all over town as this new flood in the Klondike pushed its ways to the Yukon, and practically the whole town was holding its breath.

The day after we took our walk the whistle blew at 9:11, on May 10. At once the town was in a state of intense excitement, this meant so much to everybody as well as to the lucky winners of the pools. A new crop of cheechakos became genuine sourdoughs. Some lucky individuals had small fortunes to spend and many there were who could show them how to do it.

Greater than all these was the realization that the ice was out, and soon navigation would be open again. Boats would come steaming around the turn bringing mail, supplies, and packages from the Outside as well as the occasional tourists, whose clothes and actions we would observe as belonging to a different race of beings from ourselves.

From this time on I would be very busy, packing our belongings to take to the plant and also preparing to leave the house in perfect order for our tenants. Our handy man came to take up all the carpets and clean them. While that was being done, I washed the windows and the curtains. Having decided that they would never wear out, I cut up the old cross-barred pajamas for floor cloths, thus ending ignominiously a noble career. Then, to top off my reckless extravagance, I gave the

robin's-egg-blue dress to Mrs. Churchward to make over into a
pretty dress for Annie. While John and I slept in the living
room, I finished all my labors by painting the woodwork in the
bedrooms.

The back bedroom was rapidly filling up with boxes and
trunks ready to be moved. Miss Iredell came one morning
to help me pack the dishes. On successive days my various
friends invited me to dinner. After a heavy day of sorting and
packing it was a relief to slip into a fresh dress, put John into
clean clothes and start out for dinner and the evening. Thus I
visited the Coldricks, the Pierces, the Osborns, the Thomases,
and the Nortons. We always came home alone afterward, as
it was still bright daylight no matter how late we stayed.

We had loved our little red cabin so very much and had
had such good times there that I hated to leave it, knowing that
the time would be long before we would return. On the morning of May 19, I was up early and had my breakfast over and
everything cleaned up by seven-thirty. Denny came then with
his team—big, good-natured Denny—and took our first load to
the plant. Then he came back and loaded on my piano and the
sewing machine.

My real work started then. Fred Elliott, the handy man,
and I cleaned the house thoroughly in one final going over—
walls, windows, floors, and furniture. We did not finish until
six-thirty, but the house shone.

"No matter how nice we think it looks," I said to Doug,
when he drove up to get John and me, "it is bound to look crude
to Mrs. Parmelee, just in from the Outside and not used to
Dawson houses."

Anyhow, it was as clean and bright as I could make it. However little my toiling would be known or recognized, as I turned
the key in the lock I had a right feeling about it.

The house was all mine. Not only did I own it, but it was
mine by right of possession. When a woman has washed the
windows, made and hung the curtains, cleaned the walls and
the woodwork, made up fresh sweet beds, and added whatever
touches of beauty her soul requires and she can rustle, so much

of herself has gone into that house that it is essentially a part of her. When she leaves it, it is with regret; when she returns, she opens the door upon some of herself she had left behind.

We drove away from the little red cabin, ate our dinner at Pete's (I with aching muscles) and at ten o'clock drove out to the plant in broad daylight to our summer home.

Settling the summer house was mostly a matter of putting away our clothing and making the beds because we had left the furniture in the house all winter and also some dishes and cooking utensils. The next morning I put John out of doors in a convenient sand pile and by evenings things were pretty well back to normal for the summer. It was fun to see again the fresh, cool matting, the simple homely furniture and the curtains I had put away clean in the fall. Having two sets of everything, one for summer and another for winter, was a very good idea, I decided.

I had to grow used to the new location. During the winter the company had moved our houses into a field upstream from the cookhouse about half a mile above our old location. Elsie and I were still next-door neighbors, but we were much farther away from the office and machine shops than before. Now our neighbor just downstream was the big cookhouse and bunkhouse for the men. I would not have quite such a long walk when I needed yeast.

Doug came home one noon for lunch. He peered into the water bucket standing on its small bench beside the kitchen door. "I'm just about through with this carrying water every day," he announced.

"What ho," I thought, "is this revolution? Must I carry it now?"

"I try to be careful," I said, in perfect imitation of the meek wife.

"That's okay, Bunny." He grabbed me and hugged me. "You can use all the water you want, but *I* won't carry it." He started whistling.

"Don't keep me in suspense." I was busy serving lunch.

"C.A.T. is going to put a pump in our house. Right in this

kitchen. And there will be a well underneath it." He sat down and spread out his napkin.

Such luxury on the creeks was practically unheard of. I had a pretty good hunch where C.A.T. had derived the idea. Mrs. Thomas had so often been in our little houses and seen to what lengths we went to conserve water. But I asked, "Why are *we* getting it?"

"This location is fairly permanent for the houses, so there is no reason why they should not be served by a well. We are just the lucky ones to have it in our house, that's all. The men start tomorrow."

"No more carrying water for Shelley either." This was wonderful. "I am going to write C.A.T. and thank him," I decided.

I wrote a jingle, calling it "Dancing the Kitchen Sink." There was a new dance step just out called the Kitchen Sink, believe it or not, and C.A.T. was vastly amused by my juggling of the term.

Putting down a well was not so easy as it sounded. By the time they had gone down one foot the well diggers were in solid ice. That meant that each foot of digging had to be preceded by thawing with steam, a little every day to melt the ice and soften up the ground enough so that it could be excavated. This was summer, and the well being under the kitchen, it was supposed the ground would be somewhat protected from frost, but it took just three weeks to get that well down far enough into the Klondike wash to bring water, possibly twenty feet. On the day the well was finished and the pump installed in a small sink in the kitchen, the effect of luxury was simply stunning to our imaginations, even though the waste water from the sink merely drained into a bucket underneath!

Inspired by the extra frills we were acquiring, Doug built me a new and much larger icebox at the back of the house; also an extra porch, which now extended all across the back. New mosquito netting was tacked on all the windows, the furniture was revarnished, the windows were newly washed. I gave the matting a good bath. Now we were ready for the summer.

Mr. Pretty already had fine fresh vegetables growing at the

farm. Elsie and I often walked over to see them in the afternoons when our work was done. This year John walked too,
instead of riding in his buggy.

On her little farm, just above the plant, the woman still
kept her herd of four or five dairy cows. Every day they would
graze along the roadside in our direction. Also, every day John
would manage to elude me and start out on an exploration
tour, sometimes landing right in the midst of the cows before
I could catch up with him. I was just as afraid of those cows
as if they had been tigers, but I would walk among them to
rescue John, an act of real bravery for which I never received
any credit, since Doug had been used to milking cows as a boy
and saw no reason for fear.

Finally we built a fence all around the yard so that John
could not roam into dangerous spots. Then he found out how
to lie flat and wriggle under the gate. When we discovered
what he was doing, we built a barrier under the gate and only
then could we keep him in the yard.

Elsie moved out with her chattels the day after I did, and
life commenced to run in the familiar pleasant grooves while
the peerless arctic summer came into fullness as we went about
our little routines. John called Elsie "Ah-ee," and visited her
many times a day, excitedly looking through high stacks of
Saturday Evening Posts for pictures of automobiles. Sometimes
her whole living room would be strewn with magazines, but she
was always good-natured about it and never closed her door
to the small visitor.

On the other side of us was the cookhouse, with a plowed
field between. John would toil over the furrows with his sturdy
little legs, accompanying me on the days when I went for the
cook's "jeest" to start my bread. He would return with his
sweater pockets full of cookies, so he looked forward eagerly to
those trips. On Sundays the cook made ice cream as usual for
the men, and he never failed to have enough extra so that the
Schellingers and the Ferrys could have plenty for their desserts.

What a pleasant place that cookhouse was! A large room,
the walls unfinished, with no ceiling but the rafters, and a bare

floor, it still gave out an atmosphere of cleanly comfort and cheer. Two long wooden tables, covered with white oilcloth, filled most of the room, and at one end stood the serving tables. Behind them was the big range, where the cook and his helper could work easily side by side. Wooden benches served as seats for the men. On the walls were rows of shelves to hold dishes and canned goods as well as a wider shelf where the cook prepared the bread, pies, and cookies, the flour barrel conveniently beneath it.

On the opposite wall there hung on nails ten or twelve white-enamel water pitchers and five or six granite coffeepots and teapots. Dishes were washed in a big wooden trough in lieu of a sink, the dishpans resting on a shelf underneath when not in use. The cooks had rigged up a wooden barrel on a platform above one end of the range, connected by pipes to the firebox, thus creating a crude hot-water system.

Down the center of each table was a line of catsup bottles, Worcestershire sauce, maple syrup, large tins of jam, sugar bowls, and empty tins serving as spoon holders. These were repeated down the length of the table so that one set served four to six men. At the two tables about forty men could be fed.

Mr. Pretty ordered the supplies from the Outside for the warehouse stock, which was in effect a big wholesale grocery. In turn a former Alaska Steamship steward had the job of supplying all the camps from the warehouse, distributing the goods in accordance with requisitions made out at the various camps. Only the best of food was supplied and that in abundance.

In the afternoons, between the noon and evening meals, when I went to the cookhouse for my yeast, everything was scrubbed and clean. There would be a pleasant warmth, for the big ovens would be turning out the daily supply of bread, cake, or pies. Great kettles of soup stock would be simmering on the top of the range and perhaps a gargantuan roast was being made ready for the oven, having been taken from the screened meat house just outside the back door of the cookhouse, where possibly a week's supply would be hanging ready for the meat block and saw.

Another one of Mr. Pretty's projects was the raising of pigs. They were fed from the refuse of the camps and by fall were ready to slaughter, providing a welcome change from the regular beef.

The cook and his helper were efficient and orderly, the helper serving also as waiter and dishwasher. Besides these two men, most camps employed a third man known as a bull cook, whose duty it was to chop wood for the range, carry water and do other outside chores, as well as helping inside when needed.

These men worked hard, early and late, with no associates other than the rough crews who three times a day thumped their heavy dirty boots over the floor, ate ravenously and for the most part silently, and filed out again. Seldom was there voiced any appreciation for the good food, product of hours of work and gone in a few moments. But if there were any objections, the cooks heard about it right now.

Consequently it must have been with real pleasure that they would put a few cookies into John's little starfish hands and receive in return his delighted thanks, out of all proportion to the gift. The most they would say was, "Aw, that's all right. Come any time." They stopped their work to watch him and to do whatever they thought would make him happy.

Now the summer was in full swing. Teams came and went into the yards of the big machine shops where day and night repairs were going on and heavy machinery was being moved by the overhead traveling cranes as the men whanged and banged on the steel and iron. There was also that other din, added to the steady grinding of the dredge and the rattle of the machine shop—the cleaning of the boiler flues!

A great to-do went all up and down Guggieville. Mr. Pretty, platitudes and all, had broken loose from his austere conventionality and bought an automobile, a Metz. It was coming in from the Outside by boat and was due to be delivered to him at the dock almost any day.

Up to that time the automobiles in Dawson could be

counted as easily as the bathtubs. That was fortunate for Doug, whose Devil still wanted to climb a tree or a telegraph pole at the sight of an automobile.

Mr. Thomas had a large chauffeur-driven Locomobile, big enough to hold his family. Mr. McCarthy drove an Italian car he had inherited from O. B. Perry, who had brought it in to Dawson with him from New York when he visited as general manager of the Yukon Gold Company. Mr. Perry had employed the famous onetime bicycle rider Trilby Fowler as his chauffeur and brought with him also his own secretary. These visits, when the highest-up of the higher-ups came to town, always created quite a stir in Dawson.

This Italian car, a Zust, was a racing car and utterly unsuited to the rough northern roads. Keeping it up was no end of trouble, since all the replacements must be sent for from Italy. Finally the machine shop made them right there, but even then the car was so expensive to operate that Mr. McCarthy bought a Model T Ford and used that instead, though the rough roads were no better for it than they had been for the Zust.

Mr. and Mrs. Johnson bought a Ford, which, landed in Dawson, cost just three times as much as it would have in the States. Mr. Johnson liked to drive it, and they often came out to see us in the evening during the summer. There were no other automobiles in Dawson that we knew of, so Mr. Pretty's purchase of a Metz caused quite a little excitement in arctic circles.

The Metz arrived. Mr. Pretty succeeded in driving it off the boat and then learned the fine points of handling it by driving it up and down the Hunker Creek road. When it was considered safe for him to take the ladies out driving, Elsie and I, with John, were invited for a ride. All went well until on the way home Mr. Pretty stopped too short, throwing me forward and bumping John's nose on the windshield. Like all true sourdoughs, John was a good sport and did not cry. He was so crazy about automobiles that he was willing, as the price of a ride, to suffer a little.

As the summer wore on, Elsie and I did some sewing each

day, partly for the fun we had from it and partly because the
things we made were needed. Very often, after a day of sewing,
we would have our dinners together, in the time-honored custom. The boys would come home late to find that we had
cooked up a festive meal and that they must hurry to wash
and not keep things waiting.

By that time it was definite that we were going Outside in
the fall. I was making real preparations as Elsie and I studied
catalogues as if they were oracles so that I would know what
the styles were and what my things ought to look like. Any
fashion could be palmed off on the women of Dawson, since
they would not know the difference, but I was determined to
look right when I landed in Seattle.

No matter what else we had, Doug and I must have warm
coats for the steamer trip in addition to our fur coats, which
would be warm at that time of year. John, I decided, could wear
his wool sweater and legging suit and last year's overcoat, so
that we might buy him a complete new outfit in Seattle. For
Douglass and me, I sent to Egerton Burnett, in England, for
raglan ulsters of a waterproof material known as Aquascutum.
They were made to order. Doug's was in a blue-gray hard-
finish woolen material and mine an Oxford gray as soft and
woolly as eiderdown, very thick and warm. The price of the *two*
coats was $48.50! I also ordered a tailored suit for myself in a
beautiful heather mixture of brown, rose, and blue and a blouse
to go with it at an equally absurd price—more hostages against
the day when we would need some new clothes for traveling.

It was a great day when Shelley took my order and one for
Elsie, to town. At the last minute I had ordered some blue Irish
tweed to make myself a sports suit for wear on the boat and
enough wash material for six or seven little suits for John.
When all these packages arrived, I was going to have a busy
summer.

Elsie came in one morning to find me taking apart the sewing machine and cleaning and oiling the treadle and wheel.
"What in the world are you doing?" she asked.

"You know this machine was just rented." I was underneath the machine, working oil into the treadle by hand. "The owner has suddenly decided she wants it herself. I am going to send it in by Denny this afternoon."

'What will you *do*, with all that sewing ahead of you?" Elsie was greatly perturbed. She was used to coming to my house to sew every once in a while herself.

"Haven't decided yet." I climbed out from under the machine. "Guess I'll have to buy one."

"Let's buy one together," Elsie suggested. "You can use it now and I'll have it this winter."

"It's a deal," I agreed. "I am going into town the last of the week and I'll look for one then."

I found a good secondhand machine which I fussed with until it was in perfect condition. We varnished the stand and washed the legs and treadle until it looked like new. I used to stand and admire it in my odd moments, thinking what wonderful things it was going to produce.

Garrison Costar had been sent over to Gold Run to do some special drilling for deep thawing and Clara went him, taking the baby, so we did not see her at all that summer. It took courage to move into such utter isolation with a little baby and I wondered how Clara could do it. She would be so many miles from anyone if she ever needed help.

Mrs. Thomas came out often with the children and sometimes we would all have a picnic by the river. Mrs. Osborn, with Harriet, came too, for an occasional afternoon, or Elsie and I would take John and go to Dawson for the day. We were so thoroughly acquainted by this time with the surrounding country that we were becoming less and less conscious of all the vast, unknown menace that was the traditional North. We kept going very comfortably, thank you, in our small orbits, so well adjusted to all the conditions that we took little notice of them. We worked, played and lived in our individual fields, walled about by accustomedness, giving scant thought to the wilderness beyond.

At the assay office Shelley had rigged up a convenient shower for Elsie which I too was permitted to use. This was a great improvement over the washtub-on-the kitchen-floor method. Also, while we were at the assay office Shelley weighed us on the scales used to weigh the gold. We found that John weighed 50 per cent more than the average two-year-old.

The materials I had ordered from Liberty's that day away back in the spring had come, enough for two dresses and an evening coat. I sent out to Franklin Simon's in New York for an evening dress I had seen pictured in *Vogue*, having it sent to cousin Dina in Portland so that it would be there for me when I arrived. I knew that I would need it almost immediately and did not want to bother to shop for one. With the Liberty package came another catalogue, from which I ordered gifts for Doug's family and for Margaret Strong, whom we would visit in Seattle.

I also ordered white kid gloves for Doug's sisters and mother and for myself, knowing that I could never get them in the States at such prices. There were both short gloves and the shoulder-length which was then customary for evening wear. I also ordered Dent gloves for us for traveling. John's gloves were perfect little Dents, just five inches long.

Summer. The house was filled with wild roses and bluebells we gathered during our walks in the afternoons and evenings. While I washed and ironed or swept or baked bread, the house was open to the soft winds that came from beyond our ken and to the sun that shone all of our waking and most of our sleeping hours. We all seemed to have extra vitality during those summer months. I would play the piano for hours in the evening just because it seemed wasteful to leave such loveliness and go to bed.

Elsie went over to Gold Run for a week to visit the Costars. It seemed very lonely without her. She and I were accustomed to going in and out of each other's houses all day long. John missed her too. We finally went to town and paid some visits, ending at Mrs. Thomas's. Mrs. Hardy, with whom Elsie had come into the country, and her daughter, Mrs. Pelton, were in

Dawson. We called on them, and then Mrs. Thomas took me home with Jim.

On another such trip to town I found Mrs. Osborn engaged in a trading transaction with some Indian squaws from Moosehide. The Indians would trade baskets, bags made from caribou skin and beaded, and other pieces of their handiwork for old clothes. They often visited the Dawson women to see what they could pick up in such barter.

The baskets made by the Moosehide Indians were coarse and showed none of the fine characteristics of the work done by the Alaska Indians along the Inside Passage. Strips of birch bark, folded to the shape of a basket and edged with a strip of the bark wrong side out, were a common product of theirs. These baskets were held together by a crude sort of sewing in which rawhide or strips of fiber from trees were used as thread. Often beads were strung on those fibers and incorporated into the sewing.

Occasionally baskets were made entirely from those fibers, but they were very coarse. The beaded bags made from caribou skin were soft and colorful with beads. They were crudely put together and lined with the coarsest of cloth. All summer there were bands of Indian women collecting wardrobes in return for these specimens of their work. Now I encountered them at Mrs. Osborn's.

Fortunately I had left at Mrs. Osborn's some clothes I was willing to trade just in case some Indians came along. One article was a white serge suit I had brought in with me from the States. A squaw who must have weighed at least two hundred pounds decided that she wanted it. She could hardly have been able to get one arm into it, let alone her whole self. She gave me a very nice basket for it, and each of us thought it was a good bargain.

About July 10 the things came from Belfast, mostly materials for John and wash dresses for me and also some linens. Now I could really begin to sew. I already had my new patterns, and those exquisite materials were an inspiration to get out the scissors and thread and start sewing.

20. War Clouds and Finality

BY KEEPING STEADILY AT IT I could make one little suit for John in a day, not counting working the buttonholes. On the days when Doug was away I would have one suit made and another one cut out by the time I went to bed. All were of colored materials except one white wool mohair, like fine alpaca, which was to be his best suit and would be piped with pale blue around the collar and cuffs and down the front. After I had finished all the suits, I made him three summer nightgowns, which he needed immediately. When all of John's things were done, I could begin on my own.

Not long after I had finished them, John was wearing one of his new nightgowns, which were rather long. Elsie was forever entertained by my making John's clothes too big for him. He grew so fast, they had to start out that way. At any rate John, wearing the long nightgown, started out for an evening stroll while I was busy and slipped away across the long grass in the direction of Elsie's house. He was almost there before I caught up with him and brought him back. As I was putting him into his bed I was horrified to find on the hem of his nightgown a black hornet of the huge dimensions that hornets as well as everything else in the insect world seemed to reach during those long summer days. Apparently he had picked it up in the grass, but luckily it had not stung him. No more evening strolls for John.

When Elsie returned from her week's visit to the Costars, she told me things about the loneliness in which Clara lived that I did not like to hear. People on the Outside thought we were isolated living in Dawson. Yet how much more so was Clara, living miles from any other woman, and with a baby.

"The baby got sick," Elsie went on, in her soft voice, "so Clara and I pulled it miles and miles in the wooden box on wheels she uses as a buggy. There was another woman living at a mining claim there, and we thought she might know what do so."

The picture of the sick baby being pulled over those rough roads in a wooden box on wheels was almost more than I could bear.

"The baby was better after a few days. It surely is lonesome for Clara out there," Elsie commented in her soft voice.

"She's braver than I would be," I answered. "I simply couldn't stand it." Both of us knew that was just talking. Either of us could stand anything we had to. *Company First!*

A diamond solitaire of at least two carats had been dug up at the Forks as the dredge was going through what was once the red-light district, probably the property of some former dance-hall girl. It appeared in the amalgam at the assay office. Shelley called us over to see it.

"I wish Elsie could have it," I said, trying to sound guileless. "You know the company hasn't any use for it. They'll just have to sell it. Why not give it to you?"

Elsie looked at Shelley with her big dark eyes and said nothing.

Shelley simply closed his lips in that look we all knew so well. "That would start a precedent," he told us. "We have to turn in every least thing. Lots of interesting souvenirs have turned up in the amalgam." He put the diamond away.

When I told Doug about it, he reminded me that he had to buy the gold for my wedding ring even though he had panned it from spots up on the hills where the dredge could never dig, so it would not have gone into the company coffers anyway. Still, the payment was exacted, probably for the same reason of precedent.

Marian Gifford came out one morning. "I have something to tell you, and I'm going to stay for lunch," she announced.

There was an expression in her eyes. "You're going to be married," I guessed. "Now tell me all about it."

"I don't see how you know." She took off her hat and sat down. "Yes, I am. Do you want to hear about it now or after lunch?"

"Now, silly. I'm so *glad!*" I hugged her.

I was glad, sincerely, for I liked Marian very much and thought her life was rather dull even though her father was erudite and referred to her as Mariana of the Moated Grange. I had often thought that Mariana was having rather a thin time of it at the Moated Grange and was truly delighted that she was to marry and have a home of her own.

That same day Mrs. Parmelee brought her sewing, so we had quite a party. Elsie insisted on having the lunch at her house, as I was to entertain all the office force from the plant and the Shellingers at dinner that evening. The dinner was cooked on the little stove, a seemingly impossible feat, and everybody stayed and visited until late. Each time we had such a gathering I was reminded that there would not be many more. Summer was going, and when it went, the Ferrys would be going too.

A little picnic enlivened those days of busy enterprise. Doug, driving his Devil, took John and me along pleasant, winding roads, up and up, to the Lovett Intake of the Big Ditch, source of the water for the hydraulic mines. The intake was located at Lovett Gulch on the right limit of Bonanza Creek, away up in the hills above the creek level.

There we ate our picnic lunch under the poplar trees, not large and spreading as they would be in more temperate climates but still adequate for shade. From that eminence our eyes could roam over a lot of territory. There were the operations of the creeks, curious and pantomine-like. Great streams of water from the hydraulic giants soared like majestic white plumes against the 200-foot-high face of a hill and tore into it with astonishing force, sending down cascades of mud and gravel to be separated from their gold content.

There was no sound from the dredges at that distance as they worked in the valley below the hydraulic mines, but we could see the movement of machinery and the tiny figures of men as they went about their tasks. Beyond this small center of activity our vision carried to the untamed stretches of tundra and niggerheads, leading off to the distant line of the snowy

Rockies and the unknown Back of Beyond, the real Arctic where dwelt the Ogre that came down in the winter and harried us.

As I sat there thinking of that mysterious territory which we would never see and feeling very small in the contemplation, I was forcibly reminded of how unconcernedly we lived out our little days in the neighborhood of this immense unknown, entirely absorbed in our immediate pursuits.

I myself had passed through the stage of being a cheechako into that of a sourdough. And now, with the insouciance of familiarity, I had become that dyed-in-the-wool northerner, an old-timer. I could live in the North and take it in my stride. Just when I was growing into that last stage, I must leave, to readjust to the different life of the States. That would be a good thing too, lest I become too set in this way of living. Those who stayed too long in the North were afraid to go Outside and lived on in narrowing interests and habits, fearing the more strenuous tempo of the big world.

John was playing, and Doug had stretched out for a smoke.

"Who was that lanky scarecrow with the red beard we saw at the Lovett Hill hydraulic mine on the way up?" I asked.

Doug took his pipe from his mouth and looked at me with scorn. "That, Mrs. Ferry, is Wickham, foreman of the biggest hydraulic mine the company operates, and a character. Listen to this."

I made all the motions of listening.

"You remember I told you about the visit of Earl Gray, the governor general of Canada, the first summer I was in here?"

"Yes." I nodded. I had been told of that visit and the consequent celebrations. There had been a parade, a reception at Government House, and other functions held for the earl, his daughter, Lady Sibyl and her lady-in-waiting, Lady Constance, and others. Dawson had outdone itself to fete the guests.

I had also heard of the reception at Government House when the guests, announced loudly by the earl's aide-de-camp, approached the exalted personages, bowed and backed away. And of how Doug had forgotten to be impressed, shaken hands with the earl and stopped to chat until he saw the commotion behind him and realized that he had held up the long line, whereupon he dashed out, regrettably turning his back! But what had all this to do with Wickham?

I had always liked especially the story of the aftermath of all the correct ceremonies at Government House, when there had been more celebrating all over the town. The office and engineering forces of the Guggies had shown up at dawn, their dress-shirt fronts autographed with signatures of biblical characters, right on down to Earl Gray, O. B. Perry and others, whose signatures had been skillfully faked, and last of all, old Hoot McGloot, a fictitious character who seemed always to appear at such doings.

"After the ceremonies in town the earl and his daughter were taken on a tour of the Guggenheim mining interests," Doug went on. "They took them on Dredge Number One and then had lunch at Ninety-five Below on Bonanza. McCarthy set the table with borrowed solid silver and Haviland and served champagne and grouse."

"The guests spoke more than once of the fine treatment and food the Guggies provided for their camps! I suppose they thought that Haviland and champagne were daily fare."

"You are wandering," I interjected. "What has all that to do with Wickham?"

"After lunch"—Doug tamped some more tobacco into his pipe,—"they went up to the hydraulic mines and finally Lovett Gulch. George Coffey, the superintendent of the hydraulic department, let Lady Sibyl pan, having carefully salted the gravel sample, so that she panned out about twenty dollars in nuggets. She was so fascinated with the ease with which one could become rich that she wanted to keep it up all day. While she was so engaged, the earl stopped to talk to the foreman, our aforesaid Wickham.

"The earl asked questions, Wickham answered, and they took a great liking to each other, getting along famously. When the earl turned to leave, they were old friends.

"Wickham shook hands and said, 'Well, so long, Earl.'

"The earl rejoined jauntily, 'Ta-ta, Wickie,' no doubt much taken with the democracy of the far North, as embodied in your scarecrow with the red beard."

While we had been talking, clouds had begun to gather and soon rain was pattering down in earnest. We hastily assembled John and the picnic things and started home, right in the midst of a mountain thunderstorm. Wet, but not harmed, we drove down the roads now dampened and free from dust, raindrops sparkling in the clean air as they caught the late sun, suspended from leaf and twig. So far as we were concerned, the picnic was a complete success.

It was Monday, August 3. Miss Iredell had come out to spend the day. Elsie invited me to her house for lunch, and I was to serve the combination dinner for all of us in the evening. We women talked of sewing and clothes, of trivial, personal matters, feeling secure with the future as far ahead as we cared to look.

Into that haven of isolation and peace Doug, that evening, hurled two bombshells. With his usual sense of the dramatic he built up to his climax gradually. First he announced that Garrison Costar had been put in charge of a prospecting operation at Ruby and that Clara was going with him. At once I thought of how much we would all miss Clara and what it meant for her to take the baby into such a wilderness, even worse than Gold Run.

After I had digested this for a moment or two, Doug launched his second bombshell.

"Did you know that all of Europe is at war," he asked, as casually as if he were inquiring whether I knew that the gate was open and the cows were just down the road, "and that it may easily involve the whole world?"

"Up to now that fact has escaped me," I answered flippantly, and then realized he was in earnest. My knees suddenly became weak and I sat down on the couch. The idea of war was something that people of our day thought very little about.

"How do you know? What do you mean, the whole world?" It wasn't true, it couldn't be true, just when our own little world was going along so nicely.

Doug patiently recounted the steps leading up to the embroilment of the European nations. The news had seeped through slowly, but at last it had reached even our remoteness. Its poison, like spreading gas, would in time envelop all. Deflated of all the enthusiasm of plans and vacation alike, we realized that even though for a long time the war might not touch us personally, it seemed selfish and inconsiderate to be looking forward to a winter of fun and recreation.

Since England was declared at war on August 4, every bit of news was eagerly snapped up and discussed. Meantime preparations for our trip had to go on.

Through Mrs. Johnson, who knew the buyer for Liebes and Company of San Francisco, I was able to acquire some prime ermine pelts he had bought on his annual trip north. They could be taken into the States free from duty if they were untanned. They arrived and were beautiful. I decided to have them made into a long stole, which I hoped to wear with the evening coat of blue velvet I had received from Liberty's. The war had dulled the edge of our anticipation, so that it did not seem right to have all the things I was collecting.

On our third anniversary we went to Dawson to celebrate. We called at the Johnsons' and the Osborns' and had dinner at Pete's. Then we finished with a carnival and movies at the DAAA. Simply giddy with celebrating, we drove home late but still in daylight, and our fourth year of married life had begun.

War news kept coming in, true or not, and we were in a continual state of excitement and unrest. Many Canadians in Dawson were ready to serve when Canada declared war, only a few hours after England. There was a new meaning now in our singing of "Oh, Canada," "The Maple Leaf Forever," and "God Save the King," which were always sung at public gatherings in Dawson.

Joe Boyle, mining man and dredge operator on the Klondike River at the mouth of Bear Creek, a tributary entering the

Klondike just below Hunker Creek, had announced that he would equip and send one hundred men from Dawson to be known as the Boyle Contingent. These men would be sent to Eastern Canada for training and service.

The Imperial Order of the Daughters of the Empire, to which both Mrs. Black and Mrs. Osborn belonged, began to formulate a program for war effort and service. We, as Americans whose country was not yet involved, gave monetary contributions whenever possible or whatever else was acceptable in work and assistance.

Meantime the sewing went on. I was making a dress of embroidered batiste from Switzerland between the daily routines of cleaning, washing, ironing, and meals. Doug spent part of the time at his little cabin above the Forks on El Dorado, where tall, dignified spikes of fireweed had replaced the wild roses and bluebells of early summer. Often I would take John into Dawson at the end of the day, calling on Mrs. Osborn or Mrs. Johnson. The Johnsons still liked to drive their car in the evenings and always insisted on bringing me home.

Doug would have had his dinner at one of the camps and returned home after a fourteen-hour day. Often we would find him down on his knees tending his little garden along the fence. No matter where he was or how hard he was working Doug always had to have a little garden of some sort. This one consisted of quick annuals which would grow in the brief summer—a most diminuative affair, but it gave him satisfaction and pleasure. This year a severe hailstorm in June had covered the ground with white and practically ruined the garden, so Doug was nursing it with extra care, trying to bring it back to life.

Garrison was to go down river to Ruby almost any day. The Costars came to Dawson from Gold Run in readiness and at the last minute it was decided that Clara would take the baby and go Outside with Mrs. Thomas and the children. They left about the middle of August after a short farewell visit. I did not know it then, but I was never to see Clara again.

Weeks of rain had swollen the tributary rivers and creeks out of bounds and there was talk of floods on the Klondike River as this great volume of water poured steadily into the larger river. Elsie and I were told that our houses might be flooded and that we must prepare to be evacuated.

My one concern was for my piano. I knew that in an emergency Doug could hoist all our clothing and other valuables into the attic. My trunks and some other things were already up there, but the piano was another matter: we could not take that into the attic. We finally decided to send it into town.

Mrs. Osborn had wanted a piano for Harriett and had considered buying ours when we went Outside, since we had reluctantly made up our minds to sell it rather than leave it in the rented cabin in Dawson. The possibility of a flood brought matters to a head. It did not take Mrs. Osborn long to decide when the circumstances were explained to her, and we sent the piano in by Denny. I gave all my music to Mrs. Coldrick to keep for me, a library accumulated through all my life and quite extensive.

As the days grew cooler for playing outdoors John acquired a new interest—playing cards. There was an old deck I let him have and little by little he learned the names of all the cards. He would lay them out and say them over to himself. They were a great source of entertainment, especially on rainy days. His prowess with the cards earned him the name Rowdy of the Yukon.

We had to decide what to do with all our possessions when we were Outside for the winter. There was no room for them in the Dawson cabin, not did we care to leave them in the little summer house at the plant. Packing them for storage seemed to be the only solution. Doug and I reminded ourselves, too, in the rare audacious moments when we considered such a thing, that if we should decide to remain Outside our things would be already packed and it would not be necessary to ask anyone else to pack them for us.

We had collected an astonishing amount of human miscellany while we were in the North, to be presided over by our household gods, those Lares and Penates without which no self-respecting Latin major from Stanford would think of keeping house!

My Lares and Penates were a mixed lot. The Lares were inherited from Grade A Puritan ancestors that kept me in the line of duty—practical and worthy old boys who never let me get away with anything, kept my cupboards clean and my clothes mended and presentable. The Penates were of another stripe, coming no doubt from an English line of artists and poets who saw no good in a day unless it would yield some measure of what the Lares would have called idealistic fluff.

"Come on," the Penates would nudge me on a day in autumn, "let's put on a red tam and a red sweater to match the fall coloring and go gypsying."

The Lares would step in, take me firmly by the hair and lead me to the broom and dustpan. "Get busy," they would admonish! "you know perfectly well that this is cleaning day."

I had half a mind to pack up the Lares and leave them all winter while I vacationed in the States; I would have a much better time if they were not around!

At the warehouse we found a perfectly huge wooden packing case in which some piece of machinery had been shipped. It was heavily reinforced for strength and lined with waterproofed wrapping paper, such as had been around all the packages we received from England and Ireland. This would be an ideal receptacle for all our chattels, and the one box would hold everything we wanted to pack.

It was so very large and cumbersome that we decided to leave it in the warehouse and pack it there. Then it could remain where it was until we returned to open it or until we should send for it to be shipped Outside for us. The plan seemed perfect in every way.

A little at a time, we carried things over to the warehouse to be put into the box, mostly things we were not likely to use again that year.

Our house itself resembled a tailor shop those days. John could play outdoors at least part of the time, and since Doug was usually away for dinner, I could cut out and strew scraps of cloth around with no regard for neatness until I was through and ready to prepare the simple dinner for myself and John.

A fabric I was especially fond of was brocade. I had always thought up evening wraps and such things from the brocaded fabrics I had seen in the shops of interior decorators in the States but never had utilized any of them. Now I had some of these brocades from Liberty's, fine as any dress material and soft as silk. In a moment of boldness I decided to make a dress from a piece of rich blue brocade. It did not take long to cut it out. I worked very hard to finish it before Doug arrived home from a two days' trip.

It fitted well and looked gorgeous, I thought. Then I cut out the blue tweed suit. The coat was to be of Norfolk type with a belt and a deep sailor collar and wide reveres down the front. There was not enough material for the collar!

I put this emergency aside to simmer for a while and busied myself with another part of the suit. While I made the skirt, I knew that there would be a way out and that I would find it.

Just before I fell asleep that night the solution came to me while in that borderland of consciousness in which so many best hunches come.

"I know what I can do," I said, half aloud, "I'll use John's white crib blanket and make a white collar."

Early the next morning I took the blanket out of John's little linen-lined chest Doug and I had made for his baby things that first winter. The blanket was too small for him now, a fine closely woven little white blanket with practically no nap. It was perfectly clean and proved to be exactly the same weight as the blue tweed. I ripped off the wide ribbon facing, sponged and pressed the blanket and in no time at all had the collar cut. There was enough left over for the facing of the reveres and the front also. The suit was much prettier with the white. I decided to use some white ivory buttons I had for the front closing.

Christina had sent me a length of richly brocaded blue ribbon, by lucky chance the same shade as the tweed. The ribbon was embroidered in heavy white wool, very unusual and ornate. It would be just the thing to trim a white corduroy hat I had seen at Mrs. Hammel's. *Voilà!* My traveling costume was assembled.

August trailed imperceptibly into September, with cooler days and longer nights. The ducks and geese were flying south and colors flamed over the hills, a brave putting on of pageantry before the chill silence and the long night. Doug came and went, in and out of the picture intermittently, busy, preoccupied, his mind in half a dozen places at once even when he was at home.

All the preparations he would have time for would be a last-minute assembling of enough socks, ties, and handkerchiefs, packing his suits, putting on his cap and Aquascutum coat, and being ready. All this business of scanning catalogues, sending abroad for materials—this zealous activity of sewing, this reveling in textiles and colors—meant very little to him. If I liked doing it and it made me happy, that was fine. I could draw on the joint bank account for all I needed. He continued to smoke his pipe and figure out how to buy and distribute enough wood to carry the thawing plants through the entire next year and in certain cases for several years to come.

One unsettled question caused me a great deal of uneasiness, but we could do nothing about it except keep still and hope for the best. It would be necessary for John and me to go Outside while the boats were still running, before the big freeze-up. However, according to all precedent and tradition, Doug would have to stay in Dawson until the close of the season, when all the reports were turned in and the books closed for the fiscal year, some time in November. That meant that I would have to wait in Seattle for Doug for a month or perhaps longer. We dreaded that outcome and never spoke of it.

On September 4, Mr. McCarthy told Doug he need not stay for the closing of the books if he would finish up all the rest of the season's work and reports, but could go out on the boat with me. That evening we had the gayest of gay dinners. Doug and I began to sing a new popular song, "Don't You Remember California in September?" which filled us with a strange nostalgia plus triumph. We did a few dance steps on the living-room matting to express our jubilation, John ran up and clasped Doug around the knees, wishing to be a part of whatever fun was going on.

"All right, old in-betweener," sang Doug, as he hoisted John to his shoulder and on we danced, round and round, until we were breathless with laughing and exertion.

Now we could really plan. It meant, though, that Doug would have to work even harder and for longer hours to get everything done in the remaining time. All we thought of was taking that trip together; there was little consideration that both of us would be working right up to the minute we stepped on the boat and started up the Yukon.

Mrs. Johnson was going to give a farewell party for me and a guest of theirs who was leaving after several weeks in Dawson. Everyone I knew in Dawson would be invited. Since Doug would be at the Forks for three days, I had plenty of time to prepare for the event. I intended to wear the blue brocade dress and hastened to complete the final touches.

Then I worked for three hours on salted almonds, my small contribution to the refreshments, had a shampoo and pressed my dress. John and I rode into town with Denny, sitting high in the air on the lofty driver's seat above the wagon bed. I left John with Faithful Rufino and went to Mrs. Johnson's home, attractive with asters and other fall flowers, the Johnsons having probably the most extensive and lovely gardens in Dawson with the exception of Government House.

We stood and received all afternoon. My blue brocade would have left Mrs. Astor's plush horse whimpering with envy! People kept coming in right up to the last minute. Even though I was not going Outside at once, there were many whom I would not see again and this was my opportunity to say good-bye.

Mrs. Johnson told me to get John and come back for dinner. We talked over the party, and Mr. Johnson assured us that it was the free show and good eats which attracted the many who came, and not necessarily ourselves. It was a good party, though, and he knew it as well as we did.

No matter how many things demanded her immediate attention, Mrs. Johnson always remembered others. After giving a big party that day and having a dinner guest, she still found time to do what I had seen her do on all the many occasions when I dined with them. She unobtrusively filled a large container with a generous hot dinner from her table and slipped away for a few moments to carry it to a lonely prospector who lived nearby.

Mr. Johnson was fond of John and used to roar at his antics—things he would have reproved Virginia for doing, Mrs. Johnson gently chided him. John would drink milk from his mug and then look up triumphantly without wiping his mouth and say to Mr. Johnson, "See my cream mustache?"

This never failed to amuse Mr. Johnson and made me decide to be more strict in my training. The fact that he never did that anywhere but at the Johnsons' made it more difficult, as there he was sure of approval.

The Johnsons again took me home that evening in their automobile, John asleep in my arms. After all the gaiety in town the little house seemed silent and reproachful as I deposited John in his bed and made ready for the night.

From the day of the party on, we had no more summer. There was much cold rain and raw, disagreeable weather. The nights were long and very dark, the days short and gloomy. We continued our packing, wearing heavy sweaters and shivering in spite of them. By the time our stint was over I would be chilled through.

Coming back into the house, we would build a fire in the heater and get thoroughly warm before going to bed. Those houses at the plant were essentially summer houses and not built for warmth, but we could be fairly comfortable in them by using our heaters on cold nights. Before we left that fall, the thermometer dropped almost to zero, and John had to wear his woolly sweater suit, warm shoes, and mittens when he went out to play.

Meanwhile I was disposing of the incredible amount of stuff we had acquired since we were married. Our trunks were to be bonded straight through to Seattle and opened at the customs office there instead of at Skagway, a great convenience to us. This arrangement had been made through the Mounted Police, some of whom were very good friends of Doug's.

One evening, while we were in the midst of "Now, where do you think we had better pack this?" business, Mrs. Osborn and Harriett came out to see us. Doug took them home with his Devil and had a very narrow escape on the way back which might have cost us our trip or worse. He was driving along the narrow Klondike River road, a high wall of rock on his left, while on his right the bank fell away abruptly to the river below.

He had just passed an extremely narrow place and was rounding a turn, when he met Mr. Pretty driving sedately toward him in the Metz and keeping conservatively to the center of the road in true Mr. Pretty style.

Doug's Devil reared and plunged, not up a tree this time but toward the river and away from the terrifying automobile. Most fortunately, the direct drop into the river had widened out just there into a sloping bank with a foot or two of additional ground. So instead of landing upside down in the Klondike River, Doug was able to steer the frightened animal ahead, two wheels off the road and down the bank, and once more regain the safety of the road.

It was a very narrow squeak there in the dim light of a late moon, with no assurance that the wheels on the right would not drop into empty space any second before the buckboard was once more on the road. Again we had been in luck, and life went on as usual.

Elsie and I saw each other several times a day. Nothing was said about it, but we both felt that the coming separation was an end to our happy companionship which had lasted so long and been so harmonious. I knew that never again would there be anyone quite like Elsie, with her soft voice and gentle ways, her way of saying funny things without meaning to and her rare trait of accepting people without question.

Then came the snow. September was over, and we had not many days left in the little house at the plant. Those walls had sheltered us for two idyllic summers, but now they became in effect transparent and through them we began to see dimly the California scene, the faces of old friends, and the joy of reunion with our family groups we had not seen for years.

Between stretches of wind, cold, and rain, we would have a day or two so glorious as to make us forget everything and roam the hills. The air was crisp and clear, drenched with sun and sparkling as wine. Every tree and vine on the hills stood out in color against the blue of the sky. There was challenge and delight in the whole outdoors. We wanted to go gypsying and forget all our humdrum duties.

John was such a vigorous, active child that I realized I must have some device to control him while we were on the steamer, both going up the Yukon and later going to Seattle. At that time I had never seen one, but I sketched out a design for a little harness and ordered it made at the local harness shop in Dawson. At the back, where the shoulder straps were crossed, was a ring, and into this I snapped a braided leather leash. Thus John could walk about, but I would never be afraid that he would get too close to the rail or in any other dangerous spot. The little harness was looked upon as quite a curiosity, and I was joked about it a good deal, but I did not mind because it gave me such a sense of John's safety.

On October 10 the great day came: we were to leave the plant and go in to Dawson to stay at the Yukonia Hotel until the boat left, in order to be ready to make all the last-minute arrangements. The steamer *Whitehorse* was to leave on the twelfth, the last boat out for the season.

It had been impossible for us to leave any earlier, because Doug had to remain until the dredges and thawing plants were closed down, in order to finish up all his work. I would not have dreamed of going out ahead of him in more favorable weather, especially after what Mr. McCarthy had promised us. The time had dragged on, and the river fell lower and lower, creating the danger of being hung up on sand bars as well as being caught in the final freeze-up.

Still, there was always one more last thing for Doug to do and another boat would go up the river without us. Now it was the *Whitehorse* or nothing, so we must be ready. Tributaries were already throwing fragmentary ice into the Yukon, which, added to the slush ice already in the stream, presented a real hazard. This was the season when the river could freeze overnight. It was possible for one of the river boats to be stuck on a sand bar in the low water, and then, before she could be taken off and floated again, for the freeze to imprison her there for the winter. Indeed, that very thing had happened more than once!

Naturally we were more than glad to be moving into town for the final takeoff and settling ourselves at the Yukonia, almost in sight of the river and the wharf where we would embark in two days. We were just getting nicely adjusted to the idea of ourselves and our trunks in one room, when Mr. Thomas sent word to Doug that he would have to make a trip to Stone's Wood to settle some questions that had come up and estimate the amount of wood Stone had on hand.

Doug stood there while he took in the implications of the message. He was dressed in his traveling outfit, all the rough winter things he called his digging clothes being packed and stored at the plant. The trip involved his taking his horse out of Pickering's stable, driving to the plant, digging out enough warm clothes to make the drive out to and beyond Dominion Creek, much farther than we had gone when we went to Granville that previous winter. It also meant a more hazardous and much slower trip because he would have to use a buckboard to carry the saddles he and an assistant must use in riding horseback through Stone's Wood.

There was not enough snow on the ground for sleighing. The drive would be long—sixty miles each way—and cruelly cold. He might easily be caught in a snowstorm and have a serious delay.

All this, with the last boat due to pull out at any minute if the ice in the river became worse! It began to look as if I might have to make the trip alone after all and Doug come later the long hard way by stage over the ice.

COMPANY FIRST!

All this passed through my mind as I watched Doug. His jaw tightened. He grabbed me for a quick kiss, John for another.

"I'll make it, Bunny," he promised. "It will mean going like hell. But if I'm not here, *you take that boat!*" Then he was gone.

21. We Leave on the Last Boat

JOHN AND I FOUND THE STEAM heat of the Yukonia Hotel most comfortable and the dining room, under Mrs. Segbers' management very good indeed. It was boring, however, sitting in our little room surrounded by trunks and bags, so in spite of a cold rain we went forth to seek friends and conversation. As I locked the room my glance took in our trunks and suitcases. John's things were being carried in an extra suitcase for the boat and in it was a tiny deck of "Lord Fauntleroy" playing cards and his favorite toys. Then there was the big boxlike trunk I had bought as a freshman at Stanford, a square hat trunk I now used for anything and everything but hats, and a steamer trunk of Doug's. Having that trunk there was a sort of guarantee that Doug would make the trip with me. He had to—there was his trunk!

We spent the day at Mrs. Osborn's, the last time she would see her dear godson for some time, so we were making the most of it. All day I thought of Doug, driving in that cold rain, with the fear in his heart that he would not get back in time for the boat and the resolution that he would.

All that I ever needed to say to make Doug more determined to do something was to remark that I did not think it could be done, just as I did the night he roped and tied the bed. That was enough. He would do it then or die in the attempt. Somehow I did not say it this time, although I had strong misgivings. We both felt too keenly about it, so I just kept still.

By some fortuitous circumstance it was announced that night

that the *Whitehorse* was to sail two days later than the original schedule. Was ever fate so kind in all this life? I wondered, as I stood in the Yukonia lobby that evening after the day and dinner with the Osborns and heard the news. Now Doug could surely make it back! Had he been there, we would have danced another rejoicing. Instead I grabbed John and hurried upstairs, hugging this good news to me as a living thing.

The unexpected delay came about because there was a boat-load of passengers coming up the river from Fairbanks to catch the *Whitehorse* for the Outside. From Fairbanks they had had to go in a small boat down the Tanana and wait for the big lower-river boat, the *Susie*, up from Nome and St. Michael, on its way to Dawson. At Dawson they would change again to the *Whitehorse*. Because these people were delayed in making their connections, the steamer *Whitehorse* would postpone her sailing two days. The delay made us more liable to sand-bar hazards and the fall freeze-up, but I was so glad that Doug would have the extra time that nothing else mattered.

Doug came! I knew he would. He appeared the evening before leaving time, full of good spirits and showing no effects from what must have been a very tough trip.

"I had a hell of an experience," he said in answer to my questions, "but the team was good and I went through the wood with Stone in a day. I'll tell you more about it when we are on the boat."

The trunks were already checked, bonded and on the boat. All we had to do now was to eat our dinner, relax and wait for morning. Instead of doing that, we went calling all evening on various friends and arrived at the hotel very late.

Two steamers sailed together the next morning at ten to help each other in case there was any trouble from ice or sand bars. The *Whitehorse* cast off her moorings at 10 A.M. with the Ferrys aboard, and she was closely followed by the *Dawson*. October 14 was fairly late for the last boat to be leaving. The big packet *Susie*, from Nome, lay moored just astern of the *Dawson* as the whole waterfront was thronged with passengers and their friends in the drizzling rain.

The Pierces were going out too, and many of our mutual friends came down to see us off, besides saying farewell to the last boat they would see until the following spring. The Guggies were there in force: Mrs. Osborn, Mrs. Johnson, and others we hated to leave behind. This time it was *we* who were going Outside and others who stood on the dock where we had so often stood to see the last boat pull away and breast the stream until she disappeared around the bend upriver and not even her smoke could be seen.

We remained on deck until Dawson had disappeared from our sight, feeling very much as if we were leaving a part of ourselves there in that isolated little outpost, as indeed we were. There was a powdering of snow on the hills and a raw wind with the rain. We gladly left the gusty deck for the warmth and shelter inside. The salon was warm and very comfortable, with plenty of big windows forward for observation of the river and the landscape.

After the accelerated tempo of the past weeks Doug found it good to just sit and smoke his pipe and look out at the grayed landscape as it slid by the windows. We sat in easy chairs close to the windows. Our progress was slow going upstream, but who cared?

"This is a good time for you to tell me about your trip to Dominion," I suggested. "I can hardly wait to hear all about it."

Doug tamped the tobacco in his pipe. "Might as well," he agreed.

"You know when Dredge Number Six was moved to Gold Run last year they got by for the first year on wood that was already cut. We got that at a very reasonable figure, before the wood merchants knew that the dredge was to be moved, so they did not advance the price. Not so this year. Several of them ganged up to hold up the company on wood. They cut it all ahead of time and figured they had us because there was no other wood available, and they were going to make us pay their price. They figured it was too late for anyone else to go in and cut enough wood anyway. The usual practice is to cut the wood and let it dry all summer for the next summer's use, you see. Nobody else would have time to do that now, and they thought they were sitting pretty."

"The company would have to pay out a huge sum for that much wood, I suppose," I said.

"These guys wanted over a hundred thousand," Doug said, "and the company decided to outsmart them. They told Stone they would finance him if he would go in there and cut the year's supply."

"Where would he get it?" I asked.

"As a matter of fact, those other fellows had the adjacent wood all corraled, so it meant that Stone had to go over the divide, about twenty miles into the wilderness, to cut his wood. We let him use the company equipment of boilers and hoists to haul out the wood. We advanced Stone twenty-five thousand dollars and told him to go ahead."

"I thought it was too late—" I began, but Doug went on.

"By that time it was very late to be starting such a big job, with the expectation of finishing it in time. Stone had to resort to artificial drying by burning through the woods first. Then he had to cut and trim the poles, and finally convert them into four-foot cord wood, a dishearteningly big task to undertake at the last minute. But Stone took it on.

"Then the other wood merchants began a whispering campaign to discredit and discourage Stone. They reported to the company that Stone was drunk all the time, that he was wasting the money advanced to him and that he would never be able to get out the wood on time."

"This is just like a story," I interrupted—"objective, conflict, villain, and all the rest. Go on and tell me some more."

"I intended to, before I was so *politely* interrupted." Doug grinned as he looked out at the broad expanse of river ahead of us.

"Then C.A.T. decided he had to investigate, and unfortunately I was the only man he had who knew enough about the wood business and its economics to be able to estimate the value of standing timber and wood in its various stages of conversion into fuel to see if Stone was really doing the job efficiently or was into us for twenty-five thousand without our getting full value for it."

"That's what you get for being so smart," I encouraged him.

Ignoring me, Doug went on. "I went into Pickering's and told him I wanted a team that were plenty tough. The horses would have to pull a buckboard, carrying two men and their saddles, sixty miles the first day. On the next day we would ride the horses all day, twenty miles to Stone's camp and all through his wood, then back to the Granville Roadhouse, where we would spend the night. On the third day they would have to travel the sixty miles back to Dawson."

"That meant they had to be saddle horses as well as driving horses?"

"Yes, and good ones. We would have to ride through logs, fallen like jackstraws, through iced-over bogs where they would slip and sometimes fall. Part of the time we would have to dismount and lead them, jumping them over fallen logs. I knew it would be like that, so I asked for the best Pickering had. Pickering told me he had two good horses that could stand such a three-day trip of driving and riding but was not sure I could ride one of them.

"'How about it? Are you a pretty good rider?' he asked me.

"I was so determined to get the trip over with I thought of the days on Dad's ranch when I was in the saddle every day. 'I can ride anything that has hair on it,' I told him. Right there I made my big mistake."

Just then the call to luncheon interrupted us. "More," I begged.

"After lunch," Doug promised, "while John takes his nap."

All through lunch I was curious about that big mistake. I knew that Doug could ride any horse that anyone else in Dawson could. So what?

We found our chairs again after lunch, close to our stateroom, where John was asleep.

"Now go on with the story." I felt idle and luxurious, after all the previous weeks of sewing, packing, and rushing around. Imagine either of us having time for a long conversation right in the middle of the day!

"I had quite a time saddling that horse," Doug went on. "It was five in the morning and below zero, so I laid it to the weather. When I tried to get into the saddle, I knew what Pickering meant. The horse had that suspicious hump that told me what was coming. He veered away, plunged, bucked and snorted.

"I suggested to Stone, who was with us, and to my assistant, who was no help at all, that they change horses with me, but they wisely refused. Then I thought the horse was too cold and I could lead him a few hundred yards to warm him up. I tried to mount every once in a while, with no success, until I had led that horse all the three miles to Taddy's roadhouse. We were losing valuable time and I knew by that time I could never use that horse in the woods where I would be mounting and dismounting all day.

"As well as keeping a roadhouse, Taddy supplied the meat that was used in that area, and that fact was lucky for me. A man had herded a lot of cattle all the way from Dawson to Taddy's, there to be butchered and frozen for the winter supply. That man's horse was tethered in front of Taddy's while its rider was enjoying a drink at the bar. The minute I saw that horse, I knew I had to have it, but how?

"I went inside, found the fellow at the bar and bought him a few drinks."

"A few?" I asked.

Doug grinned. "Well, enough. I made some plausible excuse that my horse was not good in the woods and finally induced him to swap horses. I got away on his, and left him there at the bar and my horse tied outside. More of that later.

"We went on, with Stone as our guide. The three of us rode and walked all day. I estimated the standing timber, so many cords, so much money; then the cut logs and the wood already made into cordwood and stacked. I can almost estimate a hundred cords of wood at a glance these days. Gosh, Bunny, it was cold!

"After a day of this sort of thing we rode back the twenty miles to Granville and I wrote up my report, finding, of course, that Stone was all right and delivering value."

"How about the other man—did he get away?" I asked.

Doug grinned. "I heard at Taddy's how he had to be helped in order to get away at all. Hours later when he went into Murray's for a drink and tried to get back on the horse, the only way he could accomplish it was to lead the horse between two cabins, where he couldn't turn, and get a man to hold him while the rider climbed up on the roof and slid down into the saddle!"

At this point I did not know just where my sympathies were. "And then?"

"When we stopped at the French girls' roadhouse at the summit, they told us about 'Such a fonny man was here yesterday. He would not get off his horse and we had to bring him his dinner and serve him while he sat in the saddle!'

"The same thing happened at Gold Bottom. That fellow did not get off his horse, I'll bet, until he reached Pickering's!"

Doug must have seen a look in my eye, for he continued with indisputable logic, "Somebody had to ride that horse, and I figured that fellow had more time than I did!"

I laughed. "It's a good story and I'm certainly glad he did, because this way you made the boat."

My journey down the Yukon four summers before had been very different from this one. Then the river was in full volume. It caught and swept our boat onward in its strong current, so that with the added power of the engines the trip had been made in almost record time.

This time the river was low and we were bearing upstream against the current, feeling our way among treacherous sand bars slowly and cautiously. This trip promised to last much longer, but it did not matter to us. Our vacation had begun, and we were together. We visited, played cards and roamed the deck with the Pierces and a couple from Fairbanks, the Achesons, whom we liked very much. John was interested in everything and no trouble at all.

There was a full load of passengers, as there always was on the last boat out: businessmen, miners, travelers, women, and children. We met the people from the lower river and finally narrowed down to our own little group. The Achesons were peppy and amusing, and their two boys were good little travelers.

The river became foggy and it was decided to tie up for the night, slowing our progress even more, but we could not risk running onto a sand bar in the dark. Our evenings were usually spent playing bridge in the salon, finishing with a dance and a late supper. Since our cabin opened onto the salon, we could look in on John occasionally and see that he was all right.

One morning we began to play a game of tag with the *Dawson*, a circumstance which clearly showed the wisdom of sending out two boats together. We were held up for a while on a sand bar, not seriously, and the *Dawson* passed us, whistles blowing and passengers cheering and shouting from the decks. It reminded me of the stories of races on the Mississippi in the early days. Not long afterward we were extricated from our predicament and on our way again.

Doug was wearing his heavy woolen sweater with a storm collar under his suit coat and an English traveling cap of the type worn by most men at that time. Over his shoulder was the strap of his camera case, because he might want to take a picture almost at any moment.

My Aquascutum coat was so warm and cuddly for the deck that I did not need my fur coat at all. Doug had left his heavy coonskin in Dawson storage, as being far too warm for any use in California. When inside, I wore the blue tweed suit with the white collar from John's crib blanket and received many compliments on it too. (The origin of the collar was not divulged!)

At night the chuff-chuff of the engines put us to sleep, the

air blowing in our windows from hundreds of miles out of nowhere, and by morning we were many miles farther away
from Dawson and the little red cabin on the hillside.

Now it was our turn to jeer at the *Dawson*. She was aground
on a bar just ahead of us as we rounded a turn. Her plight
was more serious, however, than ours had been, so we went
back and spent some time pulling her off the bar. Lucky for
her that there were two boats going out together; otherwise
she might had had to stay there until spring. Once the *Dawson*
was freed, we swept up the length of Lake Lebarge, passed
through the Fifty Mile River and late in the afternoon of the
Sixth day, steamed into Whitehorse.

There was a comfortable room waiting for us at the Whitehorse Hotel. We settled ourselves and spent the evening calling on Dr. Clark at the hospital. Dr. Clark had not seen John
since the summer of his birth and was most interested in his
progress, since, to quote Doug, "John, the Rowdy of the Yukon,
now wears four-year size of everything, including mukluks
and bear-claw necklaces."

The trip over the White Pass Railroad the following day
had memories for us all, for not one of us but had gone into
the unknown North by that awe-inspiring route. Some had
gone with trepidation; all, with curiosity and expectancy about
what the new country held in store. Now, coming out, we
knew the North in all her moods. For us she held no unknown terrors despite her harshness and her inscrutable silences.
We had every one of us fallen under her spell and forever
would we hear her calling, no matter where our paths might
lead us.

The train climbed the long grade to the summit and started
down the precipitous winding pitches toward Skagway, where
we were once again in the soft, moist atmosphere of the coastal
area with its rains, fogs, and heavy snows. At five-fifteen we
slid to a stop in Skagway. "Skagway, gateway to the North,"
I had read on my way Inside. This time we were stepping
through the gate the other way. As it would close behind us,
our faces turned toward the States, we would encounter the

rush and tumult of cities and civilization, an accelerated tempo, and an economic pressure we had all but forgotten.

We were to have two days in Skagway before our Canadian Pacific liner, the *Princess May*, was due to sail for Seattle. We went at once to the Pullen House. There were still flowers in the hotel gardens, and the little stream through the grounds rippled free from ice. In just one day's traveling we had come from frozen ground and ice-bound streams into this, to us, balmy weather.

One thing that forced itself upon me over and over again was the air and impression of luxury at the Pullen House in contrast to any hotel I had seen since I left there on my way to Dawson. I was puzzled when I remembered that when I first saw it it had impressed me as being ramshackle and crude. Thus do our standards of comparison change with our surroundings. By Dawson standards the Pullen House was indeed elegant.

I remembered how I had entered the North with confidence, because it would be HOME. Crude surroundings, hardships, small privations, had not mattered. Our little citadel had never been penetrated by the cold, had never succumbed to the rigors of living. Inevitably, in leaving, something of ourselves remained behind and that something was so innate and basic that to us the North would never be less than HOME.

After our week of restriction to boat and train, we found Skagway exciting. We explored all the shops and bought a few presents to take Outside, mostly articles of fossil ivory. Since the Pierces and Achesons were staying at another hotel, the Golden North, we invited them all to have dinner with us at the Pullen House. We had a very gay evening.

Our stay in Skagway was long enough to let us explore the whole town, which I had not had time to do on my way in. We heard stories of the gold-rush days, when Skagway was a wide-open town, sheltering every sort of desperado as well as the men who sought the North for gold. We heard reiterated tales of the hardships of the Chilkoot Trail as the stampeders packed their supplies wearily to the top of the trail, bit by bit. It was a story that would never lose its fascination, however highly colored or exaggerated.

When we saw it, Skagway was living in that past. Its tumble-down cabins, relics of the gold rush, were being cleaned up or torn down for fuel. Summer flowers, in their brief blooming, helped to create beauty to cover up the ravages of decay and neglect. Even Mrs. Pullen, with her reminiscences of the early days and the notables who had visited her hotel, seemed to be living in that past.

One could not visit Skagway and not hear of Soapy Smith, the bad man of the town, and his vicious gang. Smith was tall, plausible, handsome. The "Soapy" was derived from a little game he had invented in the States. Wrapping a five-dollar bill around one of several cakes of soap, he would offer to sell the batch at fifty cents a cake. Simpletons, hoping to acquire the bill, would buy up the soap at that price. The one with the money around it was always bought by a confederate, who showed it eagerly and thus kept the ruse going.

But Soapy's dealings were not always so innocent. Coming there in 1897, he organized a gang of tough confederates who operated under his direction to fleece the tenderfeet who came in on their way to the gold rush. Fixed gambling devices were the bait, but before they were through with a man he was often induced to drink too much and then robbed and even murdered.

Finally Skagway became so notorious that in July of 1898 plans were made to rid the town of Soapy and his gang. A mass meeting was held; and when Soapy tried to break it up, he and one of the decent men, Frank H. Reid, a civil engineer, had a gun duel in which both were killed. On Reid's grave we saw a headstone inscribed, "He died for the honor of Skagway."

So strangely is the human mind constituted that the grave of Soapy Smith, the bad man and desperado, is the one indicated as being of greatest interest to the average tourist. One cannot be said to have really seen Skagway unless he has seen that grave and lived over in his mind the lawlessness of that day.

The *Princess May* was due to sail at midnight, but we went aboard about seven in the evening of October 22. It was already dark as we left the Pullen House with our luggage and were taken down the long pier to the steamer. We found the *Princess May* very much larger and more luxurious than the *Jefferson,* on which I had come into the country. Our stateroom was on the main deck and amidships, opening into the main salon close to the stairway going down to the dining salon. We thought it an ideal location, since very little motion could be felt when we crossed the open water at Queen Charlotte Sound and Dixon's Entrance. Another feature we liked was that it was warmer than the staterooms on the upper deck and thus pleasanter for John.

We stowed away our baggage in the commodious and comfortable room, put John to bed and went out on deck. The dark, silent waters of Lynn Canal stretched ahead of us to the south, while behind us lay Skagway, dreaming in its reminiscences. Away back, behind the barrier of mountains to the north, lay the Inside. Somewhere, lost in that vast remoteness, was the tiny spot that was our little red cabin. I shivered and went back to the warmth and immediateness of the ship.

The *Princess May* was taking out the Boyle Contingent, one hundred men, equipped by Joe Boyle for service in the Canadian army. All along the starboard side of the ship was a huge banner about four feet high bearing in big letters the words "Dawson to Berlin, 7480 miles."

When they reached eastern Canada, those men enlisted in the Princess Pat regiment and went overseas almost at once. Practically none of them came back. They were a picked group of Dawson's finest, sturdy, self-reliant men who could have served their country equally well in peace as in war.

Fortunately for us the weather was mild and clear. Other late boats had encountered fog, nasty weather, and even severe storms, so we felt much favored. On deck we roamed about, took pictures and tried to miss nothing of the spectacular panorama that was passing before us mile after mile. John enjoyed the freedom of the deck, leashed to his harness and to me. In the evenings we played bridge, and occasionally a group of us would go up to the hurricane deck and sing until late at night, our voices dissolving out over the dark water as the *Princess May* carried us smoothly southward.

John's little deck of cards was a great source of amusement. He could sit on one of the suitcases and use the lower bunk for a table, spreading out the cards and playing with them by the hour. His knowledge of the various cards amazed our friends. We could not confuse him even with the jack of diamonds and the jack of hearts. He never made a mistake and was perfectly matter of fact about it, no matter how astonished his audience might be.

We stopped at Alert Bay, which I had not seen on my way in, as it is a Canadian port and not often visited by American vessels. Alert Bay is an Indian fishing village noted for its fine totem poles. We were to remain there for several hours, so everybody went ashore and looked around.

A long, wooden pier led from the *Princess May* to the shore line. I walked along, with John prancing ahead on his leash, while Doug looked for likely camera shots. As we neared the end of the pier and approached the village we began to see the Indian dwellings, each with its totem before the door. For the most part they were built of lumber rather than logs. Many were painted. Rows of fishing boats were drawn up on the narrow beach beyond. There was one street, the row of houses facing the water and then, abruptly, the hillside, covered with spruce and pine. The verdure was luxuriant, the air fresh and sweet, as we walked along the planks of the pier.

All at once I noticed a great commotion among a group of squaws gathered close to the pier. They were laughing and pointing with squeals at us as they chattered in their own language. Suddenly I knew what was entertaining them so much: it was the sight of John and his harness. They had never seen anything like that before and were simply overcome with amusement.

On the morning of October 26 we arrived at Vancouver. Here we would change boats, continuing to Seattle on the larger and faster *Princess Charlotte*. The *Charlotte* was due to sail about noon, so we had a few hours to explore the city. The Pierces, Achesons, and ourselves hired a car and drove through the extent of Stanley Park and the residential section, much impressed with the magnificent trees and verdure of the park and the wealth displayed in the homes and business section of this city, the principal western port of Canada.

We rested and had coffee at the Vancouver Hotel, and then we took ourselves and our baggage down to the *Charlotte*. Now we were just a day's trip from Seattle. Doug and I were becoming more and more exhilarated at the prospect of touching American soil again. All that afternoon we sat on deck and looked at the panorama passing before us, the journey already completed in our minds.

A stop at lovely Victoria and a stroll through the grounds and building of the Empress Hotel was delightful but did nothing to ease our impatience. We still had the longest part of our trip ahead of us. Those hours between Victoria and Seattle would seem longer and more tedious than all the twelve days we had been on the way from Dawson.

In our elation we talked to John about Seattle, the new coat and hat he was going to have, and the fun of going to Southern California, clear to San Diego to see his grandparents. Finally, after an early dinner, John fell asleep. We carried him to our stateroom and laid him on the berth, fully dressed except for his shoes, and covered him up. Then we sat on deck, immediately below our stateroom window, where we could hear him if he made the slightest sound.

The water was dark. There were no stars. Our ship rushed on. Looking out into the sea and sky and seeing neither, hearing only the hissing of the water along the side of the ship and the desultory talk of passengers nearing the destination, Doug and I sat silently side by side, encompassed in our thoughts and all that had happened in the North while we lived there. Unknowing of what lay ahead, we felt as strange coming into Seattle as if we were landing from the moon. We should have to learn anew the things people were doing, the catchwords, the tempo. Not knowing it then, we had left the North forever.

Far ahead we caught a glimpse of lights. They were strung in a great semicircle, tier on tier, an extravagant, glittering necklace, suspended across the horizon as we came closer, midway between earth and sky.

The *Princess Charlotte* swung in toward them. The lights multiplied, twinkled, grew larger, in seemingly endless array as far as we could see. Those lights were on American soil, and a new life for us.

Our hearts beating fast, we rushed inside to the stateroom.

Collect everything—John's shoes—your camera, Doug—my fur coat—

"Wake up, John darling, here's Seattle!"